Inequalities of Platform Publishing

A Volume in the Series
Page and Screen

Edited by
KATE EICHHORN

INEQUALITIES OF PLATFORM PUBLISHING

THE PROMISE AND PERIL OF SELF-PUBLISHING IN THE DIGITAL BOOK ERA

CLAIRE PARNELL

University of Massachusetts Press

AMHERST AND BOSTON

ISBN 978-1-62534-905-7 (paper); 906-4 (hardcover)

Designed by Deste Relyea
Set in Minion Pro and Franklin Gothic
Printed and bound by Books International, Inc.

Cover design by adam b. bohannon
Cover art adapted from photo *eReader on Yellow.*
CC BY-SA 4.0.

Library of Congress Cataloging-in-Publication Data

Names: Parnell, Claire, 1994– author
Title: Inequalities of platform publishing : the promise and peril of
self-publishing in the digital book era / Claire Parnell.
Description: Amherst : University of Massachusetts Press, 2025. | Series:
Page and screen | Includes bibliographical references and index.
Identifiers: LCCN 2025003774 (print) | LCCN 2025003775 (ebook) | ISBN
9781625349057 paperback | ISBN 9781625349064 hardcover | ISBN
9781685751869 ebook | ISBN 9781685751876 epub
Subjects: LCSH: Electronic publishing—Social aspects—United States |
Self-publishing—Social aspects—United States | American
literature—Minority authors—Publishing | Authors and
publishers—United States
Classification: LCC Z286.E43 P37 2025 (print) | LCC Z286.E43 (ebook) |
DDC 070.5/797—dc23/eng/20250625
LC record available at https://lccn.loc.gov/2025003774
LC ebook record available at https://lccn.loc.gov/2025003775

British Library Cataloguing-in-Publication Data
A catalog record for this book is available from the British Library.

The authorized representative in the EU for product safety and compliance is
Mare-Nostrum Group. Email: gpsr@mare-nostrum.co.uk
Physical address: Mare-Nostrum Group B.V., Mauritskade 21D, 1091 GC Amsterdam, The Netherlands

For Heidi and Jack

Contents

Tables

Preface

A few years ago, during a week focused on bookstores in a core publishing and communications postgraduate subject, my students were given an activity devised by my colleague Beth Driscoll to come up with a plot synopsis for *You've Got Mail 2*—the unofficial, un-optioned sequel to the 1998 Nora Ephron classic. The activity was intended to prompt students to think about the contemporary changes to bookselling and buying, and the power dynamics, people, companies, and technologies underpinning such shifts. The original *You've Got Mail*, a favorite rom-com of mine starring Meg Ryan and Tom Hanks, centers around the online epistolary love story and real life professional conflict of Kathleen Kelly (Ryan), owner of the independent children's bookstore The Shop Around The Corner, and Joe Fox (Hanks), nepo-baby and person-in-charge of Fox Books, a large chain bookstore that threatened to put the indie (and Kelly) out of business. Responding to the obvious, most of my students created loglines describing the threat of Amazon to our local Australian independent bookstores (the first Australian Amazon warehouse had opened in Melbourne a few years before in December 2017). From memory, and to my immense relief, no one got quite so far as to propose a romantic plotline between Jeff Bezos, founder of Amazon and CEO at the time, and an undoubtedly cool, black-clad Melbourne bookseller.

Amazon was just over four years old at the time *You've Got Mail* was released in December 1998 and its absence from the film elides the nascent impact of technology on the book industry. In fact, the young internet was highly romanticized through the intimate email exchanges of Kelly and Fox. Through these characters, the possibilities of cyberspace are highly idealized: a space to be whomever you want, to connect, and inevitably to meet the love of your life. This optimism is juxtaposed throughout by Greg Kinnear's character Frank Navasky and his sometimes farcical remonstrances of digital technologies. But as easy as it is to make fun of Navasky's exaggerated extolment and literary self-importance, were a sequel ever to exist it would likely paint the internet and digital media in an entirely different light.

Over the past few decades, Amazon and other digital technology companies have undoubtedly transformed more than the world of bookselling. Nearly all aspects of publishing and book culture have been swept up by platforms in a process Anne Helmond describes as platformization.[1] Just as Fox proclaimed his superstore would "seduce" customers with their square footage, discounts, deep armchairs, and *cappuccino*, and ultimately bring in customers by selling "cheap books and legal addictive stimulants," Amazon built its brand dominance initially by using books as a loss-leader and cemented it through the convenience afforded by innovative ecommerce systems, vast distribution infrastructures, and global fulfilment centers. And yet, as this book will show, the tension in a film dedicated to the impact of the internet on publishing and book culture need not be a shallow, one-dimensional depiction of digital platforms as the unredeemable villain. The following chapters reveal an unavoidable paradox at the heart of the contemporary digital publishing era: while platforms wield immense power over authors, publishers and readers, they also represent a promise of possibility and freedom for many.

The questions embedded within this paradox inspired this research project. I received my first Kindle e-reader in 2011, a first-generation Kindle Fire that was gifted to me secondhand in a *Frozen Planet* DVD cardboard slipcase. Around the same time, self-publishing was experiencing what many now refer to as its golden age; many authors, particularly those writing romance and other popular genre fiction were circumventing traditional publishers, publishing directly to retail platforms, selling books for a couple dollars or less and making a lot of money doing it. As a young-ish reader with very little disposable income, most of what I bought and read was self-published romance fiction, from Sarina Bowen to Alisha Rai, Colleen Hoover to Courtney Milan. Sometimes authors of other genres, like Andy Weir and Hugh Howey, made their way through too if the blurb was compelling enough and the price point low enough for me to risk a new-to-me author. At the time, most ebooks but particularly self-published ebooks were very accessibly priced for consumers at around ninety-nine cents to a few dollars. Intellectually, I understood how self-publishing provided me greater access to books and reading only shortly before I came to understand how it provided authors access to an industry. No longer were authors reliant on agents or editors or publishing houses believing in the literary or commercial value of their work to publish their work, what is often referred to as editorial gatekeeping. Authors could now circumvent traditional publishers, publish directly to distribution platforms and reach readers without a chain of intermediaries. While self-publishing was not new—indeed, Charles Dickens' *A Christmas Carol*, Irma Rombauer's *The Joy of Cooking*, and Beatrix Potter's *The Tale of Peter Rabbit* were all published independently before being picked up by traditional presses—digital platforms made the activity easier and cheaper than ever.

The new entry point afforded by self-publishing seemed a particularly important opportunity for authors from communities who had been historically marginalized and excluded from traditional publishing, including Black authors, Indigenous authors, authors of color, and LGBTQ+ authors. This idea was intricately wrapped up in the implicit promises associated with the early internet as an infrastructure built on technical and ideological openness: a technology that would fundamentally restyle the established power dynamics between legacy institutions in favor of individuals and virtual communities. But how did this access and alteration play out in practice? What were the new rules of participation and what, if any, barriers still existed? And who, if anyone, still felt restricted in this new golden era?

Despite enabling access for many, publishing platforms have failed to live up to any promise that they would herald in a democratization of cultural production. Rather, platforms marginalize authors of color and LGBTQ+ authors through their socioeconomic and techno-cultural systems, including their recommender algorithms, governance and moderation systems, classificatory logics, organizational cultures, and cultures of use. When it comes to platform publishing, platform and publishing logics *work together* to replicate old and introduce new significant barriers that perpetuate discrimination against authors of color and queer authors, with far-reaching effects across the broader publishing, media and cultural industries. But not every barrier is final, and the authors in this research show the ways in which we might navigate through.

Acknowledgments

It is quite a thing to have a book come together, and I am thankful to the many people who had a hand in this one. Thank you to Brian Halley at the University of Massachusetts Press for his enthusiasm, expertise, and guidance as well as Page and Screen series editor Kate Eichhorn for her support. Thank you also to the peer reviewers of the manuscript for their generosity, and everyone at UMass Press who worked on making this into a book. I am eternally grateful to the authors who agreed to speak with me for this research with such generosity and openness.

This research has gone through many phases and benefited from a great number of people who provided feedback, direction, and support. First and foremost: thank you to Beth Driscoll, who read multiple drafts, accompanied many thinking walks, and has provided innumerous tidbits of advice over the years. I am grateful for the incredible community of researchers I find myself part of, including Alexandra Dane, Millicent Weber, Jodi McAlister, Kate Cuthbert, Andrea Anne Trinidad, Caitlin Parker and too many others to name. It is very rare, I think, to have colleagues who bring so much joy to this work. I am also thankful to other colleagues, who contributed to this research in its earlier stages, including Danielle Fuller, Ted Striphas, Claire Squires, DeNel Rehberg Sedo, and Malcolm Neil.

A number of conversations and convenings have shaped my thinking around this work, and I am especially appreciative of the opportunities I had to talk through the ideas at academic several conferences, in particular, the Society for the History of Authorship, Reading and Publishing; Association of Internet Researchers; International Association for the Study of Popular Romance; Australian Media Traditions; and Genre Con. Some of the related ideas for this research were developed in journal articles and book chapters, and I thank the editors and reviewers of *Convergence*, *Post45*, *Overland*, *The Routledge Companion to Romantic Love* (edited by Ann Brooks), and *Post-Digital Book Cultures* (edited by Alexandra Dane and Millicent Weber). I acknowledge the support provided by the University of Melbourne, which allocated resources that allowed the research to be undertaken and the book published.

Finally, to Jack, Heather, Matthew, Jan, and John: thank you, for everything.

Inequalities of Platform Publishing

LET ME START BY introducing you to Simone Shirazi. Simone is a Black Persian American writer of young adult and romance fiction who started her writing career on Wattpad at the age of fourteen, posting stories chapter-by-chapter. She quickly built a loyal readership, particularly for her fairytale-inspired series. Her most popular title, at least by the number of readers, is *Once Upon a One Night Mistake* (*OUAONM*), a Cinderella retelling that has amassed more than thirty million reads on Wattpad since the first chapter was published in 2015. In 2020, Simone moved her writing practice to Radish, one of Wattpad's closest competitors, where she republished a serial version of *OUAONM* and has generated another forty-seven million-plus reads of this story. In 2021, approximately six years and seventy-five million total reads later, Radish published *OUAONM* as an ebook; two years later, it was still ranked an impressive #76 in Amazon's Teen & Young Adult (Kindle Store) category. Readers can now buy this story on Amazon, Kobo, Barnes & Noble, and Scribd; read it on Radish for a subscription fee; and, as of January 2023, read it as a webcomic on Pocketbooks.[1] Most publishers dream of this kind of engagement with a title, but what makes it even more incredible is the length of the title: by early 2022, Simone had written 952 chapters of *OUAONM*. In 2023, she published her first traditionally published novel, *Cross the Line*, with Pan, an imprint of Pan Macmillan.

I introduce you to Simone here, a participant of this research project whose story will feature in more depth throughout the coming chapters, because her journey encapsulates a relatively new and growing mode of publishing that is based on and around platforms. Platform-dependent authors like Simone tend to work across a broad ecosystem of digital platforms and traditional institutions, and their work is shaped by platforms' techno-cultural and socioeconomic infrastructures—from content moderation systems, payment mechanisms, and algorithms, to in-house platform staff, and so on. The astonishing length of *OUAONM*, for example, is encouraged by the serialized style of publishing and reading on Wattpad as well as the encouragement by Shirazi's loyal readers liking and commenting on each chapter. As an author who comes from a cultural and ethnic background that has historically been marginalized within both internet and book publishing spaces, Shirazi's experiences as a Black Persian American writer highlight how her success has sometimes happened despite platformed systems that perpetuate the marginalization of people of color.

This is a book about publishing platforms and the experiences of historically marginalized authors working on them. Digital platforms have transformed the book industry in the early twenty-first century, becoming increasingly central to the creation, distribution, reading and reception of books. It is fair to say that publishing is an industry now defined as much by the technology corridors of Silicon Valley, Shenzhen, and Seoul as it is by dealings in the literary hubs of New York, London, and Frankfurt. Digital technologies have been used to produce books since the 1970s–1980s when the development of early computers, networks and, particularly, Standardized General Markup Language allowed publishers to digitally produce and typeset books. But Amazon's launch as an online bookstore in 1994 represents a flashpoint in the digitization and eventual platformization of the book industry.[2] Over the past thirty-plus years, several more platforms have emerged, carving out their own spaces in the vast digital publishing landscape.

Authors and readers have built strong communities on Instagram and TikTok (known as Bookstagram and BookTok), showing off their bookish bona fides and sharing recommendations and reviews, often in front of aesthetically organized bookshelves.[3] They present book hauls and book trailers on YouTube (BookTube) and discuss favorite tropes and industry lore on Reddit. And publishing professionals long congregated on the platform formerly known as Twitter to discuss the latest literary scandal or festival and collectively generate hype around current prizewinners and new releases.[4] While these are certainly platforms used by the publishing industry (readers, authors, critics, publishers, and publishing professionals alike), this book is primarily concerned with publishing platforms; that is, platforms used in the creation, production, and distribution of books and creative writing.

There are a broad and diverse range of publishing platforms that adopt various economic models, have distinct technological infrastructures, and cater to different types of writing, publishing, and reading. Among the largest are Amazon and its competitors, Apple, Google, and Kobo. These platform companies have developed extensive walled publishing gardens, operating self-publishing platforms (Amazon's Kindle Direct Publishing and Kobo's Writing Life platforms) and, in the case of Amazon and Kobo, acting as publishers as well as managing distribution sites and the hardware and software for reading. Alongside these big tech platforms, there are several social media publishing platforms, including Wattpad, Webtoon,[5] Radish, Inkitt, Qidian, Tapas, Swoon Reads and more. These platforms are used by both recreational and professional writers, typically encourage serialized writing, and can be part of larger entertainment companies, as in the case of Wattpad Webtoon, or traditional publishing companies, as in the case of Swoon Reads, which operates as an imprint for Macmillan's Feiwel and Friends. Finally, there are other social media platforms, such as Tumblr, that are not specifically designed for creative writing but have nonetheless developed robust writing communities, and of course, fan fiction sites. These publishing platforms have popularized ebook and audiobook formats,[6] increasingly prioritize forms of authorship and reading that are social and connective,[7] and, importantly, circumvent the editorial gatekeeping of traditional publishing.

The changes brought about by digital technologies and platforms have sparked several debates among book historians, literary and publishing scholars, critics and journalists, and industry professionals. Public debates tended towards a steadfast defensiveness of the virtues of print over electronic forms, which often went hand-in-hand with angst-ridden proclamations about the imminent "death of the book." These were sometimes met with more optimistic ideas around the accessibility afforded by digital technologies that many hoped would yield a more democratized book culture.

Scholarly inquiries in publishing studies and book history have been more concerned with the impacts of digitalization on how books are produced, distributed, and consumed. The book chain of production and reception has been most influentially described by Robert Darnton in his field-defining communications circuit model, which tracks the movement of books as they move through the hands of the author, publisher, printers, shippers, booksellers (and other associated workers), and readers.[8] Several scholars have considered how digital technologies have altered this process, including Padmini Ray Murray and Claire Squires, who update the original model with modifications for digital publishing, self-publishing, contemporary changes to print publishing, and further development of the reader's role; and Karl Berglund and Sara Tanderup Linkis, who map an audiobook streaming circuit by placing platform companies at the center.[9] Both of these updates, among the numerous others proposed in the last few decades, show the "seismic shifts from print and paper to digital ink and screen," which "have resulted in new business models that challenge the prevailing hierarchies of cultural gatekeeping."[10] These shifts involve the reconfiguration, and in some cases redundancy, of several professional roles in the industry. For instance, the rise of self-publishing through digital technologies and platforms has enabled authors to publish their work without needing to be represented by an agent or having a commissioning editor believe in the literary value or marketability of their work. Instead, these authors form business relationships directly with retailers and distributors such as Amazon, Barnes & Noble, and Kobo.

Taken together, we can see how the openness of publishing platforms, which allow anyone to publish almost anything they want, have held implicit promises for many to herald in a democratization of cultural production. The arrival of Big Tech into publishing has not removed these existing barriers, but rather introduced new ones. This book investigates the contours of how platforms can act as gatekeepers, creating barriers to entry and equitable participation for historically marginalized authors through their technological, economic, social, and cultural structures.

The Platformization of Publishing and the Entertainment Ecosystem

This book is concerned with publishing platforms, which I delineate from other platforms used for creative and cultural production based on the constitutive components of both *publishing* (as a specific kind of cultural production with its own developed industry and logics, of concern to publishing studies and contemporary book history) and *platforms* (specific computational infrastructure as defined by platform studies).

In *Platforms and Cultural Production*, Thomas Poell, David Nieborg, and Brooke Erin Duffy define platforms as "data infrastructures that facilitate, aggregate, monetize, and govern interactions between end-users and content and service providers."[11] Platforms, they argue, are distinct from digital websites and applications that may use sophisticated algorithms to curate content but are not economically or infrastructurally accessible to third parties. The introduction of publishing platforms then allowed authors to publish and make money from their work independent from traditional institutions. Fan fiction sites, for example, allow user-generated content and undoubtedly exist within the broader sphere of digital writing and publishing but do not enable creators to directly earn money for their work and thus fall outside the definition of publishing platforms. This multidisciplinary conceptualization of platforms integrates perspectives from business studies, critical political economy, and software studies. In doing so, it highlights the industrial, sociopolitical, and computational aspects of platforms and makes space to consider the different functions of platforms as intermediaries, infrastructures, and data aggregators.

Publishing platforms are intermediaries that connect different constituents of book culture (authors, publishers, readers and so on) and allow them to interact. This is achieved through their programmability, which allows other companies, creators, and cultural intermediaries to build on their own products and services through APIs (application programming interfaces), or directly on the platform through user-generated content. Amazon, for instance, runs multiple platforms upon which third parties can produce and sell their books, including Kindle Direct Publishing (KDP), Audible and Audiobook Creator Exchange (ACX), and Kindle Unlimited (KU). In this way, publishing platforms operate as architecture or computing systems—layers of hardware and software. This architecture shapes the creative work that is done on it.[12] We can see this in the example of Shirazi, who used Wattpad to write upwards of 952 chapters for one book, encouraged by an infrastructure that affords serialized and social publishing. The economic and infrastructural accessibility afforded by platforms is an important feature of how they function and have achieved their dominance in the internet landscape, as companies that trade in the extraction and processing of data.

A second feature of publishing platforms is their primary business model based around the collection and exploitation of user data. Amazon collects huge amounts of data about user behavior to create predictive models and algorithms to present more relevant products, services and content to its users. Wattpad similarly commercializes on user data in several ways, including to inform acquisition decisions for their publishing and studios programs, selling trend data to third parties, and advertising. The more different constituents (users) interact, the more the platform benefits from network effects as an "increase in users, advertisers and creators makes platforms more valuable to each of the other groups, which in turn inflates the number of users, advertisers, and creators."[13] As I'll discuss in this book, although data may fold into the various business activities of publishing platforms in different ways, the breadth and detail of the data that publishing platforms collect informs the design of their products and services and has been key to their impact on the publishing field.

The imaginary of platforms as intermediaries, as simple connectors of different users, has been widely adopted by platform companies in their self-characterizations due to its tendency to render platform networks as relatively static entities that somehow escape dynamics of power. Tarleton Gillespie's popular notion of the "politics of 'platforms'" provides an important augmentation to these more technical and economic approaches. Exploring the different connotations of the term "platform"—computational, political, figurative and architectural—Gillespie positions digital platforms not just as infrastructural or economic entities but ideological ones too.[14]

The obfuscation of platforms' extractive, structuring, and enclosing nature in favor of the image of a neutral and open foundation has been operationalized by platform and publishing companies that seek to define themselves in contradistinction to one another. As Aarthi Vadde points out, the term "publisher" is often used as a definitional foil for "platform."[15] Rhetorically and practically, publishers take creative and legal responsibility for the work they put into circulation while platforms attempt to evade liability by identifying as intermediaries for information. This distinction tends to work to the advantage of platforms: "The proliferation of *platform* as an all-purpose alternative to *publisher* speaks to the term's utility for companies eluding regulation by claiming neutrality instead of selectivity."[16]

But of course, platforms are not just intermediaries for information; they structure content and users in multiple, often inequitable, ways through infrastructural and governance frameworks, their ability to set market conditions, and algorithmic sorting of content and users. Publishing platforms further complicate this rhetorical binarism, as we'll see in more detail throughout this book, as many operate as producers of creative works in addition to intermediaries and infrastructures for the creation and distribution of creative content. They are also intricately embedded within the contemporary publishing industry. The epithet *publishing* in publishing platform speaks to the influencing force of the traditional publishing industry on publishing platforms.

The interactions between traditional institutions, creative producers (authors, publishers and readers), and platforms reflect a broader process of platformization of the cultural industries. Anne Helmond first introduced the term "platformization" to describe the rise of platforms as the dominant infrastructural and economic mode of the social web.[17] Focusing on the impacts on the cultural industries, Poell, Nieborg, and Duffy define the platformization of cultural production as "the penetration of digital platforms' economic, infrastructural, and governmental extensions into the cultural industries, as well as the organization of cultural practices of labor, creativity, and democracy around these platforms."[18] As a cognate sector of the cultural industries, we can see these processes playing out in book publishing. Processes of platformization are "shaped by the interactions between particular platforms and specific cultural producers"[19] and thus unfold differently across the cultural industries. It is also shaped by specific industry logics. While the platformization of publishing may share similarities with other sectors of the cultural industries, platformed publishing responds to and is shaped by logics of the global book industry.

Platformization is not only constitutive of shifts on the platform level, nor does platformization transform cultural industries in siloes. Publishing platforms exist in a broader *entertainment ecosystem*, comprising other cultural and entertainment websites, apps, and platforms (e.g., Netflix, YouTube, TikTok); legacy institutions in the cultural and entertainment industries (e.g., Simon & Schuster, Penguin Random House, the Frankfurt Book Fair); as well as individual producers, intermediaries, and consumers. The entertainment ecosystem framework presented in this book builds on José van Dijck's conceptualization of the social media ecosystem, which presents social media platforms as operating in two configurations: as individual microsystems shaped by a range of constitutive components, and part of a broader connective ecosystem, in which platforms interact with each other in distinctive and formative ways.[20] Van Dijck's connective ecosystem provides a model to disassemble platforms to examine the technological, cultural, economic, and social components that shape activity on them, and then reassemble them to explore their position in and impacts on culture and sociality. Exploring the ecosystem in which publishing platforms are embedded reveals a network that is geared towards cultural activity and industry, and processes of platformization that are transforming the broader landscape of the media and cultural industries, including relationships between increasingly interconnected sectors.

With this ecological approach in mind, this research quite intentionally positions books as and alongside other media. This is not a new idea; several researchers have highlighted the ontological and material compatibilities and continuities between books and other media formats despite the disciplinary divide within the academy.[21] From an industry standpoint, we see how these intermedia relationships play out through adaptations of books into films or television series, novelizations, and extended universes—processes that increasingly involve platforms, as providers of infrastructure as well as brokers, developers, and acquirers of creative intellectual property. Several platform companies have attempted to corral the economic and cultural rewards of this ecosystem through processes of vertical and horizontal integration in a relentless drive towards capture and profit.

The influencing role of the global publishing industry in how the platformization of publishing and this part of the entertainment ecosystem are unfolding requires a closer integration of publishing and platform studies. How we categorize books or what we pay for them may be transmuted by publishing platforms, but these things exist relationally to established systems in the traditional publishing industry, including those that perpetuate the marginalization and inequality of certain authors, books, and readers. Activity on and by publishing platforms is only made legible then through a conceptual focus that combines platform and publishing industry studies and informed by similarly deep engagement with a wide range of issues and debates central to media studies, creative industry studies, cultural studies, and library and information studies. These include the dynamics of participatory cultures, conditions of creative labor, the effects of algorithms and automated decision-making, new forms of media globalization, and, intricately connected to these, systems of marginalization and inclusion.

Inequality in the Tech and Publishing Industries

In early June 2020, during the global Black Lives Matter protests that erupted in the wake of the murder of George Floyd and Breonna Taylor, fueled by the historic killings of Black people by police and systemic and generational racism experienced by Bla(c)k people the world over, several companies posted their support for the movement and stance against racial inequality and discrimination. On June 1, 2020, @Amazon tweeted: "The inequitable and brutal treatment of Black people in our country must stop. Together we stand in solidarity with the Black community—our employees, customers, and partners—in the fight against systemic racism and injustice."[22]

Reflecting the modish aesthetic of Black Lives Matter social media posts from commercial entities at the time, the tweet featured an image with this statement in white type on a black background. The following day, @HarlequinBooks, along with other book publishers, posted a similarly styled graphic on their Instagram account: "We stand with our Black authors, readers and colleagues. We see you and hear you. Black stories matter. Black lives matter."[23] These performative posts stood in stark contrast to the systemic exclusion and marginalization of people based on their race, ethnicity, gender, sexuality, ability, religion, and class in which these companies and their respective industries participate.

Many of the replies and quote-tweets to the post by Amazon pointed out the company's hypocrisy in relation to its business practices. To call Amazon inequitable feels redundant at this point. Inequality is baked into every facet of Amazon's operations, from its headquarters to its warehouses and platform, and has been reported on in several media and news reports. According to recent company data, 28 percent of its US workforce and 5.5 percent of its senior leadership are Black, compared to 30.2 percent of all its US workforce and 66.4 percent of senior leadership who are White.[24] In mid-2020 when then-CEO Jeff Bezos distributed a memo urging employees to cancel meetings on June 19 to reflect on and celebrate Juneteenth, the national US holiday marking the end of slavery, some pointed out that many of Amazon's Black employees work on casual contracts in fulfillment operations and could not discontinue work without risking their jobs or income.[25] Warehouse employees are staggeringly underpaid, overworked, and more often than not under surveillance.[26] The company has constantly attempted to quash unionization, and sold racist surveillance software to US police departments until June 2020 when it announced a moratorium in the wake of Floyd's murder.[27] The techno-chauvinism and discriminatory practices of Amazon are reflective of the tech industry more broadly.

Many audits of tech companies and platforms highlight how they encode and perpetuate race, gender, sexuality, and ability biases. These are important rebuttals against the idealistic discourse that dominated early internet studies, which framed the web as an inherently participatory space, untethered to discriminatory social inequalities that pervaded the "real world." The idea that computing technologies and digital networks would give rise to an utopic, democratic space stemmed from the counterculture movements of the 1960s and 1970s in which early networks were developed, as the idealism of American hippie culture, physical communes and, of course, university campuses were transmuted to the uncharted areas of cyberspace.[28] The internet, it was thought, represented a blank canvas where people were free to be whoever they wanted, live however they wanted, and say whatever they wanted.[29] Despite the growing strength of the civil rights movement around the same time, little attention was being paid to who was being included and excluded in these information societies.

The marginalization and exclusion of predominantly non-White, non-male groups continued through the late twentieth century through to the development of the contemporary platform era. In *Programmed Inequality*, for example, Mar Hicks shows how Britain lost the early dominance in computing after World War II by systematically discriminating against the women who were most qualified in the field. The development of Web 2.0, which enabled real-time, two-way communication, revitalized the utopian ideals of the early internet based on narrow conceptualizations of user groups. Henry Jenkins' theorization of the convergence culture propelled by participatory media forms focused on "predominantly White, male, middle class, and college educated" US users that he defined as the "early adopters" of the modern internet.[30] While dominant discussions of early internet use by politically minoritized groups tended to be enmeshed in deficit discourses such as the digital divide, Black techno-culture has a long and rich history. Charlton D. McIlwain's *Black Software* provides a nuanced history of the use of personal computing networks and the modern internet by Black Americans.[31] He shows how these networks have been used to further Black Americans' own personal, communal, and political interests, as well as the way computing technology has been built and developed to keep Black people disproportionately disadvantaged in society. This historical and continued erasure of women, BIPOC, gender-diverse, and queer people in the tech sector has resulted in systems that further marginalize these groups online.

Critical media and political economist approaches in platform studies emphasize the relational power dynamics between platforms and platform-dependent cultural producers. This power is felt asymmetrically across user groups, as evidenced by a growing body of research and journalistic reports that show how platforms perpetuate racial, gender, and economic inequality through their socioeconomic and techno-cultural structures.[32] Safiya Umoja Noble, for example, explores how Google reinforces racism through the social, technological, and commercial imperatives that drive its search engine results. Top search results from Google are not the outcome of an egalitarian algorithm based on citational metrics as reported by founders Larry Page and Sergey Brin[33] but rather "organized to the benefit of the powerful elites, including corporations that can afford to purchase and redirect searches to their own sites."[34] At the same time, historically marginalized groups negotiate platform power by using digital networks for their own purposes; for joy, for self-expression, and for political, connective action.[35] Power, then, does not equal sheer dominance, but rather operates "as mutual, albeit highly unequal relations of dependency."[36] This dynamic is pervasive in other sectors of social and cultural life.

Like tech, the book publishing industry is marked by cultural inequality. According to Lee and Low, 76 percent of US publishing professionals are White, 75 percent identify as cis women, 81 percent as straight, and 89 percent are non-disabled.[37] The disparity between race and gender becomes starker at the highest and lowest levels; 40 percent of US publishing executives are men, and only 51 percent of publishing interns are White. These statistics are mirrored in the UK and Australia contexts, which share North America's systemic diversity deficit.[38] Publishing's pipeline issue is clear here; the industry clearly fails at retaining and promoting people who are racially and ethnically diverse, queer, and women. As Laura B. McGrath argues, the publishing industry is discriminatory by design and an active participant in the process of racial formation and construction of othering.[39]

The overwhelming Whiteness of the industry undoubtedly impacts what it produces.[40] Literary production, reception, and consecration is intricately interwoven with gender and racial politics and book publishing industry remains, as Melanie Ramdarshan Bold writes, "characterised by a liberal, progressive, Whiteness that while not always explicitly racist is often coloured by implicit racism, unconscious biases, and micro-aggressions."[41] Publishing scholar Alexandra Dane argues that Anglophone publishing operates according to a White taste logic that is operationalized and reinforced through explicit and implicit editorial bias and capitalist imperatives that drive publishing practice.[42] Examining fiction published in the US in the postwar period, literary historian Richard Jean So argues that the literary field was defined by a "*red line* that separates White and non-White authors, depriving the latter of the resources and opportunities of publishing, reception, and recognition," a phenomenon he terms cultural redlining.[43]

The scale of the global publishing industry, which publishes millions of books each year, can render this systemic racial discrimination opaque by making patterns difficult to see and thus affording its continuation. But it nevertheless pokes through.

Across the Anglophone publishing industry, works by historically marginalized authors are pigeonholed as "diverse literature" or "books about race." They are often relegated to bottom shelves in bookstores and are systematically excluded from systems of consecration, such as literary prize lists, reviews, and festivals.[44] In romance fiction, the primary genre in which the platform-dependent authors featured in this book work, there is a long and explicit tradition of relegating books by and about Black women into separate lines, imprints and categories. The narrow sense publishers have of their audience, conceptualizing their core reader to be a White, middle-class woman, impacts the number of books by and about histori-cally marginalized people that are published as well as the relatively little compensation awarded to these authors through advances.[45] Any change is often heralded by individuals, whose efforts prove unsustainable against institutional norms. As an example, So highlights Toni Morrison's tenure as a commissioning editor at Random House in the 1970–1980s, during which the number of published Black authors increased. As soon as she leaves Random House in 1983, it "nearly instantly regresses to its pre-1970s mean."[46]

The structures that perpetuate exclusion in publishing have been most reliably identified by the authors, workers, and readers they most impact; those marginalized based on their race, ethnicity, sexuality, gender identity, religion, and ability. To unpack the power structures embedded within platform and industry environments, which have long been elided through dominant White, patriarchal narratives, it is essential to center the expe-riences, knowledges, and standpoints of those traditionally marginalized within these spaces. In technology and platform studies, Catherine Knight Steele, Ruha Benjamin, André Brock Jr., Meredith Broussard, and oth-ers argue that we can better understand and expose the many forms of discrimination embedded in and enabled by technology by deliberately inverting the techno status quo. As Knight Steele argues, the relationship with technology forged by Black women "provides the most generative means of studying the possibilities and constraints of our ever-changing digital world" and a way to rebuke the "assumption that whiteness is the standard within technology."[47]

To take this project of exposing hegemonic power within platform and publishing systems further, it is necessary to look beyond the United States. To date, explorations into systematic discrimination in tech and publishing have been most prominently explored and framed within the sociopolitical context of North America. This is understandable given the US is home to one of the most dominant tech industries and the largest, most prolific publishing territory in the world. However, an important component of debates in contemporary publishing studies is the power relations that shape a globalized industry, including an emerging regime of inequality where minor languages, markets, and literatures are rendered peripheral.[48] In tech, likewise, we cannot ignore the techno-colonialist logics that have underpinned the development of the internet and digital technologies. Centering marginalized perspectives situated within the US thus falls short of understanding the diasporic nature of Blackness or experiences of other minoritized groups globally.[49]

While this book focuses on the experiences of BIPOC and queer authors in North America due to the global dominance of the US technology and publishing industries, it also contributes to the much-needed and growing body of scholarship that decenters the West in platform and publishing studies.[50] It does so by also exploring the experiences of Filipino authors, who work in a media landscape that has been fundamentally restructured by digital publishing platforms.

Researching Publishing Platforms

Due to the heavily guarded nature of platforms' inner workings as proprietary knowledge, platforms introduce several methodological challenges as many of the technical and organizational systems that give them shape are inaccessible to researchers or hidden behind proprietary walls or "black boxes." The fast pace of technological development and near-constant change to their algorithms, interfaces and content renders them even more difficult to study. The "rapid pace of contemporary popular fiction production" likewise means that studies of popular fiction tend best to capture a particular moment in time.[51] Responding to the challenges of access and rapidity of change, I focus on author's experiences publishing on platforms using a multi-method case study and case profile approach. In doing so, I acknowledge that this research offers a particular point of view from a particular moment of time but one that highlights the importance of relationality of platformed publishing.

Amazon and Wattpad were chosen as case studies because they are prominent examples of two different kinds of publishing platforms. Amazon launched as an online bookstore in 1994 and has since expanded its operations into nearly all spheres of life (web services, food and groceries, insurance, pharmaceuticals, home security and smart devices, the list goes scarily on, at least in the US). In the book sector, it launched its self-publishing platform Kindle Direct Publishing and Kindle ereader device in 2007, purchased Audible in 2008 and launched its Audiobook Creation Exchange platform in 2011. It acquired Goodreads in 2013 (which it merged with Shelfari, another reader review platform it acquired in 2008). The company has been publishing books under its own imprints since 2009. In 2015, Amazon opened its first physical bookstore and built twenty-four across the US before they were shuttered in 2022. Amazon is, by nearly any measure, the largest, most profitable, and most powerful publishing platform in the world. To many, it represents a threat to book culture, but it is also a synecdoche of the publishing industry, with a stake in nearly all aspects of book culture, from production, distribution, reading, and reception.

Wattpad represents a different kind of publishing platform. It launched in 2006 as a social media reading and writing platform and has since developed into a global multi-platform entertainment company, advertising around 85 million monthly users. While authors and readers can write and read for free on the platform, Wattpad has capitalized on the serial storytelling native to the platform through a pan-entertainment business model. The company commercializes the intellectual property posted to the site and user engagement data by on-selling trend data or brokering acquisition deals with other publishers and production companies, republishing or adapting content through Wattpad Books (its own publishing imprint) or Wattpad Studios (its production company), arranging brand partnerships for native advertising, and through its Paid Stories programs where readers "unlock" stories with "coins." In 2021, Naver Corporation acquired Wattpad and its publishing and production enterprises were merged with Webtoon, one of the world's largest webcomics platforms. Taken together, they illustrate some of the various strategies, practices and transformations occurring in the sphere of platformed publishing.

Animating these are fourteen case profiles or "shorter cameos"[52] of BIPOC authors, some of whom identify as queer, who use Amazon or

Wattpad as a primary platform in their publishing practice, and who publish romance fiction.[53] Exploring these case study platforms through case
profiles helps to illustrate how these platforms are given form and made
meaningful through the practices of non-hegemonic users and communities.
The methods employed to investigate these case studies and profiles include
in-depth, semi-structured interviews; platform walkthroughs; metadata
analysis; and discourse analysis of terms of service and gray literature (e.g.,
industry blogs and news).[54] While the interview method can be limiting in
some research, providing partial, invested reports, the subjective accounts
of authors' experiences is precisely the point of this research. In using these
methods, I acknowledge the strengths of qualitative research and interviews
in particular in emphasizing individuals' experiences within particular contexts, an approach that draws on an epistemology of standpoint feminism
and its acknowledgement of the impact of social position impacts on how
we know and interpret the world.[55] The perceptions, experiences, interpretations, and interactions of the case profile authors described throughout
this book illuminate how the technological, economic, and cultural structures of publishing platforms facilitate or marginalize their participation
in contemporary book culture.

Finally, romance is a useful genre to examine and unpack systems of
marginalization and exclusion on platforms for a couple of reasons. First,
romance authors, publishers, and readers have been highly active in the
uptake of digital technologies and platform publishing. Some of the first
web forums centered around discussing romance fiction and sharing title
recommendations, and the uptake of ebooks and publishing platforms was
largely carried by genre fiction, primarily writers and readers of romance.
Now, romance and Young Adult fiction dominate sites of bookish production
and reception, from book lists and reaction videos on TikTok, to fanfiction
on AO3 and reviews on Instagram and Goodreads. Secondly, romance
fiction is a highly politicized genre. It has historically been denigrated for
giving primacy to patriarchal ideas of sex, love, femininity, and family, and
has been complicit in elevating White voices and representations at the sake
of diversity and inclusion.

A key example of the racial discrimination that pervades the romance
fiction genre world occurred during the research for this book. In December
2019, about six months after I interviewed her for this research, Courtney
Milan, an Asian American author of contemporary and historical romance
fiction, was censured and had her membership suspended by the Romance

Writers of America (RWA) after two authors made complaints against her to the ethics board.[56] The complaints were in response to tweets Milan wrote regarding racist stereotypes in a novel and how a former buyer for Borders bookstores, who was now an editor at a publishing company, had discriminated against books by authors of color. The board's decision to suspend Milan's membership for a year and ban her from holding leadership on any RWA committees caused outrage within the romance genre community and, eventually, betrayed more insidious discrimination as evidence emerged showing that the complaints against Milan were based on false and exaggerated information. Indeed, her tweets came after around two weeks of others engaging in similar discussions centered around the Borders book buyer.

Several authors withdrew their titles from the 2020 RWA's RITA Awards in protest and even more announced they would not renew their memberships. In January, after the president of the board and executive director resigned due to the fallout of the actions against Milan, the remaining board members announced they were canceling the 2020 RITA Awards, citing the lack of trust amongst the romance community for the organization to administer the contest fairly and inability to reflect the breadth of titles published the previous year resulting from the many withdrawn titles. By late 2020, RWA rebranded the 2021 RITA awards to the Vivian Awards after Vivian L. Stephens, a pioneer Black romance publisher and one of the organization's founders. Among the inaugural Vivian Award winners was a historical romance title that included a scene in which the hero murders Native Americans as part of the Wounded Knee Massacre of 1890 and was accused of glamorizing genocide. The scene was emblematic of the kinds of racist representations that Milan was censured for calling out in the first place, and the awarding of this title—which was later rescinded after more intense backlash—highlighted the shallow diversity of the award's name by the organization.

This series of connected controversies is indicative of systemic racism, homophobia, and other discriminatory practices embedded within the romance community and industry, and reflects a broader failure in the genre to foster inclusive spaces for marginalized authors, readers and workers. It is precisely because of these actions and representations that the romance fiction genre provides a heuristic starting point for investigating marginalization in the context of publishing platforms and the opportunity they present for change. As bell hooks argues in *Talking Back: Thinking Feminist, Thinking Black*, "we need to concentrate on the politicization of love, not just in the context of talking about victimization in intimate relationships, but in a critical discussion of where love can be understood as a powerful force that challenges and resists domination."[57] Platforms offer authors power to circumvent these traditional publishing institutions and the systemic marginalization and discrimination they perpetuate. But they also introduce new relations of power that are yet to be examined in detail.

The Structure of this Book

This book is concerned with relational and changing dynamics of power in the platformization of publishing. Platforms have incredible power in the current internet landscape: to create new avenues for creative expression, to steer users and content, to shape cultural production and civil participation, to perpetuate harm and bias. But despite their attempts at control, we can see another persistent kind of power enacted by authors who have been historically excluded and marginalized within the traditional publishing industry who build creatively and economically successful careers and communities on publishing platforms and resist unqualified domination.

Platforms and digital technologies often carry with them implicit promises that they herald in a democratization of cultural production and expression. These promises can be traced back to the mid-twentieth century and the development of pre-Web networks and their revival with Web 2.0 and social media in the early twenty-first century. The cultural practices and technical features throughout this history work to create a lore around the potential of the internet, a myth that has permeated the writing and publishing sector. Chapter 1, "The Platformization of Publishing," explores the history of digital publishing and the changing processes and logics that have resulted from publishing platforms becoming increasingly central to twenty-first century book publishing. It offers renewed consideration on how we define self-publishing in the platform era and proposes a conceptual model for the study of publishing platforms that examines their internal techno-cultural and socioeconomic structures and positions them as a component part of the contemporary publishing, media and entertainment complex. The subsequent chapters explore the platform systems of and authors' experiences on Amazon and Wattpad in finer detail, starting with the more micro and zooming out to the more macro systems that shape participation by historically marginalized authors.

Taking the new opportunities presented by publishing platforms as its starting point, chapter 2 begins to explore how platforms mediate the creation and sale of books through their infrastructures. This chapter pays particular attention to platforms' remuneration structures across the available publishing formats—from print to ebooks, audio, and serialized fiction—and argues that the business of platformed self-publishing is forcibly aligned with platform capitalist imperatives, despite opportunities presented by publishing platforms as new and more accessible entry points to publishing. While both Amazon and Wattpad present great potential for historically marginalized authors to build careers outside of traditional institutions, authors' participation is stratified across user groups and constrained by particular platform affordances and practices.

Chapter 3, "Sorting Books and Authors," focuses in on platformed classification and governance structures as two intertwined systems of visibility on publishing platforms and argues that acts of naming through these systems can perpetuate the marginalization (or invisibilization) experienced by authors of color and queer authors. Amazon and Wattpad both undermine authors' creative agency in different ways through their classification and visibility systems. This chapter further explores the visibility and circulation of books through related systems of content moderation, to which classifications and other book metadata are subject. Romance fiction occupies a particularly fraught position in relation to platformed governance as ways of denoting and describing the genre are often caught up in a broader deplatformization of sex online, which unfairly targets people (particularly women) of color and LGBTQ+ people.

Chapter 4, "From Platform to Print," takes a meso-level look at the platformization of publishing, delving into the operations of Wattpad's publishing imprint, Wattpad Webtoon Book Group (formerly Wattpad Books), and mapping the pipeline of commercial programs that underpin its acquisitions. It examines the rise of platform publishers and theorizes how this new model of book publishing integrates logics from conglomerate and platform capitalism and reflects the increasing industrialization of creativity on platforms. The data-driven approach used by platform publishers tends to replicate systems of marginalization for authors of color and queer authors as popularity data becomes a discursive strategy to justify inequitable practices around inadequate promotion, disproportionate compensation, and exclusion while simultaneously minimizing the company's responsibility to its authors.

Building on from the previous chapter, which begins to show how creative works and platform-dependent authors move off publishing platforms through republishing and adaptation deals, chapter 5, "The Entertainment Ecosystem," zooms out further to explore how publishing platforms are positioned alongside other creative, cultural, and entertainment media sectors in the global entertainment ecosystem. The links between publishing platforms and other cultural sectors and organizations are forged by both platform companies and individual cultural producers. This chapter maps Amazon and Wattpad's respective attempts to build multinational, multiplatform media organizations, focusing particular attention on Wattpad's impact in the Philippines as a synecdoche of its global pan-entertainment business model. It also focuses on the practices and efforts of individual authors, who develop their own connective and creative networks across the entertainment ecosystem. Exploring the formation of the entertainment ecosystem from these two directions shows just how central books have become in the twenty-first century entertainment complex.

Through these chapters, this book demonstrates the interlocking and embedded systems that enable or constrain BIPOC authors and queer authors in the context of publishing platforms and the broader entertainment ecosystem. The growing dominance of platforms in the contemporary publishing, cultural and media entertainment industries compounds the power they wield and ability to set the "rules of the game." But authors also gain power through the platformization of publishing and negotiate the heavy influence of platform imperatives to build careers that transverse digital and traditional spaces, and the publishing and media industries. At the heart of this book on publishing platforms, then, is a fidelity to the stories of the authors who use them.

CHAPTER 1

Digital Promise and the Platformization of Publishing

IN 1969, STUDENTS AT UCLA attempted to send the first ever message on ARPANET, one of the precursor networks to the internet. Computer programming student Charley Kline sat in front of an SDS Sigma 7 Host computer and attempted to send a simple command—LOGIN—to a computer at the Stanford Research Institute, some four hundred miles north. The system crashed after the first two letters (L and O), but this message made written text the original content of the internet.[1] Many new networks, computers and users later, there is an inconceivable amount of text online. It is perhaps surprising then, given the prominence of written text online over the early networks through to the early internet and platform era we are now in, that the publishing industry has historically had somewhat of a complicated relationship with digital media, the internet, and platforms.

That is not to say that the world of books and publishing have been averse to digital innovation. Throughout the late twentieth century, many authors and publishers adopted various digital technologies that made writing and publishing more efficient, from electric typewriters to word processors. Romance writers and readers have been among the first to experiment with these new communication technologies, and this culture of early adoption has continued in the early twenty-first century.[2] Romance fiction was a significant contributor to the explosion of self-published novels and ebooks following the launch of Amazon's Kindle ereader in 2007. In the Australian market—a significantly smaller market compared to the US and UK—self-published romance fiction titles increased by 1,000 percent between 2010–2011 and 2015–2016, compared to 290 percent in fantasy and 230 percent in crime fiction, as ebooks, ereaders, and self-publishing platforms became more quotidian.[3] The penetration of digital technologies into the book world over the late twentieth and early twenty-first centuries roused several predictions over the future of the book. The ensuing debate centered on whether these digital technologies would bring about a revolution to the way we write, publish, and read books, or would result in their regrettable demise.

The idea that independent publishing would herald in a democratization of cultural production is intricately connected to promises embedded in the early internet that it might bring about a digital utopia. Pre-Web networks were developed and connected through logics of technological openness and innovation for innovation's sake, and this ideology imbued itself into the public imaginary of the internet. When the World Wide Web was launched in the early 1990s, the internet was seen to offer users a collaborative and digital utopia modeled on the collectivist ideals of the hippie communes, post-war campus culture, and hacker networks. As Michael Bhaskar puts it, the internet was seen to "herald an opening and levelling where great visionaries would craft new democratic and libertarian social and aesthetic forms."[4] With the development of peer-to-peer networking sites and social media platforms over the early 2000s, the idea that internet technologies would fundamentally change the established power dynamics between legacy institutions in favor of individuals and virtual communities only grew stronger.

This chapter traces the promise of openness at the heart of digital publishing to the origins of the internet and explores how discourses of the early internet were reflected in ideas about the future of the book and publishing industry. In the book world, the internet has certainly opened new avenues for writing, publishing, and reading and made these activities more accessible to a larger number of people. These notions of openness and democratization are enthusiastically promoted by platforms today as they attempt to maintain public imaginaries that they afford individual freedom and equitable participation and elide the realities of their mediation. The platformization of the internet over the past few decades has highlighted the unrealized democratic potential of the internet and instead led to an increased centralization and concentration of power, primarily situated in the hands of big tech companies such as Amazon, Apple, and Google in the West; and Tencent, Alibaba, and Naver in Asia.

The second half of this chapter explores the impacts of these digital promises on publishing and proposes a conceptual framework for researching platformed publishing. In particular, it examines how processes of

platformization have altered what it means to publish a book in the contemporary landscape and offers an updated definition of self-publishing as
platformed publishing. Platforms have not only changed publishing as a
practice but restructured relationships within and between publishing and
other media sectors. Responding to these intra- and inter-industry shifts, the
final section introduces the framework of the entertainment ecosystem in
more detail. This model connects platform studies, publishing studies, and
media ecology to analyze the microsystems of publishing platforms, their
position in the broader ecology of cultural production, and the systems of
exclusion and marginalization that permeate both spaces.

The Promise of the Internet

In the mid-1990s, Richard Barbrook and Andy Cameron summarized (and
critiqued) the promise imbued in the internet and early technologies, which
were seen, however misguidedly, to "empower the individual, enhance personal freedom, and radically reduce the power of the nation-state. Existing
social, political and legal power structures will wither away to be replaced
by unfettered interactions between autonomous individuals and their software."[5] These technologically determinist ideas found their basis in the
formation of the internet, and were zealously taken up by writers, artists,
computer scientists, hackers, and capitalists alike. I do not intend to provide
a history of the internet here; indeed many others have provided detailed
and nuanced chronicles.[6] However, the creation and development of the
internet, from the building of the ARPANET in the 1960s to the explosion
of the World Wide Web in the 1990s, heavily influenced perceptions of the
contemporary internet, its content and uses.

The internet as we know it today originated with ARPANET, a computer
network set up by the US Defense Department's Advanced Research Projects
Agency (ARPA) in 1969 that was built "as a way of sharing computing time
on-line between various computer centers and research groups working for
the agency."[7] As Manuel Castells describes in *The Internet Galaxy*, ARPANET
"was envisioned, deliberately designed, and subsequently managed by a
determined group of computer scientists with a shared mission that had little
to do with military strategy. It was rooted in a scientific dream to change the
world through computer communication." Militaristic principles ensured
ARPANET was decentralized in structure and fit with redundancies, but the

developers ensured its development through standards of technological and cultural openness. This openness encouraged the patchwork and hacker-esque development of new networks and architecture, such as bulletin board systems, as well as the connection of different networks which led to the internet—the network of networks.

The values of openness and innovation among the developers of ARPANET and other early networks sprung from the university campus culture of the 1960s and 1970s in which they worked. These computer scientists, Castells argues, were "in most cases seeking technological innovation for the pure joy of discovery" and were "permeated with the values of individual free-dom, of independent thinking, and of sharing and cooperation with their peers."[8] This disposition defined how those connected to the early virtual communities participated as well: engaging in behaviors centered around personal interests, community, and an ethos of sharing. Indeed, this cul-ture of use resulted in an early intersection between the internet and book culture; according to Castells, the "most popular electronic mailing list in ARPANET was SF-Lovers for the use of science fiction fans."[9]

The culture of the internet's early development contributed to an ideology of freedom that permeates understandings and discussions of the internet today. In 1995 (and republished in 1996), Barbrook and Cameron dubbed the heterogeneous orthodoxy of the internet and emerging tech sector "the Californian Ideology," which embraced an enticing "mix of cybernetics, free market economics, and counter-culture libertarianism."[10] In their 1996 article in the journal *Science as Culture*, Barbrook and Cameron expand on the components of this ideology:

> This new faith has emerged from a bizarre fusion of the cul-tural bohemianism of San Francisco with the hi-tech indus-tries of Silicon Valley. Promoted in magazines, books, TV programmes, websites, newsgroups and Net conferences, the Californian Ideology promiscuously combines the free-wheeling spirit of the hippies and the entrepreneurial zeal of the yuppies. This amalgamation of opposites has been achieved through a profound faith in the emancipatory potential of the new information technologies. In the digital utopia, everybody will be both hip and rich.[11]

As the name suggests, the Californian Ideology is symptomatic of a deeply US set of moral judgments and values in its championing of individual freedom and economic neoliberal ideals.

The development of peer-to-peer networking and then social media in the early twenty-first century, so-called Web 2.0, gave new hope for the democratizing forces of the internet. Media theorists have long refuted the passivity ascribed to audiences, highlighting the active role they take in producing meaning and in providing feedback, but their reach always paled in comparison to the distribution power of top-down media produc-ers.[12] According to Henry Jenkins, a prominent voice in early social media scholarship, these new interactive internet-based technologies "enabled consumers to archive, annotate, appropriate, and recirculate media content in powerful new ways."[13] This individual and community activity must nec-essarily be juxtaposed against the intense concentration and centralization of power we have witnessed over the early twenty-first century, as platform companies have become central apparatuses to our economy, government, society, and culture.

Despite the strong criticisms against the so-called Californian Ideology—that the internet has only served to strengthen the concentration of power and wealth among a few corporations and (White, male) billionaires—the ideals at the heart of this ideology have an enduring kind of appeal. The belief in the promises of the internet extended far beyond the social and political realms to the worlds of art and writing as we see the promises of the early internet reflected in discourses around the future of the publishing industry, and creative and cultural industries more broadly. Specifically, that digital technologies might bring about a more equitable, participatory and democratized field of cultural production by empowering individuals and eschewing old gatekeepers.

Digital Books in the Long Twenty-First Century: Revolution or Death

The book publishing industry underwent significant transformations in the second half of the twentieth century. The paperback revolution, well underway by the 1950s, was making books more affordable for would-be readers and the industry itself was moving from the boutique model of the early twentieth century to an era of conglomeration as media companies and book publishers engaged in acquisitions and mergers. Behind the scenes and in often grassroots ways, new digital technologies were revolutionizing how books were made, produced and circulated. Projects focused on digitizing books and other literature were launched with some, like Project Gutenberg, surviving to this day.[14] From the 1980s onwards, the rise of desktop publishing software such as PageMaker, Quark Express, and Adobe InDesign made typesetting manuscripts more accessible to authors and industry professionals alike.[15] Some writers and independent publishing collectives adopted floppy disks, LazerDisks, and CD-ROMs to publish and disseminate their works. Others created hypertext literature on stand-alone, mainframe computers, with "specialized, nonlinear, and often costly authoring software such as Hypergate, Storyspace, and HyperCard."[16] These pre-Web publishing initiatives were often driven by independent producers with a high degree of tech-savviness and access to early computers and networks (usually people connected to universities). The development and mainstreaming of the Web in the 1990s led to a proliferation of digital literature and publishing, which in turn sparked constant speculation over the future of the book.

For those optimistic about the future of the book, digital technologies seemed to promise a greater degree of accessibility to the industry that would yield a democratization of what books were published and how. The idea that the internet would "empower the individual" and "enhance personal freedom"[17] by also radically reducing institutional power was taken up by some proponents of digital literature. The contradictions of this Californian Ideology were also alive and well in the book world; Amazon was at the forefront of embracing this individualist discourse, artfully replacing the individual with the customer. In a 1999 interview on ABC7 Chicago's News Views program after being named Time's Person of the Year, Jeff Bezos excitedly proclaimed that "the great thing about the internet is that the balance of power shifts to the customer."[18]

As the internet began to expand with new writers and forms of writing on forums, fan fiction sites, blogs, and LiveJournal, the promise of individual freedom seemed to be reaching fruition. Over the late 2000s and early 2010s, several success stories of born-digital writers from Andy Weir to Hugh Howey and E. L. James seemed to solidify the internet and self-publishing as a valid entry point to the publishing industry. Self-publishing went from an activity synonymous with poor quality to a space where a savvy editor might find the next global bestseller. These earlier days of internet-based writing and publishing can be described as digital collectives that, as Millicent Weber defines in her analysis of public domain audiobook production site Librivox, are often organized through grassroots communities and a volunteer-driven ethos.[19] New labor regimes emerged as self-publishing became more economically viable, a shift facilitated in large part by marketplaces like Amazon that connected self-published authors with established and widely used distribution channels.

There was also an excitement among some about the possibilities afforded by digital technologies for readers and the reading experience. For readers, mass authorship seemed to go hand-in-hand with mass authority. Reader communities first on LiveJournal and Tumblr, then YouTube, Instagram, and TikTok, have become active participants in the consumption and mediation of books. Many also predicted that digital technologies would result in making books that were more interactive, smarter, social, and personal. Some sectors of the book industry more readily experimented with these possibilities; children's publishers, for example, developed storytelling apps marketed as interactive books.[20] Not just for kids, in 2012 Push Pop Press released *Our Choice* by Al Gore, an interactive book and sequel to *An Inconvenient Truth*.[21] Although questions were raised over whether engaging with this format really counted as reading (or was it more like playing games or watching TV?), these interactive books represented the experimental promise of digital technologies and destabilization of a format that had been more or less the same since Gutenberg.

While these interactive books largely failed to really take off, the commercial success of the Amazon Kindle ereader in 2007 presented significant disruptions to the print book's dominance in the market. The digitization of books was a long time in the making: the public domain ebook repository Project Gutenberg digitized its first text in 1971, Google set up its digitization project Google Books in 2004, and the Kindle itself was modeled on the commercially unsuccessful 2004 Japanese LIBRé and 2006 Sony Reader PRS-500 ereaders. However, the Kindle benefitted from its embeddedness in Amazon's extensive service infrastructure, which offered customers the full suite of hardware, software, and ecommerce store necessary for buying and reading ebooks. In the years following its launch, ebooks experienced years of significant market growth before plateauing in the mid-2010s.[22] This growth and mainstream acceptance of ebooks was propelled in part by a growth in self-publishing facilitated by the launch of Amazon's Kindle Direct Publishing (KDP) the same year as the Kindle. Like the paperback revolution more than sixty years prior, ebooks and KDP fundamentally changed the economics of publishing, making it more straightforward and affordable for independent authors to produce and disseminate their creative works.

It was not just independent authors taking advantage of the new economic regime of digital publishing. Ellora's Cave, an independent digital publisher of erotic fiction founded by Tina Engler in 2000, experienced tremendous early success by electronically publishing texts that were not being published by mainstream publishers. Following the blueprint set by Ellora's Cave and riding the wave of ebooks' popularity, several traditional publishers developed digital-first or digital-only imprints in the early 2010s. Romance publishers were again at the forefront of this particular digital strategy; in 2012, Penguin launched Destiny Romance and Harlequin established Escape Publishing. The digital-first or digital-only strategy enabled these publishers to publish for smaller markets and titles they perceived to be riskier because they did not have to justify large print runs to maximize profit. Kate Cuthbert, the publisher who set up Escape Publishing in Australia, described how the adaptability of digital imprints combined with the economic stability of large conglomerate publishers was a boon for books that did not fit neatly into established lines, subgenres, or formats. While Cuthbert was publisher, Escape published "anything from 5,000 to 250,000 words, any genre, subgenre, cross-genre, or new genre, as long as it's romance" and, under her tenure, were "actively seeking stories that haven't been able to find a home in print: that is, riskier titles, niche titles, experimental titles."[23]

The commercial success of ebooks and ereaders following the launch of the Kindle in 2007 also gave new energy to prophecies of a different kind, namely the idea that books were going to become obsolete. This view was particularly espoused in public discussion and journalistic commentaries, with many in book-related academic fields tending to take a more moderate view that ebooks would likely coexist with print books. Despite this, predictions about the death of the book offered a productive "rhetorical starting point" for academics "to introduce their counterargument."[24] Some sub-disciplines focused on electronic writing and publishing remained interested in the nuances of what this coexistence might look like, though.

Some hypertext theorists, for instance, have argued that in addition to being easy to manipulate and circulate, digital texts could weaken the status and power of the author and run the risk of being decoupled from any authorial provenance.[25]

This discourse, which at its most extreme leans into the myth of the disappearing medium,[26] positions ebooks and print books in opposition to one another. Several researchers engaged in these oppositional debates, exploring which format offered readers a better and more effective reading experience.[27] In the broader book culture, readers who loved print books often expressed their preference by invalidating the value of ebooks, a position buttressed by Amazon's actual undervaluing of ebooks in the late 2000s and early 2010s to establish market dominance when readers could purchase them for as little as ninety-nine cents. Ebooks have often been seen as derivative from print, a by-product of producing a book that enabled publishers to go wider with distribution but were still somehow less *real* than their print counterparts. The intrinsic value placed on the materiality of print books endures even now with the discourse shifting to focus on the *look, feel*, and *smell* of print books which to many is vastly superior to digital books. What connects these ideas—revolution or death—is a firm belief that digital technologies and the internet would threaten the established order of publishing and, one way or another, forever change the book world. This change includes eroding the power of hegemonic hierarchies and gatekeepers, as digital technologies and platforms provide alternative avenues for publishing and reading.

Now, technology and platform companies are central players in the contemporary publishing industry and book culture. As Padmini Ray Murray and Claire Squires argued in 2013, the contemporary publishing industry is now "a landscape dominated by large conglomerate publishers and, increasingly, by even larger technology companies."[28] Nearly all aspects of book culture have become entangled in what Simone Murray terms the digital literary sphere.[29] Authors, publishers, and readers all participate in the production and consumption of different kinds of books, discover and buy books in online bookstores, and participate in reading and book talk on social media platforms like Instagram, TikTok, and YouTube. In terms of publishing platforms—platforms used in the creation, production and distribution of books and creative writing—both big tech (including Amazon, Apple, Tencent, and Naver) and other platforms (such as Wattpad,

Radish, and Swoon Reads) are challenging what it means to publish fiction in the digital age. It is the dual position of these digital publishing platforms, shaped by the logics of the publishing industry and platform economy, that necessitates a greater integration of publishing studies and platform studies. These fields must be conceived of together to understand how technology models are influencing publishing practice in contemporary book culture and consider reading and writing applications that do not limit themselves to forms of digital literature that closely resemble codices.

Rather than being solely a harbinger of good or bad, digital technologies and the internet have reshaped the publishing industry and book culture in messier, grayer ways. The conflicts at the heart of these early promises have become even more complex as platforms have become increasingly central to twenty-first century book publishing. What is apparent is how processes of platformization are reconfiguring established practices in the publishing industry including what it looks like to self-publish. Given the centrality of self-publishing to the authors profiled in this book, the next section provides a necessary reconceptualization of self-publishing in the platform era.

Self-Publishing in the Platform Era

Self-publishing has several, often contradictory connotations. It's for authors who couldn't manage to get a traditional publishing deal, possibly because their work isn't really any good or there's no market for it. It's a stepping stone to a traditional publishing deal, a way for authors to prove their marketability. It's freedom from the risk-averse and biased gatekeepers of traditional publishing. Or a way to retain creative control over one's work. It's just vanity publishing. It's actually independent publishing. It's all erotica and werewolves. It's all family history. Regardless of the assumption, it's hard to argue that self-publishing has grown substantially in the early twenty-first century and is now a feature of the contemporary book industry, particularly in popular fiction genres. More than thirty years since Amazon's launch and nearly two decades after the launch of its self-publishing platform, KDP, commercial self-publishing is almost entirely synonymous with platformed publishing.

Platforms have radically altered what it means to publish and self-publish in the early twenty-first century. The labor of producing a book has historically involved a relatively standardized process that connects different intermediaries that fulfill specific roles to turn a manuscript into a book. This process has most influentially been described by Robert Darnton's communication circuit, which follows a book through the different stages of its lifecycle: conception, acquisition, production, circulation, and reception.[30] This circuit describes a traditional publishing process and follows the book as it moves through the hands of the author, publisher, printers, shippers, booksellers (and other associated workers), and readers. The introduction of digital technologies over the late twentieth and early twenty-first centuries disintermediated this process, introducing new processes, roles, and hands to the circuit and short-circuiting others. Theorizing the circuit in light of processes of digitization, Padmini Ray Murray and Claire Squires argue that the introduction of new actants can work to "challenge the prevailing hierarchies of cultural gatekeeping."[31] Some of the most significant changes to the established production process have been brought through self-publishing, which bypasses traditional publishers and other intermediaries to connect the author more directly with the reader.

Self-publishing is by no means a digital phenomenon. Literary history is dotted with authors who published at least some of their works without established presses, instead using printers and vanity presses, including canonical writers such as Jane Austen, Charles Dickens, William Blake, Mark Twain, Beatrix Potter, and Irma S. Rombauer. However, the prominence of digital media in twenty-first century self-publishing has prompted many theorists to define self-publishing by its close relationship to digital technologies and distant or autonomous relationship to traditional publishing. Nick Levey, for instance, theorizes self-publishing as "post-press literature," which is "created outside of the established circles of book production," and "not only artistically significant, but also expressive of new possibilities for economic and artistic agency that arise at the intersections of the literary field and digital culture."[32] Taking a grounded theory approach, Timothy Laquintano argues that self-publishing constitutes a broad range of practices and configurations of labor but that these diverse practices share two common characteristics: first, that self-published authors produce their work without the "direct capital investment of a third party associated with the book industry," and second, that while authors many delegate tasks of book production such as editing, design, and formatting to a third party, they retain control by acting as the "general manager" of the publishing process.[33]

In defining self-publishing in distinction to the traditional book industry, these theorizations rely on an actual but nebulous understanding of what constitutes established circles of book production or parties associated with the book industry. The boundaries of what constitutes insiderness or outsiderness in literary production changes temporally and depending on genre. Self-publishing is currently very much *in* the genre world of romance and has been for some time.[34] Surely, after becoming a central apparatus in the production, distribution, circulation, and reception of books, Amazon is an associated party of the contemporary book industry whether we like it or not.

The blurriness of the distinction between traditional and non-traditional publishing is illustrated by the various activities of some traditional presses, platforms, and authors. Some traditional publishers have established their own proprietary self-publishing platforms, which they use as a virtual slush pile. These include Macmillan's Feiwel and Friends' Swoon Reads platform and HarperCollins' Authonomy platform, the latter of which was shut down in 2015 after users began to game the system through organized engagement farming. In the opposite direction, platforms like Amazon that are associated with self-publishing and the disintermediation of traditional publishing are setting up their own book imprints that follow "traditional" processes of production. Amazon launched the first of its publishing imprints more than a decade ago and, in romance fiction, its Montlake imprint has become a serious producer of romance novels. Finally, hybrid authors—who work across traditional and self-publishing—reveal how boundaries between different forms of publishing are increasingly obscured in the contemporary publishing industry.[35] These practices put into sharp relief a necessary rejection of positioning print and digital, traditional and self-publishing in a flat dichotomy.

The historical positioning of self-publishing in opposition to traditional publishing and, more specifically, free from the (bad, biased) editorial gatekeeping of traditional publishing has encouraged a conflation between self-publishing and autonomy. The reliance on digital platforms to create, distribute, and read self-published literature, however, undermines such idealistic claims of agency. As Laquintano argues, self-publishing is now "intensely mediated" as "the work of authors is distributed across digital platforms of giant corporations and small start-ups, through an emerging cottage industry of support services, and through the authors' mediated

engagement with the peer-to-peer energy of readers in participatory culture."[36] Based on his inspection of the terms of service (ToS) of Amazon
Kindle Direct Publishing, for example, Mark McGurl likewise argues that
"there may be frankly lower standards at KDP than at Knopf, but there *are*
standards, and they take their bearings from the absent presence of the
customer as reader."[37] This mediation is most acutely executed by platforms
and platform companies, which structure creation, production, and reception in explicit and implicit ways.

As the title suggests, this book is concerned with the forms of self-
publishing that are based on and around platforms. In theorizing self-
publishing in the platform era then, we must recognize how digital technologies and platforms (and the companies behind them) have not only
facilitated a massive growth in self-publishing but rendered authors who
choose to self-publish on them and their readers increasingly *dependent*
on them. Authors who self-publish commercial popular fiction, in particular, are not autonomous from big industry, but have simply replaced Big
Publishing with Big Tech (at least temporarily).

The ingress of digital technologies and platform companies into publishing continues to raise questions over what *counts* when it comes to
publishing. This uncertainty is deeply intertwined with debates around
what constitutes a book, and whether ebooks really count as real books.
Even among the early adopters of the romance genre, several camps held
steadfastly to their position that ebooks meant poor quality and that print
was vastly superior. As Christine Larson notes, "RWA would not accept
[ebooks] for consideration for the RITAs" and romance blogs and other
review publications refused to review them.[38] While ebooks most closely
resembling traditional print codices have become a more acceptable part of
the contemporary market, purist readers have a new target in audiobooks. If
the intangibility of audiobooks produced by traditional publishers is enough
to discount them to some, digital-born literature—including hypertext
fiction and electronic literature, fan fiction, and serialized writing—seems
to have no hope of ever really signifying.

This question over which formats count heavily influences ideas of what
it means to self-publish. To date, self-publishing has primarily been associated with authors who work independently from traditional publishers
to produce particular kinds of bookish objects: print books, ebooks, and,
increasingly, audiobooks. But the increasing dependency on platforms

to self-publish popular fiction requires a consideration of the publishing forms and formats enabled (or enforced) by platforms through their interfaces. What counts as self-publishing in a platform context must expand beyond codices and the ebooks that most closely resemble them to other platformed kinds of writing and publishing including serialized fiction on sites such as Wattpad, Radish, and Webtoon. Like established self-publishing authors, this form of publishing is increasingly professionally oriented and commercialized.

As an evolving space, what is most useful is a flexible definition of self-publishing that prioritizes a practice ontology rather than one that defines self-publishing by its technological conditions or relative position to traditional book culture. Laquintano's second characteristic of self-publishing that describes these kinds of authors as "general manager[s]" indicates the kind of production activities that are necessary to be considered a self-publisher (such as managing the production) and those that may be delegated to others (such as editing, design, formatting). This delineation usefully distinguishes self-publishing from vanity publishing in which authors pay a fee to delegate all production responsibility. This practice-based conceptualization builds on from Alison Baverstock and Jackie Steinitz's definition of self-publishing as a process by which authors take primary creative and economic responsibility for the production of their work.[39] This simple definition is useful in that it is broad enough to cover different kinds of self-publishing practices, including those authors who engage in self-publishing collectives or as micro-publishers, wherein a (usually small) group of authors work together under a colophon but remain economically and creatively responsible for publishing their individual works, as well as both print and digital formats. It also does not preclude self-publishers who hire professionals to perform production services and tasks such as editing, cover design, or typesetting, but does not conflate individual agency with autonomous production.

The view of self-publishing outlined here prioritizes the activities and practices of authors rather than placing a priori boundaries around the activity based on certain formats. As Michael Bhasker has argued in his theory of publishing, "publishing is not necessarily to be equated with book; if anything, it is some kind of activity, a role to be played."[40] But how do platforms allow this activity or role to be played? Historically, self-publishing has represented an important avenue for participation for many BIPOC and queer authors who have turned to this mode of publishing due to their historical marginalization and exclusion in institutional spaces. Publishing platforms certainly afford these authors more straight-forward ways to participate in the contemporary publishing industry but do so in complex and heavily mediated ways.

Self-Publishing as an Opportunity for Change

During an interview for this research, an author described an experience from her first Romance Writers America (RWA) conference. A bookstore had been set up in one of the small hotel conference rooms, with shelves brought in to display books by authors on the program and other RWA members. At the back of the room, laying flat on a table, were the books published by Black authors. This relegation of BIPOC authors is not limited to spaces of bookselling. Traditional romance publishers have historically published works by Black authors under race-specific lines and imprints and marketed them by their difference to hegemonic Whiteness, beginning with Rosalind Welles' 1980 *Entwined Destinies*, the first Black-authored mass-market romance novel: as ethnic romance, Black romance, multicultural romance. The establishment of racially focused imprints—including Kensington Arabesque (which ran from 1994–1998 when it was sold to BET Books and stopped being a race-specific imprint), Harlequin Kimani (2006–2018), and Kensington Dafina (2000–ongoing)—undoubtedly helped to demonstrate a market for non-White romance stories. However, they also limited the opportunities for BIPOC authors within and especially beyond these dedicated imprints.

Farrah Rochon, who has published her work traditionally and independently, described the race-specific romance imprints of having "one or two . . . Black romance authors, but it was really you had all these authors vying for these very few spaces."[41] Black authors, she said, "just didn't have places to publish" and so many turned to digital self-publishing. Suleikha Snyder described independent publishing as much a necessity as it was a choice:

> because, you know, women of color were not given seats at the table . . . and indie publishing and self-publishing was where we had to go. Ditto for queer authors writing queer romances. Digital publishing was where you had to start because it wasn't

until these print publishers, the big [publishers] . . . it's not until they realized they could make a profit that they were willing to take a chance.[42]

The growth in self-publishing and rise in popularity of self-published titles not only enabled historically marginalized authors to prove they were marketable as authors, but also that their books featuring people of color and queer people were marketable too.

Romance is often perceived as a genre that promotes patriarchal ideas of love, relationships, and marriage. Whether or not this is the case—and I would argue that it is definitely not *always* the case—romance fiction has historically been very heteronormative. Practically speaking, the generic convention of romance fiction needing to feature a central love story has historically meant a heterosexual love story. Courtney Milan expressed how this exclusionary practice was reinforced for her by her publisher, who pushed back against her including queer characters in her novels:

> In my initial books that I did with Harlequin I had a handful of characters, side characters who I was thinking to myself "oh this person is probably gay" but I didn't say it because . . . I was getting so much pushback from [Harlequin] . . . we had people explicitly saying, like, "don't write about x, y or z because you don't want to offend your readers." I heard that so much: "We don't want to put gay people in books because you don't want to offend your readers."[43]

Self-publishing provided Milan the freedom to explicitly include more diversity in her characters, and she met this opportunity with gusto: "as soon as I could get out it unraveled, like 'Everyone's gay now!'"[44] Perhaps one of the best examples of this is *Hold Me*, a contemporary romance novel featuring a bisexual hero and trans heroine, which was published in 2016 when there were exceedingly few bisexual male characters and even fewer trans characters in romance.[45]

The market orientation of traditional, commercial publishers reinforces rigid ideas of what readers do and do not want (even what offends them) and therefore what authors and narratives will or will not be successful. Where large, profit-driven traditional publishing houses tend to avoid anything perceived as risky, independent publishers have been able to ignore established truisms of what kinds of narratives can be successful. This results in some authors leaning into the kinds of products that are more or less avoided in traditional publishing: racially and culturally inclusive characters and narratives, queer relationships, longer series, and microgenres, for example. A good example of this is Ruby Dixon's Ice Planet Barbarians series, which consists of twenty-two books self-published between 2015 and 2021.[46] Berkley Books acquired the rights to republish the print books in 2021 after the series gained a large following on BookTok, the book reading community on TikTok, and topped multiple Amazon bestseller lists in May 2021.

Katrina Jackson pointed to the work of Theodora Taylor as another example of the way that self-publishing allows authors to invest in longer series that may not fit with preconceived ideas of marketability held by traditional publishers. Taylor's most famous romance series is 50 Loving States, which—as the name suggests—includes a title for every US state. This series, according to Jackson, consists of "stuff that you maybe couldn't get away with in traditional publishing, with characters you couldn't get away with, with storylines you couldn't get away with."[47] Typically romance series consist of titles in the same subgenre, but those in 50 Loving States transverse subgenres: "there's a time travel werewolf shifter romance . . . that becomes a dragon romance at the end of that series . . . there's a Russian romance [and] a whole thing about ruthless billionaires." These books exist in the same universe and span decades, Jackson tells me; "at this point [Taylor's] writing the grandchildren of a couple that is in a previous series. It's at that point, that series is set like 30 years in the future." Series of this length are a classically difficult sell for traditional publishers as the publication of sequential books in a series is typically contingent on the sales numbers of the books before them in the series (except maybe for brand name authors like Danielle Steel). As Jackson succinctly put it, "no one would let [Taylor] do this at Berkeley or whatever, it just wouldn't happen." But, as she said, "self-published authors are like 'who's going to stop me?'"[48]

The freedom to write to perceived gaps in the traditional book market was a theme emphasized by Wattpad authors too. Many of the authors I spoke to wrote stories that didn't always neatly fit into popular genres or subgenres or included themes that weren't prevalent in traditionally published books. For Ivey Choi, this included stories that were

> more reflective of what I wanted to see in writing, and for
> me that meant a lot more people of color, a lot more queer
> representation, a lot of stories that explore feminist [themes]
> and like the #MeToo movement. And that's kind of where I
> think my niche market now is.[49]

The market Choi was writing in proved not to be too niche on Wattpad; the popularity of some of her stories led to her being invited to the Stars Program (later rebranded to the Creators Program).

The engagement Choi experienced on her inclusive stories corroborates some of the reader statistics shared by Wattpad. For instance, Wattpad's 2020 Year in Review report declared that users spent more than 725 million minutes reading stories tagged #LGBTQ (up 58 percent on the previous year, apparently) and more than forty-five million minutes reading stories tagged #CelebrateBlackWriters. These numbers likely correlate with the sociopolitical context of 2020, which saw publishers, platforms and other entities promoting Black authors and books and anti-racist reading lists after the murder of George Floyd and subsequent global Black Lives Matter protests. However, they do track with longer trends of diversity on Wattpad such as that shown by publishing scholar Melanie Ramdarshan Bold in 2016, who found that many of the most popular authors on Wattpad at the time wrote stories that featured diverse gender identities, pansexuality, and themes of intersectional feminism.[50] In this way, Wattpad presented—and seemed to actualize—a publishing space that seemed to push back and at times subvert the narrow conceptualizations of who constitutes a reading public held by traditional publishers in North America and the West.[51]

The opportunity to break from traditional notions of the market was true in other locationally specific ways. Working in Iloilo City in the Western Visayas region of the Philippines, Sol Tuberosum saw Wattpad as a means to write fiction she couldn't see being published in her country. This includes queer characters who have been historically globally marginalized.[52] But, as explored in more depth in chapter 5, Filipino is the dominant language in the traditional publishing industry in the Philippines and for Filipino stories on Wattpad, which is not a language she has. She has Hiligaynon/Ilonggo, the regional language where she lives, or English but the former is not widely used on Wattpad, so in the interest of developing a larger readership, Tuberosum writes in English. Here we see the complex overlay of platform and traditional publishing markets which writers must negotiate, as well as subtle but important shifts in how markets are conceptualized on different publishing platforms, depending on whether their primary business model relies on a product or attention economy.

There is also an evolving interplay between platform and traditional publishing markets in the way they inform one another. This is perhaps most evident in the way traditional publishers have become more attentive to the popular authors and books in independent publishing spaces, at times working to capture the associated economic success for themselves. As self-publishing became an economic powerhouse in the early 2010s, publishers and acquisitions editors started looking to platform bestseller lists for new authors to sign. As Farrah Rochon described:

> towards the end of [my traditional contract], right when I was, I'd have to say two books left, I found out that the assistant editor, she would find her new authors by every morning, going on Amazon and seeing which self-published authors were doing really well and contacting them, so it switched from authors submitting to publishers to the publishers . . . going to them, [which was] a complete one-eighty.[53]

Self-publishing became a way to build an existing audience and prove marketability, which could lead to a traditional publishing deal. Simone Shirazi, for example, who began writing and publishing on Wattpad in her teens had one novel published by Radish (one of Wattpad's competitors) and published her debut print novel with Berkley in 2024. This pathway is not uncommon: several authors I spoke to referenced Alyssa Cole, Alisha Rai, and Rebekah Weatherspoon, who all began their careers self-publishing and are now traditionally published, with Rai securing a film deal for her romance novel *Partners in Crime* in 2023.

But the growth of independent self-publishing as an increasingly commercially viable option for authors altered the power dynamic between authors and traditional publishers in other ways too. According to Milan, it increased the power traditionally published authors wielded to push back against unfair treatment and decisions they felt did not best serve the creative work.[54] This shift in power was perhaps at its height in the early 2010s, when the growth and then-untapped power of self-publishing was at its highest. Milan stated that one of the biggest changes during this time was the loss of fear by authors:

> When we first started there were so many rules we had that were basically like "be afraid of your publisher," like "don't be a diva." If you get a cover, just smile and say "I love it," even if it sucks . . . and, you know, never complain about anything, always be happy and like "oh yay, great, oh look a contract for half as much as the last one, awesome!" And I think that that fear has disappeared, and in many ways I think it's been good for both traditional publishing and self-publishing because authors are now saying "yeah, this cover's not going to cut it. I'm looking at what's going on in the marketplace and this thing is not good enough" and "we can do this, this and this, and here are some comps and you should up the saturation on this" and, like, they come back and it's like, it's actually moving to a better product.[55]

This power to improve the degree of collaboration between publisher and author, particularly around how books are edited, designed, and marketed, is especially important for BIPOC and LGBTQ+ authors, whose works have historically been marginalized through practices of editorial bias that have been (often poorly) disguised as pragmatism and market orientation. Talking of book covers, Jackie Lau, an Asian Canadian author, explained her experience of a traditional publisher's reticence to accurately represent the racial identities of her characters on her photorealist covers:

> Often when you work with a publisher, depending on the situation, sometimes they'll say "well, White people on the cover sell better," and you'll have to fight to get someone on the cover who actually looks like your character. . . . With one book, I had an East Asian hero and they sent me a[n image] . . . they're like "oh is this guy okay?" and he was almost certainly not East Asian. He wasn't White, but like . . . [my character] looks like Daniel Dae Kim but 20 years younger, and it was like, no, this is nothing close.[56]

Lau managed to get the publisher to change the cover image through her resistance to the initial cover model and through some work of her own. "I forget exactly," she said, "I think I just sent them an example from like two seconds of searching on ShutterStock, and I'm not sure that's the one they ended up giving me but eventually they did use one that was pretty reasonable for the character."[57]

The resistance of traditional publishers to accurately portray people of color is not specific to romance fiction. Anamik Saha, for example, highlights the clichéd representation of South Asia on the covers of books published in Britain and Europe.[58] But this established practice by traditional publishers was a contributing factor to Lau's decision to self-publish; so she did not "have to fight to have people that represent their characters on the cover. So when I do the covers now, I don't have to worry about that."[59] However, although a stock image site provided Lau a way to fight for better representation within her traditional publishing house, she soon found it limiting in her self-publishing practice. Finding a wide variety of stock images that include people of color is a specific challenge for independent authors. Lau said she spends "a lot of time trying to find appropriate stock photos" because

> there's only sort of a small number, and so like I now recognize every time someone uses an East Asian guy on the cover. Like I almost certainly recognize the model or the photo because I just, I've seen them all . . . so once I've written like a couple dozen books then I'm going to be in trouble.[60]

This difficulty is compounded when trying to find images that depict interracial and queer couples, suggesting that representations of intersectional identities and relationships are in meager supply in stock image repositories.

Despite the autonomy associated with platformed self-publishing, it is not untethered from all exclusionary practices associated with traditional publishing. Rather, the marginalization of BIPOC and queer identities is layered, interwoven into different activities of book production. This contextual relationship highlights the systemic nature of inequality in book publishing and culture, shaped by sociopolitical realities and organizational and economic structures. The political economy of traditional romance fiction publishing, where the market is often used as a foil for editorial choices, intersects with that of publishing platforms. As the experiences of authors described here shows, self-publishing book production is also intrinsically linked to established logics, practices, and structures of traditional book publishing as well as within the broader platformed media ecology.

Platformed Publishing in the Media Ecology

In conceptualizing publishing on platforms, this book positions books as media and, importantly, as part of the media ecosystem. This is not a radical approach, nor a new idea. Books mediate information in their own textual ways and sometimes form the basis of other media forms in the adaptation industry.[61] Many traditional publishing houses have parent companies in the multinational media conglomerates of Viacom, News Corp, Bertelsmann, and others. And scholarly research has highlighted the ontological and material compatibilities and continuities between books and other types of media despite the disciplinary divide within the academy.[62]

The relationship between books and other types of media is drawn even closer through processes of platformization, which has reshaped the creative and entertainment industries and restructured relationships within and between the publishing and media sectors. As explored in detail in chapter 5, the bookish sides of Amazon and Wattpad sit within much broader platform companies that participate in multiple media industries, breaking down whatever siloes remained between them. Where Amazon has built a vast infrastructure across media and service sectors through intense vertical and horizontal integration, Wattpad has developed a pan-entertainment model focused on commercializing the authors, data, and intellectual property on its platform. Moreover, popular content on these platforms can move beyond the social media sphere, to be republished by traditional print publishers or adapted for film and TV through both formal and informal partnerships. Books, in short, are part of a broad entertainment landscape. This final section builds on these ideas and introduces in more detail the ecosystem framework explored in the rest of the book. This framework draws together publishing studies, platform studies, and media industry studies, and positions platformed publishing in a broader ecology of media and cultural production and consumption, which I term the entertainment ecosystem.

The relationship between platforms and media, and platform studies and media studies, is relatively well established. There are many references both in and out of scholarship to the growing interconnectedness of Hollywood and Silicon Valley, as the industries associated with these geographic areas become increasingly enmeshed with one another.[63] Investigating social media entertainment, Stuart Cunningham and David Craig, for example, argue that platforms like YouTube, Facebook, and Instagram have given rise to a new creative industry operating at the intersection of the screen and content industries. Platforms, they argue, have given rise to new forms of screen media, new industry players and creators, and new systems of production and monetization. At the same time, they have impacted the norms, principles and practices of established or legacy screen media companies which now have to contend with platformed digital streaming.

From a scholarly and consumer perspective, it is easy to see why platforms and platformization has been so often conceived of in relation to traditional screen media. Platform studies is connected to digital media studies as a cognate discipline, and audiovisual media platforms such as Netflix, YouTube, and TikTok have upended film, TV, and entertainment viewing to a greater degree than digital technologies have impacted reading. Regardless of the relative impact, a similar perspective must be brought to contemporary publishing studies and this book adds to the emerging scholarship that has begun this cross-disciplinary work.[64] Incorporating digital publishing platforms into theorizations of contemporary book publishing more fully acknowledges the contours of media production and book culture in the early twenty-first century as well as the growing interconnectedness of the publishing, platform, and media industries.

I draw on media ecology to conceptualize the emerging relationships between these industries forged through processes of platformization, as well as the dynamics between older and newer institutions operating within them. The scientific logics of the natural ecosystem were first introduced to media studies by Marshall McLuhan and Neil Postman in the 1960s and 1970s as a model to examine the complex interactions between different media forms and their contexts. An ecological approach positions media *as* environments—that structure modes of production and reception—and media *in* (social, cultural, and political) environments. From this perspective, new media forms are not simply additive but evolve and disappear relationally to established forms, practices, and technologies. To take an old bookish technology as an example, Gutenberg drew on innovations in moving type from China and Korea that had existed for centuries when developing the printing press. Likewise, manuscript culture did not cease with its introduction and its impacts of mass-produced texts on advancing literacy, religion, politics, and lifestyles were by no means immediate. The printing press became one technology, albeit an impactful one, within a diverse literary culture. Media ecologies then may be viewed as technical, sociopolitical, and historical systems that are constantly emerging, adapting, and changing, as are their impacts on media producers and consumers, and media as cultural artifacts produced within specific political and historical contexts.

Media ecology is a particularly useful frame for analyzing cultural production on platforms. Platforms themselves are part of large, often walled gardens; tech ecosystems and data infrastructures are propped up by a range of websites, apps, servers, software, and hardware. The programmability of platforms, which allows them to be customized by outside developers and users through application programming interfaces (APIs), has made them central to the infrastructure of the internet.[65] As these platform ecologies intersect with established creative institutions, they introduce new modes of production and reception which work to transform the cultural industries. But, as Cunningham and Craig show in their analysis of social media entertainment, platformed cultural production also exists in relation to legacy cultural industries, which may be considered as part of the broader media ecosystem. Media ecology further provides a foundation to put authors, readers, platforms, and institutions in dynamic relation with each other and allows for a consideration of cooperative intermedia relationships and emerging media forms that exist within this dynamic sphere of creative production. In adopting it here, I acknowledge that the entertainment ecosystem presented in this book is not only framed by the lens of the case study platforms of Amazon and Wattpad, but also mutable to change over time and by centering different platforms or participants.

Here, I find Carlos A. Scolari's work of expanding the ecology metaphor particularly useful.[66] Scolari considers how theorizing processes of media evolution, extinction, survival, and coevolution might help us understand how and why particular media forms and platforms evolve as and when they do. Like ecosystems of the natural environment, media ecosystems are dynamic entities, subject to periodic disturbances and containing potential for resilience. This metaphoric extension is also useful for reflecting on the evolution and evolutionary choices of platforms, their users, and their response to disruptions within the system. For example, what affordances have Amazon and Wattpad introduced or abandoned in the interest of survival? How do these platforms fit into the media environment in which it exists? What features of legacy media institutions have evolved or become extinct through processes of platformization?

Media ecology has previously been applied to studies of social media platforms. In particular, I draw on the work of José van Dijck and her connective media framework that brings together actor-network theory and political economy. In *The Culture of Connectivity*, van Dijck theorizes social media platforms as operating in two configurations: as individual microsystems, comprising a range of constitutive components including technology, users/usage, governance, ownership, business model, and content; and a larger connective ecosystem, in which platforms interact with each other in distinctive and formative ways. By disassembling social media platforms into their "constitutive components," this model explores how platforms are techno-cultural constructs and shaped by socioeconomic structures. Reassembling them into an ecosystem of "inter-operating platforms," she argues, works to recognize how they interact with and are shaped by one another in various ways, and which "norms and mechanisms undergird the *construction of sociality and creativity*" on individual platforms.[67]

In this book, I explicitly extend van Dijck's connective ecosystem frame to theorize a broader *entertainment ecosystem*, which encompasses platforms for cultural production and traditional media sectors, including publishers and entertainment studios. The term entertainment ecosystem was introduced by Elizabeth Fife and colleagues in reference to the mobile entertainment ecosystem, a similar theorization to van Dijck's connective ecosystem of platforms, and in adapting this term I acknowledge the centrality of mobile applications to platformed cultural production. Positioning platformed book production in a dynamic relationship with traditional sectors of the book industry enables an analysis of the cultural logics that shape the production and reception of books on platforms. In this way, an ecological framework has heuristic value for investigating the technological, economic, and sociocultural contexts in which books and authors circulate online and a consideration of cooperative intermedia relationships and emerging media forms that exist within this dynamic sphere of creative production.

Conclusion

The contradictions at the heart of platform publishing—namely, that platforms both enable and constrain self-publishing authors in various ways—was highlighted in a discussion I had with Simone Shirazi. When we spoke in November 2020, she had been working at Radish as a story lead writer for a few months where she was actively working with her team to improve the diversity and inclusiveness of romance fiction on the platform. Being a story lead, she said, "gives me the opportunity to really highlight these diverse stories and show that we're not just about White, cis, straight stories."[68] This priority for diversity was supported by Radish. She added:

> This is stuff that comes from the top down being like, "We want diverse voices, and we want diverse stories. We also want to have fun with it. We want to show that these stories don't have to be about, like, trauma or anything like that. They can be about just having a good time and finding love and romance and all of that kind of stuff."[69]

I found this outlook heartening but was also wary. On the one hand, I was excited by the duty to diversity and inclusion Shirazi seemed to embody in her own writing practice and the positive messaging from Radish. On the other, I was increasingly disillusioned by Wattpad, another platform that had historically put diversity and inclusion at the forefront of their branding but that repeatedly failed its authors of color and queer authors.

Our conversation also happened at a time when many companies were doing their best to signal their commitment to anti-racism in response to the global Black Lives Matter protests in mid-2020. Publishers and platforms were being moved by the cultural momentum of the Black Lives Matter movement. In the book world, the needle had also been pushed forward by collectives of authors and readers advocating in other publishing-specific campaigns for racial and cultural equality such as #WeNeedDiverseBooks and #PublishingPaidMe. I was also struck by how Shirazi's autonomy to contribute to editorial and curatorial decisions that were likely to be more inclusive is further evidence of how platforms allow or encourage particular kinds of activity, communication, and interaction. What happens if Radish decides that diversity and inclusion is no longer a priority? What happens when the individuals on platforms or working within platform companies are at odds with platforms' organizational, technological, or governance structures?

In some ways, the promises heralded by digital technologies and the internet are being realized in the context of platform publishing. Authors are provided with alternative ways to publish and are no longer reliant on legacy publishers who have been (at least mostly) responsible for their systemic exclusion in the book industry. These authors are afforded greater agency to publish on their terms: to write what they want, to choose their own covers, and so on. But the expected utopia is far from realized. Platforms ultimately control the practice of self-publishing in a myriad of significant and opaque ways, and while platformization leads to a further un-siloing of cultural and media industries, it also leads to an increasingly intense centralization of culture. The following chapters explore in more detail how digital technologies and platformed publishing are changing the experiences of publishing and, particularly, how they both enable and constrain authors and their works through particular economic, technological, cultural, and organizational structures.

CHAPTER 2

Platformed Book Markets

Creating and Selling Books Online

ECHOING THE PROMISES OF the early internet and later peer-to-peer networking, platformed self-publishing holds implicit possibilities for a democratization of publishing. Platforms offer authors alternatives to the historically marginalizing and exclusionary pathway of traditional publishing, including alternative revenue structures. The commercial success of many self-published authors in the early 2010s, including Colleen Hoover, E. L. James, Hugh Howey, and Andy Weir, seemed to confirm the lucrative potential of independent digital publishing. Suddenly, you didn't need the backing of one of the Big Five publishers, with all their cultural and economic capital, to be a financially successful author. All you needed was an internet connection, an idea, the perseverance to write, and a readership. The platformization of publishing has also undoubtedly introduced new forms of dependency. Self-published authors are now dependent on platforms to publish their works and engage in book culture, where participation is stratified across user groups and constrained by certain technical affordances. Today's self-publishing practice and book culture is governed by platform-owned-and-operated markets that prioritize a platform capitalist model of datafication and surveillance. Rather than upholding these implicit promises, then, platforms impose particular infrastructures for publishing. These structures enable new forms of book publishing, including serialized stories that do not resemble traditional codices, as well as new revenue systems that seemed to be more transparent and equitable compared to those offered in traditional publishing.

While the accessibility of publishing platforms presents important entry points for many authors who have been historically marginalized from the traditional publishing industry, publishing platforms dictate specific modes of participation in contemporary book culture. They create frameworks that determine what authors can create, how their works are produced and remunerated, and how they engage with readers. By examining the political economies and architectural infrastructures of Amazon and Wattpad, this chapter shows how the promises and opportunities heralded by internet technologies and platformed self-publishing, particularly for BIPOC and queer authors who have historically been marginalized and excluded by traditional publishing institutions, are balanced with strict conditions of engagement imposed by platforms through their remuneration structures, proprietary markets, and affordances that shape writing and book design. Through interviews and website analyses, this chapter explores the economic structures of platformed publishing offered by Amazon and Wattpad, and how these platforms shape how books are created.

Books under Platform Capitalism

In contexts of platform publishing, the business of books is forcibly aligned with platform capitalism. Throughout the late twentieth century and into the twenty-first, digital networks have introduced new modes of working, set new parameters for social, cultural, and economic interactions, and become the central apparatus of a supranational market system.[1] Technology companies like Google, Apple, Microsoft, Facebook, and Amazon, all major players in the platform economy, are having transformative effects on the organization of societies through the disruption of markets and labor relations and transformation of social, civic, and democratic practices.[2] The penetration of platforms into nearly all spheres of personal, industrial, and governmental life has given rise to a regime of platform capitalism whereby technology companies have become key economic actors and the basis on which economies and industries operate. In other words, platform capitalism describes a system in which digital technologies constitute the central apparatus of a supranational market system and transform forces of production and structures of work.[3] This has resulted in radical decentralization, flexibility, and acceleration of work and the broader market through vast economic restructuring and the computerization of productive systems.

Platform capitalism coexists with other, more established forms of capitalism including, in the book industry, conglomerate capitalism.[4] Under these coexisting supranational systems, some aspects of longstanding forms of capitalism endure under platform capitalism—private ownership, wage labor, and commodity markets, for example—while other aspects—types of property, assets, and capital—are transformed by digital networks and technologies.

Platform capitalism gives rise to a mutually dependent but tenuous relationship between platform companies and its users. Platforms rely on users for network effects, where the value of platforms arises from the increase in and profitable connection between content (user-driven production), attention (the number of users), and interactivity (the connection between users). Data is at the heart of platforms' economic models, and this system is closely associated with surveillance capitalism.[5] The accumulation, monitoring, analysis, and exploitation of user data is the central business of platform companies. Several concerns related to surveillance capitalism rightly focus on the accumulation, exploitation, and safety of users' personal data, but datafication is having significant impacts on the creative and cultural industries too. The accumulation, monitoring, and analysis of personal data is transforming practices of traditional institutions in the cultural industries, too, while also cementing the dominance of the Big Tech companies that control these processes. But through platformization, individual cultural producers and cultural industries alike are becoming increasingly reliant on tech platforms for key processes, rendering users both reliant on and the subjects of this economic model.

The economic imperatives of platforms are articulated through business studies and political economy. From a business studies perspective, platforms are theorized as multi-sided markets, or matchmakers, that connect different groups (or sides) within an economy, such as riders looking for a ride with drivers looking for passengers, or readers looking for books with authors who have published books to sell. By providing the hardware and software foundation for individuals, businesses, and civic organizations, platforms are driving a major shift in how capitalist firms operate all the while imposing particular "economic rules" under which these businesses and industries operate.[6] This approach tends to flatten the relationship between different sides of the platform, treats platforms as relatively static entities, and positions platforms as simple intermediaries connecting different market constituents. Therefore, while a business studies perspective provides considerable nuance into the economics of platforms and underpinning businesses, less attention is paid to the way platform economies impact power relationships between actors within this system.

Political economy sheds light on these dynamics, highlighting how platforms and networks are imbued with and reinforce unequal power relationships between platform companies, producers, and consumers. A foundational feature of platform capitalism is the dominant power platforms hold in disrupting markets and transforming labor relations. At the same time, the labor and material of platform work are often rendered invisible behind the seemingly intangible connectivity between authors, content, and readers. As platforms consolidate their power, platform-dependent cultural producers will increasingly struggle to "defend their position and interests" against them and contest inequitable treatment.[7] Several authors I spoke to articulated the bind they faced in their dependency on publishing platforms; they lamented the rigid power a platform like Amazon held over their publishing practice, how it was impossible to know *what* went wrong when things did go wrong or do anything about it, while also acknowledging its importance to their careers as it generated the majority of their sales. The dependency of self-published authors on platforms necessitates deeper investigations into how platforms are reshaping the ways in which books are created, produced, and sold through their architectural and economic structures.

The Kindle Economy

Self-publishing exploded in the late 2000s and experienced a period of seemingly exponential growth over the early 2010s, driven in large part by two interlinked developments by Amazon: the introduction of the Amazon Kindle device, and launch of the Kindle Direct Publishing (KDP) platform. While other companies had released ereader devices, the launch of the Kindle ultimately became what Simon Rowberry terms "the 'iPod moment' of ebooks," marking a "transitional moment in the acceptance of ebooks" and "legitimizing force that boosted the form into the mainstream."[8] This mainstreaming was encouraged by the increased availability of ebooks at this time as many authors turned to KDP to self-publish their creative works. Bolstered by the rising popularity of its Kindle platforms, Amazon set the conditions for the self-publishing and connected ebook market that continue to this day.

KDP offered the first streamlined service for authors wanting to self-publish, eliminating the need to have an agent, publisher, or even editor or printer on side. KDP allows authors to produce, publish, and disseminate their works through a simple webform-like interface called Kindle

Create. After signing up or logging in through their existing customer Amazon account, authors simply choose which book format they want to create—print or ebook—and fill in the relevant metadata information: book title, series information, author information, description or blurb, rights, keywords, categories, appropriate age range, and so on. They then upload their manuscript document, which can be pre-formatted or formatted automatically by KDP. After a review period of varying lengths (more detail on this in the next chapter), the book is made available on the Amazon store. The whole publishing process takes less than five minutes, according to Amazon, and requires exceedingly little technical expertise or publishing proficiency on the part of the author, allowing, in theory, anyone to publish almost anything they wish.

Autonomy and the associated idea of authorial control is central to the branding of KDP. A far cry from the relational power dynamic between authors and traditional publishers described in the previous section, Amazon highlights the creative choices afforded to authors: "everything from content to price is totally up to you," a promotional video that appeared on the KDP homepage in 2021 exclaimed, including writing book descriptions—"because after all, *you're* the author"—and choosing categories—"again it's your call!"[9] Independence in self-publishing is relative, though. Despite the tenor of the sales pitch, self-publishing authors are highly dependent on the platforms on which they choose to publish and disseminate their works and certain choices are encouraged through economic incentives and infrastructural and technical affordances.

Amazon incentivizes certain price points by offering higher royalties to books of different file sizes and between different price points. For example, KDP authors are offered a 70 percent royalty option for books priced between $2.99–9.99, unless they are certain file sizes and prices and then receive 35 percent (table 1).[10] Given most authors would prefer more royalties, these incentives contribute to a setting of standards across Amazon's marketplace. While not as bad as the predatory pricing strategy Amazon implemented in the first few years of Kindle ebooks, which saw many priced for free or ninety-nine cents and helped to cement their market dominance in the ebook format, these pricing standards have a similar impact on how ebooks are valued across the book industry.

Amazon maintains this control by monitoring the prices of titles on other digital marketplaces through spiders, web crawlers, or internet bots, that systematically scour the web pages of competitors such as Apple Books,

Google Play, and Kobo. According to Xio Axelrod, if an Amazon spider finds a different price for the same title on another platform, it will automatically adjust the price on the Amazon product page to match. This platformed interdependency undermines authors' agency in setting prices. Axelrod added that other platforms also undermined the prices she would set; Google Play, for instance, would often set "random" prices and "if an Amazon spider sees that, they'll put your book up as that [on Amazon] and you're like where did this price come from?"[11] Amazon furthers its control over self-published authors through its terms for KDP Select, a program that authors must re-enroll in every ninety days but demands books be exclusive to Amazon. KDP Select enables authors to run advantageous promotion deals, including ones that allow authors to list their book for free for five days out the ninety-day enrolment period or offer discounts for a limited time. Books enrolled in KDP Select are also made available in Kindle Unlimited (KU), Amazon's subscription-based content library of ebooks, audiobooks and magazines that launched in 2014.

Table 1. File Size and List Prices for Books that Receive 35 Percent Royalties

File size	Minimum list price (USD)	Maximum list price (USD)
<3 megabytes	0.99	200.00
3–10 megabytes	1.99	200.00
>10 megabytes	2.99	200.00

KU subscribers pay a monthly fee of $9.99 to access the library; they can read as many books as they like per month but are only able to have up to ten downloaded on their Kindle devices or apps at a time. For the first year, authors who had books in KU were paid per book loan but for the past decade or so, they have been paid from the KDP Select Global Fund, a predetermined monthly "pot of gold" that is divided between all KU authors based on the number of pages from their books read by readers. Amazon alters the unit of sale in bookselling through this pricing model, from whole books to single pages and, in doing so, fundamentally alters the commodity market to which books have historically been subject. This new market structure has led to bad actors taking advantage, predominantly through a practice known as book stuffing, which involves filling an ebook with extraneous content so readers must view more pages (for which authors are paid) to be able finish the book.

Amazon entirely controls this market through opaque decision-making and rules that determine who gets paid how much and when. Amazon determines what counts as a page, something that becomes reflowable when read on differently sized devices (the amount of text on a Kindle ereader page is different to the amount shown in the Kindle app on my smartphone, for example). It also determines what counts as a page read; if readers read too quickly, their time spent on each page may not register as an eligible "read"). Significantly, Amazon determines this information without sharing it with KU authors or readers. The company also changes the value of the available funds each month (it was $2.5 million in July 2014, $49.5 million in December 2023, and peaked at $49.6 million in August 2023) and thus alters the value of a page from month to month (in December 2023, the payout per page was $0.00437).[12] There are limits to how many pages per book an author can be paid for (up to three thousand page reads per book) and bonuses for the top one hundred authors with the most page reads each month, introducing a top-down hierarchy in an otherwise relatively equal-opportunist lending library.

Kindle Unlimited presents authors access to an in-built audience of readers who, due to the perceived economic value of subscriptions (where access to the content library is a fixed cost, getting your value for money means consuming as much content as possible), tend to be more likely to try books by new-to-them authors. KU can also be especially effective for authors who write series; getting readers hooked on the series available on KU means they may be more likely to purchase the next books in series, which authors can distribute widely across retailers. Of course, the exclusivity demanded by KDP Select and Kindle Unlimited limits authors reaching readers who are not part of Amazon's ecosystem and, in doing so, prevents authors from engaging in other price-related marketing strategies.

While Amazon no longer allows authors to permanently distribute their books for free on Amazon, it is possible to use its competitive price matching spiders to do so. Books can be listed as free on Amazon outside of KDP Select/KU if the web crawlers identify a title as being listed for free on another retail platform. Katrina Jackson, who publishes romance and erotica but has a day job in another industry, told me that she would like to make the first book in her Welcome to Seaport series permanently free on Amazon.[13] This title was in KU when we spoke and the exclusivity requisite of this lending library meant that to make it permanently free to readers she would have to take the title out of KU, publish it on another platform, set it to be free there and then hope that Amazon made it free too. Of course, this strategy would only last as long as other platforms allowed authors to set the price—even a price of zero—without it being algorithmically altered to suit various platform imperatives, demonstrating the interdependency of publishing platform infrastructures.

Despite the frustrations Amazon inspires in some authors and readers, its dominance in the market, aggressive vertical and horizontal integration, and accessible platforms means that it has become somewhat of a necessary evil for self-publishing authors. While other companies have introduced platforms that compete with Amazon's ebook and print publishing processes, Amazon remains one of the only financially profitable and technologically accessible options for authors to self-publish audiobooks, making the structures by which they can do so especially significant.

Self-Producing Audiobooks via Audible ACX

If the ebook boom was the story in the early parts of the 2010s, the audiobook boom is the story of the later part of the decade. While still a relatively smaller part of the overall book market, the Audio Publishers Association's annual sales surveys show eleven straight years of double-digit growth in audiobook sales between 2012–2023.[14] The popularization of audiobooks correlates with the widespread uptake of the smartphone and the closely connected growth in entertainment streaming, including video, music, and podcasting.[15] Digital platforms have facilitated the growth of noncommercial audiobook production; Librivox, a popular platform on which volunteers create and share public domain audiobooks, "empowers the amateur, the general public, to participate in literary production."[16] But for independent authors wanting to tap into this market segment and commercially publish their works as audiobooks, Amazon's Audiobook Creation Exchange (ACX) platform is one of very few options.

Despite their recent popularization, audiobooks have a long history. In the first sustained research into audiobooks, Matthew Rubery tracks the history and development of recorded literature over the twentieth century, beginning with "talking book" records that were introduced in the 1930s by the American Foundation for the Blind and Library of Congress Books for the Adult Blind and visually impaired adults and veterans injured during World War I.[17] From the 1970s, audiocassettes began to replace records until the late 1990s brought with it digital technologies and the internet that disrupted these formats. The digitalization of recorded literature or audiobooks, particularly from CDs to digital files disseminated by streaming platforms like Audible, has radically boosted their market share.

The history of digital audiobooks, though, is almost synonymous with Audible. Audible Inc. was originally founded in 1997 when it introduced its Audible MobilePlayer, the first portable audio device to hold direct downloads with a capacity for two hours of audio. Over the next few years, it introduced a subscription membership model, providing Audible customers access to its content library for a flat monthly fee, started a weekly audio show featuring Robin Williams, and launched internationally in Germany and then the UK and France. In 2008, Amazon acquired Audible for around $300 million, tapping into and building on the company's history of popularizing digital audiobooks. In the last decade and a half, audiobooks have seen substantial market growth, correlating directly with technological and economic developments including the widespread uptake of the smartphone and the closely connected growth in streamed music and podcasts.

The introduction of the ACX platform by Amazon in 2011 has enabled greater participation by independent authors to also stake a claim in this increasingly popular segment of the book market. ACX is an online rights marketplace and production platform that connects independent copyright holders (authors) and audiobook narrators/producers and, as such, facilitates access to a form of book production that has historically been very costly. While traditional publishers who could justify the expenses associated with the production and distribution of physical audiobooks have been a mainstay in the market since the days of records and cassettes, self-publishers are relatively new to this sphere and wholly reliant on platforms as intermediaries of their participation.

The introduction of ACX certainly contributed to the growth in the audiobook market; in the year after its launch, there was a tenfold increase in the number of audiobooks on Audible.[18] This growth was encouraged by two strategies adopted by Amazon in the early days of ACX, which incentivized authors to produce audiobooks via the platform. The first strategic arm targeted high-profile authors and their agents. Audible and other audio companies began investing heavily in unsold rights and rights not retained by print publishers. According to Boris Kachka in an article for *Vulture*, Big Five publishers were reluctant to relinquish the audio rights they held and so Audible began offering authors "an eyebrow-raising amount of money" in the hopes that agents of brand-name authors would strategically sell the print rights of titles they represented to independent publishers that did not have their own audio divisions and the audio rights to Audible.[19]

The second part of the strategy involved promoting a program to authors who either self-published or retained their audio rights that offered them $1 for every audiobook sold if they signed up to ACX independently from a traditional publisher, a predatory pricing scheme that worked for Kindle ebooks in the early 2010s. This second strategic move has had another significant impact on how we should understand the work of independent authors. In addition to needing to be writers, marketers, editors, and publishers, those who choose to self-produce audiobooks must also perform (or employ) the professional roles of scriptwriter, producer, and director.

At the time of data collection, only two authors I spoke to, Courtney Milan and Xio Axelrod, had used ACX independently to publish audiobook versions of their titles, despite the marketplace being integrated with the KDP interface. As Axelrod described, "once your book is in the Amazon system, you can claim it on ACX and put it up for production."[20] Within ACX, authors post a section of the script and actors can record files of them reading it in a disembodied digital audition. When creating an audiobook

> some people will not rewrite the book but alter enough of the book and say abridged or unabridged. It's like an abridged version where they take out a lot of the dialogue tags or something like that, so it flows easier for narration. I don't do that. But some people do. But you can put up a piece of script and the actor will read it and record, and you can listen to a bunch of auditions to people reading the words and it's just kind of fun . . . All of the production is on the narrators' side. All I do is say "this is what I want" and then they send me the chapters to listen to and I listen through to find errors, you know, stuff like that. Or say, "hey, can you read it differently, this way?," like being a director. And then once they send me the final file, I listen, everything's cool, I hit approved, and then they

upload it from their end. They do all the editing. They do everything on their side.[21]

In other words, once the narrator is hired, they are responsible for the entirety of the audio production process, including recording and editing. Authors can offer direction and request that parts are corrected and re-recorded if necessary. Once the author signs off on the final version, the narrator uploads the finished version to the Audible marketplace.

However, authors do not have to engage fully in the ACX marketplace to publish audiobooks via Audible. Courtney Milan, for instance, first used ACX to find narrators for her historical romance novels and, after finding a narrator she liked, she began circumventing the platform and organizing the production of her audiobooks with her narrator, Rosalyn Landor, directly.[22] Milan's eventual bypassing of ACX points to the way authors negotiate their relationship with Amazon and undermine the platform's dominance in the self-publishing sector. Amazon retains its power by simplifying the process for KDP authors who option their rights on the ACX marketplace, including through its economic model.

Through its operations, ACX fundamentally rearranges the economic system of audiobook production. ACX offers two models for self-publishing authors to fund the production of their audiobooks. The first option is a royalty share, whereby the authors and narrators each earn 50 percent of profits for the duration of the copyright period (in the US, this is the life plus seventy years after the death of the creator). The second option is for the author to pay narrators upfront for the production and every finished hour of the final audiobook. According to Xio Axelrod, this rate could be "anywhere from $25 to $1000, depending on how experienced the person is."[23] The first audiobook she produced, *The Calum*, a title around 35,000 words, cost her approximately $700 upfront. As a digital marketplace, ACX enables independent producers to compete in a historically costly form of creative book production.

ACX converges the book publishing and performance sectors of the creative industries. Previously, the chain of production for audiobooks comprised several professional intermediaries. As a blunt mapping, authors wrote a book and owned the audio rights to that book, their agent would pitch the book to publishers who would license the rights, the publisher would then contact voice actors' agents, actors presumably auditioned, and they would record and produce the audiobook in a recording studio that was either internal or external to the publishing house. The professional roles on the performance side are also restructured as ACX performers tend to also fill the producer role in the creation of audiobooks.

Narrators participating in the ACX marketplace include film, TV, and stage actors, including those from the Screen Actors Guild (SAG), voice actors, radio personalities, recording artists, singers, journalists, and other media professionals who have rarely, if ever, had to work as producers of the media they perform for. The first narrator Axelrod used for *The Calum*, for example, was a news broadcaster. ACX fills the knowledge gap that it creates by making agents, publishers, and producers redundant through its educational service ACX University (ACXU), which was set up as a website but now operates as a YouTube channel. While it is possible that narrators may have deals with producers to do this work, the norm seems to be that performers expand their professional skills and retrain as producers as well.

ACXU was launched in 2013 as a free audiobook production education targeted at new producers. While lessons started in classrooms at Audible in Newark, New Jersey, ACXU is now an annual series of weekly webcasts posted to YouTube. Amazon also offers workshops in drama programs at the University of Southern California, Boston University, Columbia, Juilliard, Stella Adler, New York University Tisch, and other US universities as well as a partnership with the London Academy of Music and Dramatic Arts for paying students.[24] The changes to the chain of production through the consolidation of roles in the performance sector are reflective of those in the book industry, and speaks to broader industry processes of convergence and employment trends under late stage capitalism.

ACX eliminates the need for agents and publishers in this chain by brokering relationships directly between performers and authors and other rights holders, following a broader political economy of increasing gig and service work. In this post-Fordist system, ACX necessitates performers to diversify their skills and offer a range of services, for which Amazon provides the training all while engaging in a gig economy in which performers must bid for work. Like other platform-dependent workers, ACX creators are distanced from the platform for which they work both physically and through contractual labor arrangements, which contributes to their obscurity and precarity. This digital gig economy weakens the bargaining power of workers while the inbuilt anonymity of this organizational structure can facilitate conditions for discriminatory hiring practices and regimes of economic inclusion and exclusion. There is another geopolitical inequality at play in this platformed labor regime as ACX is only available to authors and narrators in the US, UK, Canada, and Ireland, which reinforces the Western hegemony of the global book industry.

The platform capitalist structure of Audible and ACX ensures its market dominance by vertically integrating systems of audiobook production and providing the technology that constitutes the central apparatus of the market system. But Audible further subverts the traditional audio publishing production chain by producing its own original audiobooks. The first iteration of this was launched in 2012 when Audible launched its A-List Collection, a series of audiobooks of mostly public domain literary classics narrated by Hollywood stars including Claire Danes, Samuel L. Jackson, Diane Keaton, Colin Firth, Anne Hathaway, Nicole Kidman, and Kate Winslet. Most of these are no longer marketed or even searchable under the A-List Collection, except for *The End of the Affair* by Graham Greene and narrated by Colin Firth, which won the 2013 Audie Award for Audiobook of the Year. The A-List collection is a clear attempt to legitimize the format and platform through the exchange of cultural capital from high profile actors, a strategy that developed into Audible Originals.

The Audible Originals collection launched in 2018 with literary classics read by Hollywood actors, including Jane Austen's *Emma* narrated by Emma Thompson and Louisa May Alcott's *Little Women* narrated by Laura Dern, in an obvious revamp of the A-List experiment. Over the years, the Audible Originals list has grown to include other novels licensed by Audible as well as shorter-form audio-first books written by popular authors. The first of these audio-first titles in romance fiction was Alyssa Cole's *The AI Who Loved Me*, narrated by a multicast including Regina Hall, Mindy Kaling, and others. Alyssa Cole is a Black romance author who began her career self-publishing before signing with a traditional romance publisher.[25] Through Audible Originals, Amazon acts as a traditional publisher or producer, acquiring authors with high cultural and symbolic capital in their respective genres to build a competitive and commercial list of audiobooks. This approach is representative of a broader strategy by Amazon to acquire popular, and prestigious cultural content that is distributed exclusively on their platform.

The changing market conditions imposed by Amazon through the Kindle and Audible platforms is perhaps the starkest example of its impact on the production of books, altering established remuneration structures in the book industry and converging labor regimes of historically separate industries. But platform infrastructures also shape how books are written, created and read. Like Amazon KDP and ACX, Wattpad sets the remuneration and format conditions by which its authors publish their work. On Wattpad, professionalization and commercialization are deeply intertwined through the platform's partner program.

Making Money through Wattpad's Creator Program

Wattpad launched the Stars Program in 2015 as an accelerator program, an increasingly prominent kind of platform incentive and monetization scheme. Rebranded as the Creators Program after the acquisition by Naver, this incubator scheme creates a semi-enclosed writing industry, where both opportunities and remuneration are predominantly controlled by Wattpad and which serves the company's business models.

The eligibility requirements and support provided to authors in the Creators Program reflects the commercial nature of the program. In order to qualify for the Creators Program, Wattpad users must have at least one story that is 40,000 words or more; is written in English; has been updated by a minimum of 500 words at least once in the last previous two weeks and at least six times in three months; and does not fall into the fanfiction, random, poetry, or classics categories.[26] Additionally, they must meet engagement hurdles, having at least one story in an eligible genre with a minimum number of readers that has spent more than five minutes reading the story within the past year—what Wattpad terms Engaged Readers. The required number of Engaged Readers varies depending on the genre, ranging from 9,000 for general fiction to 100 for horror. As part of the Creators Program, writers must publish a minimum of 500 words per week, and have access to editorial support; educational resources for writing and creative workshops; a community Discord; creator coordinators and talent managers; and opportunities to pitch stories directly to the content team. Wattpad Creators are also subject to near-exclusive consideration by Wattpad for the Paid Stories and Futures Programs, Wattpad Webtoon Book Group, Wattpad Webtoon Studios, and brand partnerships.

The Wattpad Creators Program is a kind of partner program, an increasingly prominent monetization scheme in platform markets and the creator economy in which select creators are able to earn money from their content and channels directly through the platform. Monetization from partner programs often comes from a share of advertising revenue, as in the well-known Facebook and Instagram Creator Program, YouTube Partner Program, and the TikTok Creator Fund. Partner programs such as these work to incentivize creators to produce a consistent stream of high-quality content and enable platforms to regulate which creators are able to monetize their content through access requirements. Radish takes quality assurance to another level by regulating access to the production side of the platform entirely, requiring potential writers to apply to publish on the platform— more akin to the Netflix model than YouTube model, according to its CEO.[27] Regulating access to partner programs, though, is a "non-trivial governance challenge for platform owners: On the one hand, if the eligibility criteria for creators are too restrictive, their effectiveness as an incentive device will be limited. On the other hand, if they are too open, then their control function will be compromised."[28]

There have been several revenue sharing and monetization opportunities for writers in Wattpad's Stars and Creators Programs. In 2017, Wattpad ran a program called Wattpad Futures, which enabled select Stars to earn a percentage of revenue from the programmatic advertisements that appear to readers on the webpage and between chapters of stories on the application. According to Simone Shirazi, who was part of the Futures Program between 2017–2019, remuneration all depended on reading time: "I think if you read for about 10 or 15 minutes or something, you'll encounter an ad."[29] The split between writers and platform was fairly even: Shirazi earned 49 percent of the ad revenue while Wattpad earned 51 percent. Returns were based on the traditional advertising metric of CPMs (cost per mille, where mille is French for thousand), which was reportedly quite low on Wattpad. Writers in Futures were also subject to a threshold they had to reach per quarter to be paid—around $50 or $100, per Shirazi's memory.[30] If writers did not reach that benchmark, Shirazi said the money "would keep rolling over until essentially the program ended or you made enough to be paid." She continues, "for some writers, they could have been in the program for a year, and they never hit payout."[31] Thresholds also exist in traditional print publishing; the contract for my first short scholarly monograph stipulates that I will only receive royalties after the first x copies sold, for example.

Thresholds also favor logics of popularity, though even these benchmarks are not straightforward or transparent for authors. As Shirazi recounted, "Gosh, let's see. During that time span [2017–2019], I think I gained about 20 million reads across . . . I think I had about five stories posted at that point. That amounted to a few thousand dollars. I can only imagine if you're only getting about a couple hundred reads a day that you weren't going to make much money off of that."[32] This model, which very explicitly links popularity with compensation, means that authors with larger readerships, especially those writing in popular genres, will be more commercially successful. It also means the algorithms that surface stories, making them more or less visible to potential readers, have a significant impact on which authors are more likely to earn money through this program and accrue the kind of success that informs acquisition decisions in the publishing and studios programs.

While the introduction of the Creators Program seems to have put an end to Futures, another monetization scheme has remained in a new iteration: Paid Stories, previously Wattpad Next, now Wattpad Originals. Wattpad introduced this program in 2018 as Wattpad Next, a beta test originally available in the US. It expanded to South America and Spain in early 2019 before being rolled out globally in July the same year when it was rebranded as Paid Stories. Authors who were invited to take part in Paid Stories could earn revenue from readers unlocking chapters to their serial stories using prepaid virtual coins. This program mirrored the business model of Radish Fiction, Wattpad's newest competitor at the time, which offered readers access to stories on a subscription basis.

While authors in the Creators Program are likely to commercially benefit, they are still entirely dependent on Wattpad and the changing conditions of monetization the platform company offers. Writers in the Stars and Creators Programs, as well as those who aspire to them, are afforded little security in earning money from their creative work on Wattpad and thus experience a high degree of precarity. Theorizing the nested nature of precarity platform-dependent creators experience, Brooke Erin Duffy and colleagues argue that unpredictability is often experienced in relation to changes in markets, industries, and platform features and algorithms, including in

> evolutions in audience tastes, advertiser demands, and sources of competition . . . in the ecology of platforms on which creators produce and circulate content . . . and in the platforms themselves, ranging from transparent changes (e.g., new features) to more opaque changes (e.g., changes to the algorithm).[33]

We see this nested precarity reinforced on Wattpad, where the structure of, access to and opportunities presented by the Wattpad partner program have changed several times since its introduction around 2015. Wattpad Creators and hopefuls must contend with changing eligibility requirements and monetization schemes on top of changes to visibility algorithms and broader market trends in publishing. Of course, cultural work has always been autonomous and precarious, at least to some degree, but the negative effects of these conditions are exacerbated, not remedied with the platformization of cultural work. The vulnerability of this position is compounded further for writers from historically marginalized groups, who have experienced racism on the platform and within the Stars Program.

Writing within Wattpad's Sociocultural Infrastructure

Wattpad authors who have been part of the Stars or Creators Programs are provided with a level of insider knowledge on how best to write on the platform. These authors initially learnt to successfully write on the platform by being immersed in the platform's architecture and community, through "observation and seeing what worked for other people."[34] Upon joining the Stars Program though, Shirazi found that Wattpad began instructing these authors on what works on the platform:

> It wasn't until I was invited to join the Stars Program, probably in the last two years that Wattpad has been more open about "this is what works on our platform" and "this is what's happening behind the scenes and use these tags and take advantage of these rankings" and stuff like that.[35]

Wattpad now also provides free writing resources on their platform, outlining topics such as how to get started on Wattpad, the basics of web novels, planning, and the "storycoaster."[36] Platforms shape reader markets through their interface design, economic structures, affordances, and interactivity. When it comes to publishing platforms based on the technological and ideological foundations of social media, Wattpad shows how interactions between writers and the platform company, writers and the interface, and, importantly, writers and readers shape production experiences.

Wattpad prioritizes a serialized form of writing, which is inscribed into the interface of Wattpad, shaping how works are created and consumed by its users. Through the platform's editor interface, authors are encouraged to upload their stories one chapter at a time. And this is the format by which other users read it; each chapter is displayed individually on a web or app page and readers move to the following chapter by clicking "next" at the bottom of the page. Like reading on a Kindle, these pages are reflowable, adapting to whatever kind of screen being used. Limiting the amount of text per page renders stories easier for users to read on computer screens and, more importantly, mobile devices through which most social media usage occurs.

While nothing technically prevents authors from posting whole stories in a single chapter on Wattpad, the formatting affects how readers engage with texts. In one of Wattpad's first official partnerships (established in 2007), for example, works from Project Gutenberg, an ebook library for public domain works founded in 1971, were uploaded in their entirety in single chapter spaces on Wattpad. Going against the site architecture in this way meant that the first and only chapter of each Project Gutenberg book on Wattpad can take up to several hours to read. Practically speaking, if the reader does not read the story in a single sitting (or leave the window open in their browser), they would have had to scroll down to find their place rather than being able to use the more convenient method of navigating to a numbered or titled chapter. When Wattpad took over the management of classic texts originally posted by Project Gutenberg, the texts were split into their original chapters, following the intended use of the site architecture. They were also reposted under accounts named after the original authors, which means that among Wattpad's more than 90 million global users you will be able to find ones ostensibly belonging to Charles Dickens (who has five stories and nearly 30,000 followers at the time of writing), Jane Austen (seven stories and nearly 100,000 followers), and Mary Shelley (one work and just over 8,000 followers).

Serialization affects how authors write and can impact what kinds of stories do well on the platform. Many Wattpad stories are plot-heavy and high-drama. Readers often express wanting entertainment, excitement, and/ or a payoff in the comments of each chapter and authors often respond by introducing and resolving tension quickly in each chapter. Cliff hangers are also a common occurrence at the end of every chapter, as they were in Victorian serial fiction. The ways in which the architecture of platforms influences styles of writing is also evident in the Instagram poetry of poets such as Rupi Kaur and Lang Leav, where short text is posted within or alongside an often-illustrated image or video according to the platform affordances and conventions. With publishing space being rendered virtual on Wattpad, stories have near-infinite potential for serialization, as demonstrated by Simone Shirazi's 900+ chapter story *Once Upon a One Night Mistake*.

For the relatively young Wattpad authors I spoke to—all except two were in their twenties, which reflects the young user base of the platform as well as the earning potential for young authors within a platform publishing sphere—serialized online storytelling is something they have become accustomed to reading. Shirazi, who "grew up on the internet and . . . serialized fiction" describes how this "shaped [her] writing style." She said,

> I've been conditioned over, I guess, about 15 years to write in that serialized format, which is relatively short chapters, but a lot of them, and posting chapter-by-chapter. Making sure that you write chronologically essentially, and you have that update ready to go and you just keep going with it. I think you want to have that little cliffhanger at the end of every chapter, so you get people to come back and read the next one because you never know who you're going to lose along the way. When you're updating a story, consistency is the key or else you will lose a lot of people as I've seen because I have been a lot less consistent lately because real life gets in the way.[37]

Serialization, which impacts the way stories are written to contain short-chapters and cliffhangers, thus also shapes the conditions of connectivity between authors and readers. For Wattpad writers who become part of the Stars/Creators Program, the advice around writing in a serial format becomes even more specific and algorithmically aligned. Ivey Choi, an Asian American author who became a Wattpad Star around 2018, said that Wattpad's advice to Stars was to "post a chapter close to [or] between 2000 and 2500 words, [and] try to update weekly."[38]

The serialized publishing structure of Wattpad plays a significant role in the data economy on which the platform relies. According to Aarthi Vadde, the serialized format of Wattpad "yields more site visits and enables a constant stream of conversation around a work."[39] Breaking up a novel into shorter segments helps to determine popular content by providing more nuanced data to the platform's algorithms, including where readers drop off or stop reading, time readers spend reading, when they read and how often they read, as well as higher levels of engagement such as liking, commenting, and voting. These metrics in turn inform the recommendation and discoverability algorithms on the platform as well as Wattpad's commercial business models. This nuanced reading data helps determine which texts are republished into books, adapted into films and television series, and sold on to other publishing and media companies.

The information generated through these opportunities for interactivity by readers can be important for authors too. Wattpad's reading interface allows users to comment on stories, both inline and at the end of each chapter. This constant stream of conversation around a work contributes to algorithmic filtering as well as the sharing economy ethos of the platform's community and brand. This participatory affordance has been previously theorized by Melanie Ramdarshan Bold as a digitized return to social authorship, in which the roles of the author and reader become more fluidly intertwined as readers engage in editorial feedback and the circulation of texts.[40] She argues that the feedback system on Wattpad is a "collaborative process with readers providing feedback on installments . . . [who can] also act as editors."[41]

The experiences of the Wattpad authors I spoke to indicate that this feedback is not as productive as may seem at first glance. Claire Kann noted, for example, that often "the feedback from readers isn't a critique. If they're not trying to make your work better, sometimes they're just mean."[42] Kann has chosen not to engage with readers on Wattpad, for the most part except "if there's like a question, about a story that or there's a typo or something, I'll reply to those, but for the most part, I still don't engage there." Rather than being productive editorial advice, comments on Wattpad tend to include "lots of praise, a little critique, advice, wishes for the story's direction, and random comments."[43] Emotive language seems to be the dominant form of expression in Wattpad comments rather than constructive writerly feedback.[44]

Despite these trends, some authors still found guidance in the reader comments on Wattpad. At times, Shirazi found the feedback from readers reassuring as it let her know "whether or not what [she's] writing is something that people like and people want to see more of . . . just knowing that someone is interested in this and someone is reading it and someone's engaged with it is extremely really encouraging."[45] But it could also have a dark side. In fact, several authors I interviewed spoke of experiencing targeted harassment and negative comments on their stories, particularly in relation to the representation of non-White characters and feminist themes.

Choi described experiencing a significant amount of "toxic comments" on one of her stories that explicitly featured intersectional feminist themes.[46] Initially, reader engagement was positive because her existing readership knew and expected this kind of story from her. At some point, though, the story was featured on the Wattpad homepage. With this visibility, the story amassed a whole new readership, and this was when the first wave of comments came through. When the author looked at the profiles of many of the commenters, she found that most were teenagers, who were perhaps still learning about the history of feminism and feminist issues, but there were also a few commenters that she deemed to be extreme cases, including users who had neo-Nazi and other hate symbols in their profile banners, and whom she reported.

In another instance, Shirazi experienced trolling, targeted harassment, and death threats over two straight White protagonists not ending up together in a romance story. In her words, the harassment from readers was from

> people who just didn't like what I was writing, but it wasn't in a sense of I'd written something offensive. It was just that two straight White characters didn't end up together. It didn't have the sweeping romantic ending they wanted. It was in the sense of the content wasn't up to their standard of "happy." . . . It wasn't because I'd done something traditionally problematic or offended a group of people or anything like that. It was just in the sense of, "You didn't give me this happily ever after that I thought I was promised," when in actuality it was never promised, that they feel the need to take that out on you, because, "You're the one controlling the story, but if you don't give us what we want, we're going to riot." That's what set off a lot of the hate and harassment for me.[47]

The story this harassment was centered around included the tag #Romance on Wattpad as well as popular romance fiction tropes such as #EnemiesToLovers and #FakeDating. This response might also then highlight the permeable genre conventions of online fiction but the equally insistent genre expectations of readers who were expecting a Happily Ever After (HEA) or Happy For Now (HFN) ending for the protagonists associated with romance genre fiction, which this story does not include. But taken with Choi's experience as well as reports and open-letters from several authors who resigned from the then-Stars Program in mid-2020 citing racial harassment, inequitable treatment, and marginalization, the problem is clearly not unique to the nuances of this story.

While Wattpad allows users to hide inline comments, there is no way to disable the commenting function completely. This means that by posting a story to Wattpad, authors tacitly agree to this interaction with readers. It also means that there is limited recourse for authors to protect themselves if this interaction becomes harmful. According to both authors, Wattpad's Trust and Safety Team did not do a lot when they were experiencing this targeted harassment, despite both being Wattpad Stars at the time, Shirazi was part of the Paid Stories Program, and both had direct access to some Wattpad staff. As one said:

> It takes a lot for them to actually get involved. I've had people send me essentially direct death threats. Wattpad's like, "Well, could you just explain the situation a little more?" I'm just like, "Well, what do I need to explain more than showing you the screenshot of someone saying they're going to come to my house and kill me?" They obviously don't always mean what they say, but when somebody is in your private messages, telling you, "Oh, go kill yourself" or "Oh, I'm going to kill you," that's something that needs to be handled better, I think, and I understand it's a huge platform and it's hard to detect tone over the internet and stuff like that, but words like that, I think that's valid, worthy of an investigation at least.[48]

These rather confronting experiences demonstrate that despite creating spaces for authors to publish more culturally diverse and socially progressive stories, free from the traditional gatekeepers that have historically excluded these under the guise of market orientation, platforms do not always provide a safe environment for authors to do so. As will be explored more in chapter 4, Wattpad has historically leant into its identity as a platform, as opposed to its role as a publisher, emphasizing the discursive imaginary of platforms as intermediaries in an attempt to evade responsibility and liability for what is published on their servers.

Platform Paratext on Amazon

As with writing on Wattpad, Amazon shapes how books are designed and produced through the KDP and Amazon Marketplace interfaces. Book design constitutes an important step in the production process, turning a manuscript into something we recognize as a book. Those involved in the design of a book are responsible for arranging what literary theorist Gérard Genette terms the paratext; the elements that "surround" a text, such as the author's name, title, preface, illustrations, and so on. [49] These liminal devices present the text in particular ways, working to "*make it present*, to assure its presence in the world, its 'reception' and its consumption . . . as a book."[50] Paratext accompanies a text, though at relative distances to it; they exist as peritexts (elements that are physically part of the printed book, such as titles and blurbs), and epitexts (elements that are not physically part of the book, such as author interviews or advertisements). Together, paratexts act as "thresholds" to a text that mediate readers' experiences, inform their interpretations, and dictate their access.[51]

Platforms and digital technologies have transformed the creation, appearance, and function of paratext in various ways. The introduction of new book formats (ebooks, audiobooks, serialized online writing) and containers (ereaders, smartphone applications, websites) has prompted renewed conceptualizations of paratext, including where and how they manifest. Ellen McCracken, for instance, shows how ereaders eclipse the role of the front cover and front matter of books "by setting the book to open on the first page of the main body of the text."[52] In cases where the cover is absent or plays a diminished role, she argues, readers must access it elsewhere—going backwards through ebook pages or on a separate webpage, for example. Simon Rowberry likewise considers how paratext manifests in Kindle ebooks, which feature displays that "have converged toward a minimal interface: Kindle for iPhone 6.7 allows users to view just the main body, and the Kindle 7 discreetly displays the location information in the footer."[53] As these changes in the book interface demonstrate, platforms challenge "the unity of a discrete book" as well as establish new boundaries between text, paratext, and context.[54]

As these reconceptualizations show, locality is central to theorizations of paratext; the prefix para signifies the textual elements that exist alongside, near, and apart from the text itself, "something simultaneously this side of a boundary line, threshold or margin, and also beyond it." Paratexts occupy a liminal position between what is text and context, what Genette refers vaguely to as "beyond text."[55] However, this boundary line is significantly challenged in contexts of platformed publishing where digital rights management and other systems creates a technical inability to separate books from the digital environments in which they are discovered, sold, and read. Examining audiobook streaming, Karl Berglund and Sara Tanderup Linkis argue that "the distributor plays a crucial role in the framing of literary works" in digital spaces, and thus "a complete analysis of "books" as material objects . . . should also cover the streaming service platform and the hardware used for consumption."[56] The technical inability to separate books from the digital environments in which they are discovered, sold, and read that prompts Berglund and Tanderup Linkis' extended analysis of the book-as-object also applies to book publishing and distribution platforms for print and electronic books, such as the dot.com domains for Amazon, Apple, Kobo, Wattpad, and so on. As the container of the book changes in its various digital and platformed formats, so too does the forms of its paratext. It is not only the distribution and circulation platforms that influence the development of paratext, but for those that offer it, the production side as well.

I conceptualize these situated book design elements as platform paratext, which are generated through platform-specific technical affordances, interfaces, and contexts. To investigate how Amazon may be influencing the paratext self-published authors create, I analyzed the Amazon product pages of case profile authors using a grounded approach informed by website analysis. Website analyses have been used primarily in business studies as a method for usability and prototype testing.[57] This method positions the medium and text of websites as analytical objects and analyses the website's media environment (the internet and application ecosystem), its textual environment (hardware and software), and its textuality (written elements, static image elements, moving image elements, sound elements, and the coherence and formal relations between them).[58] My use of this method is informed by Johanna Drucker's theorization of interface as a "boundary space" that can be read as an object and a space that constitutes activity, a conceptualization that marries nicely with paratext.[59] Product detail pages follow a relatively standard template for all products sold on Amazon, though input into data fields (e.g., title, description, author) varied widely between authors' books suggesting that there is no standard for filling many of the data fields. All data were collected from the Australian Amazon store on a clean browser in early 2024, with screenshots taken for posterity.

One of the most obvious examples of how platforms alter paratextual elements is with regards to cover design. As platforms—especially Amazon—have become a primary point of book sales, covers have become increasingly designed to look good as tiny thumbnails on screens and not just on bookstore shelves or display tables. This means that where fine details once thrived (splashy prints, bright colors, contrast), Instagrammable or Book-Tokkable covers have taken over. In the case of romance fiction, the popular shirtless-male-torso covers of the self-publishing boom of the early 2010s has given way to a mass of illustrated covers. For authors writing BIPOC and LGBTQ+ characters and relationships, illustrated covers are one way to address the lack of diverse representation in stock image libraries described by Lau and Jackson in the previous chapter.

Illustrated covers are divisive in the romance genre world, though; apart from individuals' aesthetic preferences, they have been criticized for increasing the representation of historically marginalized groups visually without actually including the *people* from those communities. For Mina V. Esguerra, who self-publishes as part of a collective called #RomanceClass, using photorealist covers was an important move away from the illustrated chick-lit-style covers—pink, vector art—that she had on her traditionally published novels and increase the visibility of Filipinos in romance fiction. But she had a similar problem to Lau and Jackson: "there just aren't enough cover-worthy romance stock photos with Filipinos (or Asians even)."[60] In response to this problem, Esguerra, with other members of the #Romance-Class community, set up an ongoing project where authors pool resources, both financial and skill-based, to do semi-regular photoshoots with local actors.[61] These grassroots efforts are distinct in both the Filipino and Western romance industry, driven by collective goals rather than current market logics that give primacy to illustrated covers regardless of the sociopolitical implications because of their synergy with platform environments.

Another key paratext that has changed in response to the platform context is the subtitle data field. On Amazon, the title must faithfully reflect the title associated with the ISBN and cannot be changed after publication, but the subtitle can be edited and updated. This editability has resulted in publishers and authors, particularly those working in fiction, using the subtitle field in more creative and capricious ways. Many self-published authors I spoke to use the subtitle field to give information about the series in which the title appears; for example, the subtitle to Courtney Milan's *The Duchess Affair* is, at the time of writing, "The Brothers Sinister Book 1."[62] Increasingly, though, the subtitle field is used by traditional publishers and independent authors as a space for a tagline of sorts, which might include either as an endorsement for the author or book or extra information about the content or narrative of the book that operates as an extension of the blurb. Farrah Rochon's novel, *The Dating Playbook*, which is published by Headline Eternal (an imprint of Hachette) combines all three: "A fake-date rom-com to steal your heart! 'A total knockout: funny, sexy, and full of heart' (Boyfriend Project)."[63] What connects each of these strategies for the subtitle is that they operate as an extra site of recommendation to the reader about the author and/or book. This is both an implicit recommendation through intertextuality ("If you like fake dating stories, you'll like this book!") as well as technical recommendation in the subtitle field offers an extra space to include keywords that improve the discoverability of a title through Amazon Search and promote sales through comparisons with familiar favorites.

A significant feature of platform paratext is their editability. Except for the title, most paratextual elements that appear on Amazon product pages can be updated or changed either by the author (including the cover, subtitle, or description) or algorithmic processes (such as the order of reviews). As tethered appliances, any updates to the product pages or files through an author's KDP dashboard results in the ebook being updated on readers' devices.[64] In some ways, this tethering can be beneficial by providing authors the opportunity to fix grammatical errors found after publication or update their title list in the front matter, for instance. It has also been used to update covers in attempts to make older titles more marketable within current trends. For instance, the paperback version of Jaci Burton's *The Perfect Play*—a title that was among the first to popularize the shirtless male torso romance covers of the early 2010s—was updated in early 2024 with an illustrated cover and re-marketed to new readers.[65] The use of this editability affordance can be controversial though, if it is used in a misguided way (for example, some argued that adding an illustrated cover to *The Perfect Play* inappropriately disguised the sexually explicit nature of the novel), or by undermining readers' preferences (if they purchased a particular ebook for the cover, for instance). The mutability of digital texts and paratext also has significant implications for book historians, textual criticism, and bibliography, as these changes often occur with little or no trace.[66]

The increasing prominence of publishing platforms in the production, circulation, and distribution of books necessitates further research into their impacts on design practices in publishing. This is particularly important given the relationship between book design, user engagement, and automated decision making systems such as visibility algorithms, which can have significant effects on authors' sales. As will be explored in the next chapter, books' paratext—including their covers—also become subject to content moderation on platforms, which can disproportionately negatively impact people writing about BIPOC and LGBTQ+ communities.

Conclusion

In June 2020, amid the global Black Lives Matter protests and performative allyship of publishing companies as they shared anti-racist reading lists and statements of solidarity with the Black community on social media, the hashtag #PublishingPaidMe went viral on Twitter. This grassroots movement, started by Black young adult author L. L. McKinney on June 6, called for authors to share the advances they had received for their books. Information from the hashtag, which was collated in a spreadsheet, exposed the racial disparity in what authors were paid.[67] Highly prolific and celebrated Black authors such as Jesmyn Ward, N. K. Jemisin, and Roxane Gay reported having to fight their way to higher advances, even after they won awards and their earlier books demonstrated strong commercial appeal, while virtually unknown White authors reported getting huge advances on debut novels. The disparity in advances illustrates the commercial confidence traditional publishers have in books by and about historically marginalized people and, in turn, indicates how much (or rather, how little) they are likely to invest in the marketing of these books. The historic lack of transparency around inequitable advances and publishing deals—knowledge that has circulated as known secrets among many for years—has worked to further marginalize BIPOC and LGBTQ+ authors in book culture.

Publishing platforms provide an alternative for authors to these and other disparate treatments in traditional publishing by enabling them to self-publish more easily and cheaply. Self-publishing, which has exploded in the early twenty-first century in large part by the access granted by platforms, is often conflated with a more autonomous publishing practice. And while relative to traditional publishing houses authors are afforded greater creative control over their works and transparency around remuneration, platforms heavily mediate authors' publishing practice through their economic and technical infrastructures. Put differently, both Amazon and Wattpad present great potential for historically marginalized authors to build careers outside of traditional institutions but do so in ways that benefit their own bottom lines, subsume publishing under platform capitalism, and render self-published authors, along with contemporary book culture more broadly, increasingly dependent on proprietary platforms.

A clear way that platforms engender dependency is through market dominance. Many authors I spoke to who sold their books via Amazon did so primarily because the platform accounted for most of their sales but otherwise distributed widely across platforms. Despite attempts by Amazon to encourage exclusivity to the platform, wide distribution has become an important strategy to minimize dependency on Amazon as well as reach more readers. Katrina Jackson was the only author I spoke to who chose only to publish on Amazon due to its convenience. Describing her experience, she said "Amazon doesn't always feel good, but at this point it feels easy."[68] In her monograph *Buy Now*, Emily West argues that these two features are interlinked; Amazon has gained market dominance because of its branding of convenience, and can be economically convenient because of its ability to delegate sections of its business as loss-leaders.[69] Amazon is easy to use in nearly all aspects of consumers' lives and thus difficult to get away from. Under these conditions, authors may negotiate their creative praxis on digital publishing platforms but are ultimately bound by the specific publishing and remuneration structures built into platform interfaces that control the rules of participation with little regulation and competition. This is not to say that authors simply submit to the rigidity of platform structures. Indeed, many engage in strategies that purposefully circumvent platform-controlled spaces, for instance by engaging in activities that platforms provide infrastructure for *off-platform*. These circumnavigation strategies become incredibly important for BIPOC and LGBTQ+ authors targeted by automated platform systems based on their identities.

CHAPTER 3

Sorting and Moderating Books

Systems of Algorithmic (In)visibility

IN 2009, APPROXIMATELY 57,000 LGBTQ+ themed books disappeared from Amazon's search results page, bestseller lists, and sales ranks, a vanishing act that occurred after an Amazon employee reportedly mistakenly marked books classified as gay and lesbian as "adult" material.[1] Despite Amazon quickly correcting the mistake, the incident revealed that Amazon's search engine results, sales rank, and bestseller algorithms are moderated processes. It also shows the close links between the classification of cultural objects and their governance. Determining how books are classified also determines what we do with them, where they go, who they are supposedly made for, and who can access them. Library and information scientist, Hope A. Olson refers to this as the power to name; a power that often reinforces an unquestioning acceptance of common presumptions that reflect a mainstream view.[2] This power is especially impactful on the organization of information and cultural objects created by and about groups who have been historically excluded or marginalized in society and the cultural industries based on their gender, sexuality, race, age, ability, ethnicity, language, and/or religion.

Publishers and other institutions in the book industry have held this power to name and the related power to organize titles for a long time. Publishers choose industry standard BISAC (Book Industry Standards and Communication) codes for titles and organize these titles under imprints and lists. Bookstores stock a select catalog of books and arrange them under meaningful labels, including BISAC codes and other descriptors. And libraries have been shelving books according to the Dewey Decimal (DDC) or Library of Congress (LCC) classification system since the late nineteenth century. The need to sort and classify materials has only grown in the abundance of the digital age and this work is increasingly done by computational processes. As literary and cultural studies scholar Janice A.

Radway has argued, books "do not appear miraculously" in people's hands, but are, rather, "the end product of a much-mediated, highly complex, material and social process."[3] Platforms alter these processes, controlling abundance through strategies, including the design and implementation of automated or semi-automated classification and governance systems. This chapter explores how platforms mediate the discoverability and visibility of books through their classification and governance systems, and the power enacted by and negotiated between these platform systems and self-published authors of color and queer authors.

The data presented in this chapter were collected through original interviews, a walkthrough of platforms and their terms of service, and metadata analysis, and these latter methods warrant some detail. To go in order, the walkthrough method draws on ontologies from science and technology studies and cultural studies and involves performing a critical analysis of an application or website—in this case, Amazon's collection of terms of services pages. It entails systematically engaging with an interface to "examine its technological mechanisms and embedded cultural references to understand how it guides users and shapes their expectations" and a "step-by-step observation and documentation of an app's screens, features, and flows of activity."[4] This method has heuristic value for establishing a user-centered approach to analyzing apps or platforms' intended purposes and idealized users and uses.

The methods employed for collecting and analyzing metadata related to platform categorization and governance systems necessarily differed for Amazon and Wattpad as access to key metadata and information varied across the two platforms and over the research period. When I began collecting metadata of book categories from Amazon in 2019, I used a platform called Sales Rank Express, which collected and collated book metadata from Amazon through its application programming interface (API). This included information on a title's price, filter status, categories, (linked) paired titles, and so on for Amazon's US and UK stores. At this time, Amazon also showed the categories of books in the far-left column on the books' product pages on its website, which enabled a comparison between how a book was categorized on the backend (through Sales Rank Express data) and where it appeared on the front end (on the homepage). Likewise, I could compare the status of any flags or filters (i.e., for adult content) through Sales Rank Express with the impact it had on the visibility or searchability on amazon.com. In early 2020, Amazon changed access to its API and data could no longer be extracted through Sales Rank Express. Later that year, the list of categories and departments on amazon.com also disappeared, rendering this method for mapping categories useless too. By this stage, I had fortuitously collected the data for all my Amazon case studies. Unfortunately, without access to Amazon's API through Sales Rank Express or Amazon's affiliate program (through which access to the API is still available), reproducibility of this data collection method is not possible. Any further category metadata for books was collected using the "Book Category Hunter" tool on the website Nerdy Book Girl that uses the Amazon API and shows some of the categories books are organized in on the US marketplace, but no similar tool is available for adult filter flags.[5] Some further information on title categories were provided by authors in interviews.

Wattpad data remains more publicly accessible. On Wattpad, categories were collected by scraping tags listed publicly on story homepages.[6] When posting stories to Wattpad, authors choose from genre categories, such as romance and teen fiction, but can also free-text tags to boost keyword discoverability through the platform's search engine. Tags may still follow traditional subgenre descriptions or tropes, such as paranormal or enemies-to-lovers, but tend to be more idiosyncratic because they do not have to follow established categories. Wattpad tags were open coded and analyzed using a thematic analysis for common topics and themes. A comparative analysis between Amazon and Wattpad categories presented an opportunity to consider the way digital classification systems work to position and present books by historically marginalized author groups, and whether user-generated categories radically reinvent or subvert classification systems that subjugate historically marginalized groups.

The classification and governance systems on Amazon and Wattpad prove that the curatorial and gatekeeping roles ascribed to traditional publishing do not disappear online. Rather, these roles are replaced by technological mechanisms and policy formations, such as platform terms of service (ToS), review systems, and classification algorithms, which disproportionately affect authors from historically marginalized communities and, in doing so, reinforce structures of othering and discrimination evident in traditional book culture.

Structuring Marginalization in Book Classification Systems

Classification or knowledge organization systems are useful tools across cultural industries. They constitute the rules and regulations by which objects are grouped together into defined relationships, and when effective, allow for easy access to information. Book classification systems on publishing platforms can be read in context with contemporary print publishing and bookselling and traditional knowledge organization systems, such as BISAC, DDC, and LCC codes. As new knowledge organization systems often inherit, adapt, expand, or narrow terminologies from established systems, traditional knowledge organization systems offer an interpretative schema for analyzing their logics and hierarchies.[7]

Classification systems on publishing platforms adapt traditional systems of knowledge organization in the way they subjugate writing by and about historically marginalized groups. These systems are socially and culturally situated, shaped by who is doing the naming of information, what is represented or left unnamed, how information is organized relationally, and how access is granted to subjects—decisions that affect the circulation and reception of knowledge and cultural objects, and in which political biases and consequences are embedded.[8] As Olson puts it, knowledge organization systems do not "just passively reflect the dominant values of society in some neutral or objective manner, but selects those values for expression."[9] This selection, and the naming of the selection, is always a political act: a way of structuring and denoting reality, and cementing a certain (often hegemonic) perspective or worldview.

The relegation of particular subjects is in-built into the structure of traditional knowledge organization systems that are built around, and build, linear and hierarchical relationships between subjects based on an Aristotelian logic. Library classification systems tend to relegate books by and about historically marginalized groups under subject headings lower in the hierarchical structure or as other. For example, the literature class in the Dewey Decimal system includes divisions for American, European, English, Latin, and Greek literatures, with more specific subordinate classifications under each. African literatures, Literatures of North American native languages, and Literatures of East and Southeast Asia, as examples of literatures outside the White colonialist North, conversely, are positioned as the specific subclasses under the 890 Other Literatures division. BISAC subject headings, developed by the Book Industry Study Group (BISG) and used widely throughout the North American publishing industry, mirror the hierarchical structure of library systems.

BISAC is organized around subject headings based on literal descriptors that are linked to a nine-character alphanumeric code. For example:

- FIC000000 Fiction / General
- FIC002000 Fiction / Action & Adventure
- FIC022110 Fiction / Mystery & Detective / Cozy / Animals
- FIC082000 Fiction / Own Voices
- FIC027000 Fiction / Romance / General
- FIC027180 Fiction / Romance / Historical / Viking.

The maximum depth is four literal descriptors, with each part or level separated by a forward slash (/); e.g., (1) Fiction / (2) Romance / (3) Historical / (4) Viking. Publishers classify books according to these subject headings and booksellers typically, but do not always, organize their stores around first-level subject headings, such as art, history, fiction, young adult, travel, etc. As a subject heading system, BISAC is useful for the publishing industry as it aligns more closely with genre systems and resembles reader-interests.[10] As books may have more than one BISAC code attributed to them, they may be organized differently or in multiple places in different bookstores, increasing points of topical access and opportunities of discoverability to the same title.

Like library classification systems, though, BISAC subject headings encode Whiteness as the default or "General" category and set non-hegemonic genders and sexualities against an assumed cis-male, heterosexual norm. While first-level categories are organized around general topic content—art, bibles, biography and autobiography, cooking, drama, fiction, history, juvenile fiction, juvenile nonfiction, poetry, and so on—the second, third and fourth-level identifiers begin to mark out marginalized identities. Hegemonic political identities—Whiteness, maleness, straightness—are subsumed into the "General" or narrative-based subgenres. In romance fiction, for instance, there is no classification for books by White authors or that feature White characters. Rather, these books are sorted into FIC027000 Fiction / Romance / General or related to the setting (e.g., Contemporary, Historical, Holiday), characters' occupation (e.g., Firefighters, Rock Stars, Billionaires), subgenre elements (e.g., Erotica, Fantasy, Paranormal). In the

2024 edition, several descriptors based on tropes were added, presumably in part due to their increased usage in marketing and on BookTok (e.g., Fake Dating, Alpha Male, Enemies to Lovers). While books by and about historically marginalized groups may be coded under these trope-based subgenres, there are also several identifiers based on racial or sexual identity:

- FIC027300 Fiction / Romance / LGBTQ+ / General
- FIC027390 Fiction / Romance / LGBTQ+ / Bisexual
- FIC027190 Fiction / Romance / LGBTQ+ / Gay
- FIC027210 Fiction / Romance / LGBTQ+ / Lesbian
- FIC027600 Fiction / Romance / LGBTQ+ / Nonbinary and Genderqueer
- FIC027400 Fiction / Romance / LGBTQ+ / Transgender
- FIC027520 Fiction / Romance / LGBTQ+ / Two-Spirited & Indigiqueer
- FIC027470 Fiction / Romance / Polyamory
- FIC049060 Fiction / Romance / African American & Black
- FIC027500 Fiction / Romance / Hispanic & Latino
- FIC027510 Fiction / Romance / Indigenous
- FIC027230 Fiction / Romance / Multicultural & Interracial.

The explicit naming of political minorities and non-naming of White, cisgender, and heterosexual identities is not exclusive to the fiction or romance categories. Those writing biographies, autobiographies, social science, literary collections, poetry, and drama also have their works categorized according to this system. However, some groups that are included as second level identifiers in the fiction and other categories are excluded in romance subcategories. These include texts by and about Asian & Asian American people (FIC054000 Fiction / Asian American) and disabled people (FIC079000 Fiction / Disabilities & Special Needs). The absence of these subject headings under romance fiction further marginalizes books about and authors who are part of these communities.

As several critical race and internet scholars have demonstrated, the internet is also a racialized space, where ideas about race, ethnicity, and identity more broadly are encoded through technological structures.[11] What possibility is there, then, for publishing platforms to transform discriminatory systems of book classification? Unfortunately, but perhaps unsurprisingly, in the case of Amazon, there is very little chance. Employing a similar top-down categorization system to BISAC codes, Amazon replicates hierarchical logics that marginalize culturally diverse subjects and authors through its classification system.

How Books are Organized on Amazon

Books self-published via Amazon's self-publishing platform Kindle Direct Publishing (KDP) are subject to two classification systems that operate relationally. First, authors classify their books from a list of "browse categories" on the KDP platform and second, upon publication, Amazon translates these and other metadata to determine the placement of titles on its online storefront. The connection forged between top-level categories, more descriptive subcategories, and placement categories creates a path that determines how books are named and where they appear on the platform. The KDP browse categories use similar subject headings to BISAC, but do not faithfully copy them. Additions to Amazon browse categories include popular self-published genres like Yaoi, also known as Boys Love, a genre of fictional media originating in Japan that features homoerotic relationships between male characters, signaling the increasing prominence of popular online genres in publishing platform systems. More importantly, Amazon's browse categories replicate acts of subjugation in traditional classification systems by designating literature by and about culturally marginalized groups as other from a "General", unspecified but supposedly White, classification.

Some authors I spoke to for this research described instances where the information on their Amazon author profile determined how their books were classified. All the authors that participated in this research had books classified in categories based on race or ethnicity and all Amazon authors interviewed—Courtney Milan, Jackie Lau, Suleikha Snyder, Xio Axelrod, Katrina Jackson, Melissa Blue/Dakota Gray, and Farrah Rochon—had at least one book classified as "Multicultural" on the US site. All books by Jackie Lau, an Asian Canadian author, and Suleikha Snyder, an Indian American author, were classified as Multicultural, while only one by Courtney Milan, an Asian American author, was classified this way. Katrina Jackson, Melissa Blue/Dakota Gray and Farrah Rochon, all Black authors, also had books that had been classified as Literature and Fiction > United States > African American. It is possible that the positioning of books in the African American literature category is Amazon's translation of authors who choose the

African American romance browse category when they entered the metadata into KDP. However, the exception of books by Xio Axelrod, who is also a Black author, in this category suggests that it is not just browse categories that dictate this positioning. Based on evidence provided by Axelrod, author data is also a determining factor in the categorization of books on Amazon.

When Axelrod first started self-publishing her books on Amazon, she listed a few in the multicultural romance browse category.[12] Multicultural/ interracial romance is a smaller category on Amazon, so it takes fewer sales to be ranked higher in the bestseller and top seller lists. While the size of subgenres—measured by the number of authors writing and titles available in them—like African American romance and multicultural and interracial romance is an indictment on the opportunities for authors of color in the publishing industry, listing titles in these subgenres can be a useful marketing strategy for authors to reach their readers, and conversely for readers of these subgenres to find books they are interested in.

Axelrod eventually decided she wanted to move her books from the smaller category of African American romance to larger categories that are not based on race. As she said, her goal "has always been to sell my books. I want as many readers as possible from as many backgrounds as I possibly can because my stories are universal. Everyone's story is universal."[13] To make this switch, she reclassified her titles on KDP, changing the romance browse category from "Multicultural" to "Contemporary." Contemporary romance is one of the largest subgenres of romance fiction with one of the largest readerships so "even if [the book is] lower on the totem pole," Axelrod said, "it still gets exposed to a wider audience."[14] Except, Axelrod said, Amazon kept sorting her books into the African American Literature and Multicultural Romance categories, including "books [she] never tagged" that way.[15] She would log on to Amazon KDP, take the books out of the categories she did not want listed, and Amazon's knowledge organization system would move them back, and she would start again. Axelrod said that this back-and-forth finally stopped when she changed her author photo from a portrait of herself, a Black woman, to her logo, an illustrated heart with two people embracing and her name in white on a dark purple background.

The possibility of Amazon changing categories that authors input is flagged on a KDP help page, where they state that

> We [Amazon] reserve the right to change the categories of a book at any time to ensure a positive customer experience.

> The categories you add and the categories shown online may
> not always match. Your book may be added to additional or
> different categories to improve the customer experience.[16]

However, Axelrod's experience suggests that categories based on ethnicity and race follow authors of color into online spaces, whether they want them to or not, and Amazon's platform capitalist logics give supremacy to one kind of user (customer) experience over the autonomy and experience of another user (authors, as publishers and content creators).

Further, it shows that in addition to metadata provided by self-published authors, Amazon appears to use profile data of authors, including author photos, biographies, and metadata linked to other books from the same account, to determine how books should be categorized in its ecommerce system. This could be considered a form of techno-cultural redlining. While the term redlining was first used to describe the practice of banks refusing mortgage loans to customers who lived in neighborhoods associated with racial minorities, scholars have since used it to describe how other institutions perpetuate this kind of discrimination. In platform studies, Safiya Umoja Noble has described processes of technological redlining whereby people from racial minorities are discriminated against through technical systems such as Google Search.[17] Similarly, Richard Jean So has used the term cultural redlining to describe the marginalization and exclusion of people of color from the cultural industries, particularly publishing.[18] Amazon continues a tradition of redlining in the book industry through its classification system, which replicates systems marginalization evident in traditional systems of book classification. In doing so, and in employing an opaque system whereby classifications are determined based on an amalgam of metadata, Amazon's classification system undermines the autonomy of self-published authors, and impacts the discoverability and potential sales of their titles.

Metadata associated with authors' identities also seem to impact book classifications and recommendation algorithms on Amazon. Authors' profile data impact the network of related titles on Amazon, including books that are paired through "also-bought" and "also-read" recommendations. Also-bought recommendations were launched on Amazon's marketplace in 2004 and are the platform's recommendation system that shows up on books' sale page and after customers make a purchase. They read something like: "Customers who bought this item also bought . . .". Amazon's recommendation algorithm is based on a relatedness metric based on differential probabilities; "item B is related to item A if purchasers of A are more likely to buy B than the average Amazon customer is."[19] While the precise algorithm is not publicly available, also-bought recommendations are based on a complex matrix of data including categories, customer purchase and view histories, and, for books, linked or paired titles that are nominated and/or paid for by the author or publishers. Also-bought recommendations on a given book title page are often from the same genre or subgenre. In other words, on a contemporary romance book page, the also-bought recommendations are more than likely to also be contemporary romance, and novels on a sport romance page are likely to be other sport romances.

When Amazon changed the classification of Axelrod's books from Contemporary Romance to Literature & Fiction > United States > African American, the titles that showed up as also-bought recommendations on her books' pages also changed from similarly categorized books within the romance genre to books by and about African American people from a variety of genres including history and biography. When Axelrod changed her profile photo, the also-bought recommendations on her product pages changed back "almost overnight" to romance fiction titles.[20] Amazon categories therefore do not only affect the visibility, placement, and movement of individual books—they also contribute to the formation of book assemblages that indicate relatedness and thus reinforce conceptions associated with certain book categories and genres in a kind of "algorithmic imagination."[21] This particular assemblage by Amazon, which prioritizes identity over genre, reinforces the false notion that books by and about people of color do not fit neatly into popular, mainstream genre categories and are only produced for a small, niche audience with shared identity. Romance fiction titles featuring LGBTQ+ characters have also been subject to disparate organizational rules whereby identity-based attributes have resulted in books being filtered into unrelated subject classifications, a point I'll return to shortly.

While the author's identity may be a determining element in publishers choosing BISAC codes—Fiction / World Literature is intended for works written by authors commonly identified as being from a specified country or region (outside the US or UK), for instance—the increased datafication of books and authors on publishing platforms means that determinations relating to identity are exponentially more complex and increasingly automated. The distinctive treatment of books by and about marginalized people in Amazon's classification system impacts both authors and readers. Subject representation in classification systems is as much an exercise in controlling access as it is in naming and hierarchizing cultural objects.[22] As the largest platform and retailer for self-published authors, how books are classified, organized, and grouped on Amazon has a significant impact on the careers of self-published authors. Amazon replicates established patterns of knowledge organization systems that position books by and about people of color and LGBTQ+ authors against a White, cisgendered, heteronormative norm that is subsumed under a "General" classification. Amazon also introduces new modes of naming based on the datafication of author profiles on its platform.

Even this is not a straightforward process, though. The metadata collected for books by the authors I spoke to showed discrepancies in book categories across formats and geolocation stores. Take Courtney Milan's contemporary romance title *Hold Me*, for example, which shows different categories for the same book across the Books and Kindle departments. In the Books department, *Hold Me* is categorized as Contemporary Romance, Multicultural Romance, and New Adult and College Romance. In the Kindle department, it is categorized as Contemporary Romance, Multicultural & Interracial romance, LGBTQ+ Romance / Bisexual Romance, and LGBTQ+ Romance / Transgender Romance. The differences in categories across the departments for a title with the same ASIN (Amazon Standard Identification Number) demonstrate the inconsistency of the categorization process and the role of other metadata in determining title classifications, particularly for categories denoting representations of marginalized populations.

Until around 2022, in order to have a title appear in the LGBTQ+ sub-categories, the title's search metadata needed to include specific keywords. According to a table on a KDP help page in 2022, in order to appear in the LGBTQ+ categories, specific keywords needed to be input by authors in the metadata section (table 2). The title, author, and descriptions on the print and Kindle versions of *Hold Me* are the same so it is unlikely that the keywords for each format are different and thus result in the differences in categorization. The difference between formats suggests that metadata is translated differently by the Books and Kindle departments in the process of determining title categories and placement. The organization of books on Amazon's marketplace is determined through an opaque system that incorporates title metadata, including keywords, descriptions, and author information in addition to browse categories.

Table 2. KDP Help Page Advice on which Keywords to Use
for Books to Appear in LGBTQ+-Related Placement Categories

Amazon.com Placement Category	Keywords
Lesbian, Gay, Bisexual & Transgender eBooks / LGBT Studies / Bisexuality	bisexual
Lesbian, Gay, Bisexual & Transgender eBooks / LGBT Studies / Transgender Studies	transgender
Lesbian, Gay, Bisexual & Transgender eBooks / Politics	lgbt, gay, lesbian, transgender, bisexual
Lesbian, Gay, Bisexual & Transgender eBooks / Romance / Bisexual Romance	bisexual
Lesbian, Gay, Bisexual & Transgender eBooks / Romance / Transgender Romance	transgender
Lesbian, Gay, Bisexual & Transgender eBooks / Science Fiction & Fantasy / Fantasy	lgbt, gay, lesbian, transgender, bisexual
Lesbian, Gay, Bisexual & Transgender eBooks / Science Fiction & Fantasy / Science Fiction	lgbt, gay, lesbian, transgender, bisexual

Keywords and phrases in a variety of metadata fields heavily influence the placement of titles in Amazon's bookstores. This includes technical information about a product, such as file size and type, language, publication date, ISBN (International Standard Book Number) and/or ASIN, as well as title information provided by authors, including the book title, subtitle, book description (blurb), keywords, series information, publisher information, and author information. The way these metadata are used to determine placement is extremely opaque for authors who are dependent on Amazon for their careers. As the table above suggests, keywords are a blunt instrument to determine placement in particular categories. The same keywords—bisexual, transgender, LGBT, gay, and lesbian—are advised for different genre categories. Theoretically, other category information helps to determine the placement of bisexual romance in Lesbian, Gay, Bisexual & Transgender eBooks / Romance / Bisexual Romance rather than Lesbian, Gay, Bisexual & Transgender eBooks / Science Fiction & Fantasy / Fantasy.

However, some books by the case profile authors in this research that featured LGBTQ+ characters were listed by Amazon in categories entirely extraneous to their genre or subject matter. These oddball categories differed across geolocation sites. On the US Amazon store, the Kindle version of *Adonis Line* by Dakota Gray[23] (a pseudonym of Melissa Blue) is surprisingly listed under the Arts & Photography > Photography & Video category, though this was the only instance among the case study authors of a nonsensical category on the US site. On the UK site, however, many books featuring LGBTQ+ characters by Xio Axelrod, Katrina Jackson, and Courtney Milan were categorized as Society, Politics & Philosophy > Social Sciences and University Textbooks > Social Sciences. The titles listed under this category included: Milan's *Hamilton's Battalion*[24] and *Mrs. Martin's Incomparable Adventure,*[25] Axelrod's *When Frankie Meets Johnny*[26] and *Love is All vol. 3,*[27] and Jackson's *Small Town Secrets*[28] and *Bang & Burn.*[29] These are also the only books also categorized as Gay & Lesbian > Literature from the sample on the UK site. It is striking that the same keywords (e.g., transgender, bisexual) can result in a book being sorted into romance fiction as well as LGBTQ+ studies and politics categories without much differentiation between the genres. Theoretically, contextual keywords and categories should minimize, if not eliminate, the possibility for LGBTQ+ romance fiction to be categorized as textbooks or study materials, but in practice this is obviously not the case. This may be an unintentional, unidentified, and/or unresolved error, but it is further proof that Amazon organizes books about LGBTQ+ people and relationships differently to those that feature cis-heterosexual relationships. Books by and about people of color and LGBTQ+ people would thus be doubly marginalized in Amazon's system, as titles that fit into associated identity-based categories are subject to intersecting filtering biases.

The additional importance of this other metadata in a data-centric online context has led publishers and self-published authors to adapt the conventions of these fields. Subtitles on Amazon, for instance, increasingly include marketing- and keyword-rich subheadings such as Xio Axelrod's *The Girl with Stars in Her Eyes*, which includes the subtitle "A story of love, loss, and rock-and-roll (The Lillys Book 1)" on Amazon.[30] This trend is more popular among books published by multinational publishers; for example, on the Australian Amazon site, *The Other Black Girl* by Zakiya Dalila Harris, published by Bloomsbury publishing, includes the subheading "'Get Out meets The Devil Wears Prada' Cosmopolitan" as part of the book's Amazon title, emphasizing the symbolic capital associated with a book having been reviewed in Cosmopolitan.[31] Sally Thorne's *The Hating Game*, published by Piatkus, an imprint of Little, Brown, includes the subheading "TikTok Made Me Buy It! The Perfect Enemies to Lovers Romcom" and represents an increasing number of titles using TikTok as a selling point in the subtitle. *It Ends with Us* by Colleen Hoover, published by Simon & Schuster, and a breakout TikTok book throughout 2021–2023 adopts a similar subtitle to Thorne's novel: "TikTok Made Me Buy It! The Most Heartbreaking Novel You'll Ever Read."[32] Subtitles provide additional heuristic searchable keywords, such as the series title (e.g., The Lillys), themes and tropes included in the story (e.g., Love, and Rock-and-Roll), and marketing recommendations and buzzwords (e.g., Cosmopolitan, TikTok) that improve potential discoverability as well as the placement of books in niche microgenres.[33] As forms of digital paratext, they also influence how readers approach and read these stories.

The development of controlled vocabularies through subject headings aims to improve accessibility to content libraries by applying identical and consistent top-level subject headings to their catalog representations. However, a controlled vocabulary limits the system of representation, constructs a universality/diversity binary, hides exclusions under the guise of neutrality, and "disproportionately affects access to information outside of the cultural mainstream and about groups marginalized in our society."[34] Universalized (Western) norms historically have been built into systems of classification and knowledge organization but also become universalized through them. As can be seen with the impact of metadata on Amazon's placement of books by historically marginalized authors, free-text functions can create more classificatory possibilities—a possibility put to the test on Wattpad.

Collective Categorization: The Potential of Tags on Wattpad

Wattpad adopts a dual approach to categorizing the millions of stories on its platform that combines a top-down subject heading taxonomy with elements of a user-driven tagging system, or folksonomy. Folksonomies are user-generated systems of classifying and organizing content online into different categories using electronic tags, most often associated with fan fiction sites. In contrast to the hierarchical nature of other taxonomies that are structured like trees with branches for specific topics, folksonomies and tagging systems can be interpreted as piles of leaves, composed of non-hierarchical clusters of information.[35] Tags enhance the search function on Wattpad and in this way somewhat resemble the keywords used by Amazon's classification algorithms. Tags are also explicitly connected to stories on their landing pages and thus act as interpretive paratext as well as navigational aids. As English and fan fiction scholar Maria Lindgren Leavenworth notes in relation to paratextual elements on fan fiction sites, while some "tags work similarly to how fictions are arranged in a bookstore, signaling a connection to known genres, others are specific to the fanfic text form and as they are placed in close proximity to the text itself, signal both how the text should be read and how it should *not* be read."[36] While there is a common lexicon of tags on different sites, the ability to free-text tags offers a potential for a wider interpretive schema and more inclusive classification system.

On Wattpad, tags are essential to classify texts with descriptors that indicate diversity and inclusion. When posting a new story to Wattpad, authors select a category from a drop-down menu, which can be augmented with tags using a free-text function. Categories reflect major publishing/genre categories—such as action, adventure, fantasy, historical fiction, mystery and thriller, non-fiction, romance, science fiction, poetry, teen fiction—and subgenres, like paranormal and vampire. Notably missing is any category that relates to marginalized identities; there is no LGBTQ+ or "Diverse Lit" category to choose from on the author end, despite both appearing in the browse menu on the site's homepage. Stories are linked to these categories through user-generated tags.

Tags may be used in a variety of ways by authors beyond signaling genre or category. Tags can also be used as meta-commentary and as expressions of emotion and affect.[37] The tags on stories by the case profile authors demonstrate what this looks like for some marginalized identities and representation. Across the twenty-one stories by the authors I interviewed, the most common tags include *youngadult, love, romance, humor, teenfiction, adventure, life, drama,* and *Filipino*. Several tags—and variations of tags—are used to indicate diversity and inclusion by all authors. These include: *celebrateblackwriters, civilrights, diverse, diversity, weneeddiverse-books, poc, interracial, arab, islam, philippines, filipino, westphsea, taglish, tagalog, bisexual, bi, girlxgirl, gxg, lesbian, uselesslesbian, gay, gaydisaster, lgbt, lgbtq, lgbtpride, writtenwithpride,* and *lgbt-themed.* Some of these fit within relatively established lexicons of representation, such as *weneeddiversebooks* and *gxg*, the former a term popularized through a social media campaign that began in 2016 by a non-profit children's literature organization, and the latter a popular shorthand for lesbian-themed literature on fan fiction sites. Others are idiosyncratic to certain authors and texts. For example, Sol Tuberosum includes the *uselesslesbian* tag on her apocalyptic story *Wish Granted* as a reference to her "hopeless romantic klutz" main character.[38] At the time of writing, only six other stories used this tag on Wattpad. The greater freedom afforded by a folksonomy system represents a more inclusive approach to indexing as authors can articulate their individual vocabularies and identities and prioritize aspects of the text that they feel are important.

The variety of tags denoting diversity and inclusion, with many variations often appearing on the same story, show that writers are embracing the opportunity to classify their work with non-hegemonic descriptors. With no limitations on the number of tags and an ability to include a variety of lexical descriptors, authors can include words or phrases, including slang, that have specific meanings for marginalized communities. This ability for self-determination is especially important for texts by authors from marginalized communities that have been subjected to relegation in hegemonic classification systems like DDC, BISAC, and Amazon categories. Wattpad authors require a high level of community knowledge of the platform and its reader audience—knowledge of which tags are widely used and searched for and by whom—in order to successfully use tags as a discoverability tool.

Despite the opportunities afforded by a folksonomy system, the way tags are incorporated in Wattpad's visibility algorithms is unclear. For Ivey Choi, it is "a big gripe of me and my friends . . . that the tagging system is, like, broken." She explains: "if you search, like, paranormal, bad boy, fantasy, werewolf or something like that [then] you'll be able to find very specific books that match exactly what you're looking for, but . . . I don't think they really offer a good way to see what's trending in young adult fiction, what's trending in romance."[39] This suggests that tags are more useful for readers looking for certain kinds of stories rather than those searching to serendipitously find something that interests them. This makes it hard for authors to reach new readers and may keep authors from marginalized backgrounds in narrow spheres.

This difficulty is compounded by the opaqueness of the relationship between tags and visibility on the homepage, where carousels of featured stories have become a primary site for readers to discover new stories. For the first five years or so, Wattpad's homepage featured stories that reflected user-driven popularity metrics; most-read, most-starred, and so on. As Wattpad begun to actively commercialize the user content and data through its pan-entertainment business model, the homepage increasingly featured platform-curated story carousels that fed back into its monetization programs, such as carousels titled "From our Stars," "Paid Stories," "Published by Wattpad Books," "Wattpad Studio Hits," and "Available in Bookstores." The curtailment of the role of popularity metrics in the categorization of stories on the homepage has occurred simultaneously with a decrease in social functionality on the site. The news feed, chat function, forums, and other social connectivity features have been reduced to a narrow window of user engagement, including commenting, liking, and not much else. The top-level menu option on the homepage has gone from housing links to forums to a single link to the Watty Awards page, an award that itself has gone from being fan-voted to being judged by a selection of Wattpad staff.

The changes to the platform's organizational system since around 2015, which includes an increase in curatorial selection on the homepage, has made discoverability feel more inaccessible for many of its authors. As Simone Shirazi said, "I was never a huge reader on Wattpad, but now I just don't even know how to find books that I will actually like, because everything is like Paid Stories and more Paid Stories, honestly."[40] Discovery on Wattpad is now more likely to be facilitated through platform-mediated visibility mechanisms such as trending and bestseller lists, just as on Amazon, or featured carousels of thematically-similar stories on the homepage. The minimization of social functionality that generates user engagement seems at odds with a platform whose business model is based on user-generated data. However, what we have seen on Wattpad over the last seven years or so is not an elimination of the data, but rather its privatization and strategic commercial redeployment. The folksonomy tagging system provides Wattpad an opportunity to gain insight into audiences, trends, evolving language, and emerging popular microgenres that Wattpad commercializes by on selling this trend data and adapting popular content through its own programs and partnerships. The tagging system therefore works for Wattpad as much, if not more, than it does for authors.

While some carousels on Wattpad's homepage are organized around genre or lead readers to Wattpad's commercial programs, many also reflect the broader popular culture and media environment in which stories are written. It is not uncommon to see seasonal featured lists on Wattpad, such as "Spooky SZN" (October) and "Scorpio Season" (October–November). Intertextual media tags also proliferate as writers are encouraged to include tags of bands, media texts and celebrity names on fan fiction and other genres if celebrities' likeness have been cast onto the characters (i.e., if characters are meant to look like celebrities even if they do not portray them). Wattpad also connects stories to popular culture and media events through curated categories, or "handpicked" in Wattpad's vernacular, on the homepage. In January 2021, when season one of the historical romance series Bridgerton was trending on Netflix, Wattpad featured a carousel of historical romance fiction stories under the headline "In The Mood For Historical Fiction?" This reflects a broader trend by cultural and entertainment platforms and apps (from creative writing to video streaming) to organize content with a focus on affect and experience through microgenres.

This experience-based or affective categorization is evident on other cultural and entertainment platforms and apps (from writing and publishing to music or video streaming), which increasingly organize content into microgenres based around affect and experience. When the final season of Succession premiered on Binge in Australia in 2023, the tags on each episode page featured easter eggs from the episodes; Episode 2 had category tags *drama*, *business*, and *scandal* alongside *disgusting brother*, a reference to the self-characterization of the relationship between Tom Wambsgans (played by Matthew Macfadyen) and Greg Hirsch (played by Nicholas Braun). On my personal Netflix account at the time of writing, there are carousels entitled "Irreverent Sitcoms," "Casual Viewing," "Gal Pals Movies & TV Shows," "True Bromance," and "Food for Hungry Brains" (this latter one featuring documentaries).

Categories and classifications have historically been used by producers to communicate genre to potential audiences and produced through the textual form as well as marketing and reception. The affective, experience-based categories on cultural and entertainment platforms that have attention economy business models and thus more reliant on creating valuable user experiences, highlight the degree to which consumers have become central to the construction of genres. In other words, these categories demonstrate the increasing *interconnection* between marketing, textual form, and reception in the organization of content on digital platforms. These genre processes do not happen in isolation of media sectors though. As is evidenced by the Bridgerton-inspired categorization example on Wattpad, there is a growing intertextuality between media sectors in the formation and understanding of affective, experience-based genres. This interrelationship demonstrates the growing connection of popular culture across platforms and media spheres in the entertainment ecosystem explored more in chapter 5.

Wattpad has promoted itself as a platform that has "democratized storytelling for a new generation of diverse Gen Z writers."[41] The use of the terms "democratized" and "diverse" implies a values-based project of transformation, but this ideal has been undermined by mundane capitalist interests. While a folksonomy tagging system allows more agency amongst authors to categorize their creative works and may thus be seen to be a more democratic form of knowledge organization, writing and reading on the platform is ultimately shaped by corporate interests. Wattpad mediates the power of a folksonomy logic through algorithmic and editorial hierarchization of featured content in featured carousels and search results, often to the detriment of BIPOC and queer authors who have historically been marginalized in capitalist publishing systems.

While categories based on race and sexuality can be a useful marketing tool that help readers find the books they are interested in, Amazon and Wattpad's classification algorithms can be a crude and reductive interpretation based on the book and author metadata. Books classified with these categories face even more barriers to publication and discoverability through the platforms' content moderation systems. What happens when a classification ascribed to a product contravenes the platform's ToS, for instance? Or, more pressingly, what happens when classifications result in automated processes that perpetuate the marginalization of historically excluded groups?

Naming, Moderation, and Visibility

As the example at the beginning of this chapter shows, there is a close relationship between how we classify cultural objects and how we treat them. Classification systems are tools of access; they determine where we see objects and if and how we can retrieve them. In physical book settings, this often means if and where titles are shelved, what other books they sit with, and how close they are within reach. The story of Xio Axelrod reclassifying her books against automated processes that put her books in categories she didn't want demonstrates how book classifications interact with sorting algorithms, including related titles that show up as also-boughts or bestseller lists. On publishing platforms, the classifications and metadata of book titles are captured under and subject to content moderation. This section examines how publishing platforms' governance systems moderate books and, in particular, its impact on cultural products by marginalized creators.

Governance structures are an important part of the platform ecosystem. How platforms regulate content and users through ToS, end-user license agreements (EULAs), and moderation systems materially impacts users' experiences. As Tarleton Gillespie points out in *Custodians of the Internet*, although platforms often position themselves as open, impartial, and non-interventionist spaces, governance is necessary online in order to protect "one user from another, or one group from its antagonists, and to remove the offensive, vile, or illegal."[42] Platforms have a duty to ensure behavior on their sites complies with external laws and regulations, and filter or remove content that is antithetical to these frameworks as well as the platform's internal policies and brand.[43] These policy documents are spaces in which platforms articulate and construct value. This section investigates Amazon's governance structures by conducting a walkthrough of Amazon's terms of service and conditions of use, which stipulate the legalities around privacy, intellectual property, and acceptable content. It also explores how the platform moderates content it deems to breach its conditions of use through interviews with affected authors.

Books disseminated via Amazon are subject to both human and computational moderation systems. Amazon applies a proactive automatic detection review system that uses word and image filters to assess the cover, description, author, title, categories, and tags to regulate books published and sold via its sites. This method matches new content with known violations.

At the scale of books published and sold on Amazon, Amazon likely uses its automatic detection software, Rekognition, to perform this programmed review. If the automatic detection software flags content for violating ToS (e.g., copyright, hate speech), if customers report books for issues, or if authors or publishers submit requests for review of a content moderation outcome, Amazon will also conduct a retroactive human editorial review. This human element has proven to be inconsistent, perhaps partly due to differing interpretations of ambiguous platform conditions of use by moderators. Ascertaining when, how, and why moderation teams intervene reveals important information about how users and content are treated differently on Amazon and how platforms may perpetuate harm through biased systems of moderation.

What is Considered "Adult Content" in Romance?

Self-published authors must first self-determine if their books contain adult materials when publishing a book on Amazon. During the set-up of their books through KDP, authors are asked: "Does the book's cover or interior contain sexually explicit images, or does the book's title contain sexually explicit language?" Accompanying this question is a checkbox: check *yes* if true; leave unchecked if *no*. Amazon now provides some further detail regarding what constitutes sexually explicit images (e.g., nudity or sexual poses) and language (e.g., words or phrases that refer to sexual acts, etc.), but at the time of data collection, the question stood alone without contextual information. If authors checked *yes*, the book's visibility and movement would be limited on the site. Knowing this or perhaps having different ideas of what constitutes adult content in different genre contexts, authors may not have always checked this box. Regardless of their choice, their books could still end up marked as containing adult materials and suppressed within Amazon's marketplace.

As with all books published and sold on Amazon, when Katrina Jackson published her novel *Her Christmas Cookie* on KDP, it went through a content review.[44] This review, conducted initially by Rekognition, can take anywhere between four hours and three days after which, if no violations of the ToS are found, the book is made available in the Amazon store. If the book is found to breach Amazon and KDP's terms of service, the book is prevented from being published on the platform. This is what happened to Jackson's novel, which was deemed to contain inappropriate content on the cover. The cover features a circle black and white photo-style image of a woman, bordered by a red Christmas-themed background, with the title, subtitle and author name in white. The woman in the image has tightly curled dark hair and dark skin. She is sitting down and looking away from the camera, her shoulders and upper arms are bare, and her torso and legs are covered by a white sheet. Despite the relatively small amount of skin depicted, Amazon's Rekognition software determined that the cover image contained adult material (likely nudity) and prevented *Her Christmas Cookie* from being published via KDP.[45]

How this book ended up flagged may have something to do with how Amazon's Rekognition software works. Rekognition is a deep learning convolutional neural network that can identify and analyze text, objects, people, scenes, and activities in images and video content. As a machine-learning tool, it compares content under review to a large library of images and videos, including those previously tagged as "unsafe," and labels similar content. Automatic detection tools are also typically programmed to identify body-like shapes, texture, and/or depth within the image. Likewise, some recognition tools consider the text surrounding the image, including captions, user comments, or the name and metadata of the image file. Flags of unsafe content are labeled in a two-level hierarchical taxonomy of categories. The four top-level categories are explicit nudity, suggestive, violence, and visually disturbing. Under each top-level category are a few second-level categories. Explicit nudity can be further classified as nudity, graphic male nudity, graphic female nudity, sexual activity, illustrated nudity or sexual activity, or adult toys. Suggestive content can be further classified as female swimwear or underwear, male swimwear or underwear, partial nudity, or revealing clothes. As is evident, Rekognition has a limited vocabulary to describe content that may potentially contain "adult" materials.

Rekognition and other automatic detection software can be confused by unusual lighting conditions, images that include colors that may be confused with skin tones and clothing that interrupts areas of skin tone, including, potentially, Jackson's novel *Private Eye*, which has a similar color palette across the whole cover and had not been flagged as adult content.[46] It may also present inconsistent results with images that include naked skin but are not objectionable such as baby photos, beach snaps, or artistically or historically significant works. In 2016, for example, Facebook removed a copy of the Nick Ut's Pulitzer prize-winning photo "Napalm Girl" posted by a Norwegian journalist for violating the site's terms of service, and in 2018, it removed an image of the Venus of Willendorf after its moderation protocol mistook the image for an advertisement that depicted nudity instead of an image of the sculpture.[47] Rekognition may also be limited in detection in black and white images, which may have compromised the review of Jackson's novel.

Automatic detection tools are also unequipped to consider the context of images or their relationship to established genre conventions. Jackson is the author of fourteen romance novels and novellas, all solely published and sold through Amazon. Many of Jackson's book covers feature a similar image: a Black woman, sometimes a torso shot fully clothed, sometimes a profile shot with bare shoulders. In the context of contemporary romance fiction more broadly, Jackson's covers tend not to be overly suggestive. Since the 1970s and 1980s when romance fiction first began including explicit descriptions of sex, romance covers have tended to pictorially indicate the intimate content inside. Fabio, the long-haired, shirtless male cover model who graced many romance fiction covers throughout the 1980s and 1990s resonates well beyond the romance reading audience, as does the "clinch" cover trope that shows a couple embracing, often with lots of skin on show and in the early 2010s covers featuring naked male-presenting torsos abounded as self-published romance fiction and new adult romance fiction proliferated. Despite the decontextualized sphere in which automatic detection tools operate, Amazon Rekognition now has incredible power over shaping genre conventions.

These technical calls on acceptability unfairly target depictions of marginalized people. When asked why she thought the review had a negative outcome, particularly considering some of the conventions of romance fiction covers historically, Jackson responded, "I think it's because she's Black, to be honest . . . I think it's because she's a Black woman."[48] She refers to Elia Winters' *Three-Way Split* as a comparison, and the standard that is generally accepted in romance fiction and by Amazon; a cover that contains the clinch and naked male torso conventions described above as well as a White woman scantily clad in lingerie.[49] Despite Winters' cover representing content that Amazon's automatic detection software could deem unsafe— large, uninterrupted areas of bare skin, for example—the cover had not been moderated by Amazon Rekognition. While this comparison or Jackson's experience with *Her Christmas Cookie* is not generalizable—there are plenty of romance novel covers with Black women who are suggestively dressed, including by Jackson—this incident does point to the way that computer vision and automatic detection software perpetuate inaccuracies and biases against people of color.

Along with other automatic detection software by companies like IBM, Microsoft, and Facebook, Amazon Rekognition is relatively imprecise at identifying skin tone and nudity and substantially less accurate in identifying darker-skinned individuals, particularly darker-skinned women, compared to lighter-skinned people.[50] These biases are often inherited from the human raters who train the data on which machine learning tools like Rekognition are based.[51] Research on different social media platforms by several scholars has demonstrated that content moderation disproportionately and uniquely impacts women and mainly women of color. Twitter was shown to knowingly permit a disproportionate level of abuse to Black women, Instagram has previously restricted hashtags related to women of color, like #MixedGirls and #MexicanGirls, and Tumblr no longer allows images of "female-presenting nipples."[52]

The difference in outcomes for *Her Christmas Cookie*, *Three-Way Split*, and even *Private Eye* may be attributed to the humanistic element of Amazon's review system. It is possible that *Her Christmas Cookie* was flagged by Rekognition and then went to a human content moderator to review and was still deemed to be adult material, and just as possible that the others were also flagged by Rekognition but deemed not to be adult material by human reviewers. The possibility of this two-step system is why the initial review period may take anywhere between four to seventy-two hours, as the content works through the system to be reviewed by a person. Jackson notes that *Her Christmas Cookie* "took a long time to go up for pre-order primarily because I think whoever was looking at it was trying to figure out if it was lewd content."

Books may also go through a human review if authors appeal content moderation decisions. Jackson appealed the flagging of *Her Christmas Cookie* as adult content with Amazon's author services division, but this human-centered method also proved to be inconsistent. Reporting instances where terms relating to marginalized identities are flagged has mixed results; some Amazon author service representatives will say books go against the terms of service while others will report the initial decisions as errors. Jackson said that she went back and forth with Amazon's author services for two or three weeks and "the answer changed depending on who I was talking to, because you never talk to the same person unless you call and, even then, it doesn't work." She added, "we're pretty much at the whim of whoever is reviewing the content."[53] Where automatic detection tools might offer a blunt interpretation of the acceptability of content, humanistic approaches are designed to safeguard the implementation of incorrect outcomes. However, the subjective nature of acceptability or objectionableness combined with purposefully vague definitions of "adult material" does not necessarily reduce biased content moderation outcomes that can in turn have profound impacts on authors' careers.

As indicated by the example that opened this chapter, whether a book is flagged for containing adult material has a considerable impact on how it exists within Amazon's online marketplace. After going back and forth with Amazon's author services, *Her Christmas Cookie* was eventually published on the platform. However, it is only visible on Amazon through hyper-specific, narrow search parameters or via Jackson's author profile page. Jackson first alerted me to this, telling me, "If I search my own name every other one of my books shows up except for [*Her Christmas Cookie*] . . . even if you search for it explicitly, you might not see it."[54] Metadata collected through Sales Rank Express showed that despite this novel becoming available on Amazon after Jackson's appeal to the author services team, the title was still flagged as adult material.

The adult content flag affects the discoverability of books through Amazon's search function across different geolocational stores, particularly between different departments. The algorithm responsible for Amazon's search results page is A9, which ranks products based on factors such as keyword relevance, conversation rate, sales history, ratings and review, price and product images. Customers are presented with different search results depending on the keywords they use and the Amazon department within which they conduct their search. When I tested the discoverability of this title, I could see *Her Christmas Cookie* in the Books and Kindle Store department in all geolocational sites, but only if the author and title were used together as search terms. If I searched with just the title or author in the Books, Kindle, or All Departments, results varied—appearing on a subpage, as the last result after titles by other authors, or not at all (table 3).

**Table 3. Search Results for *Her Christmas Cookie*
by Katrina Jackson on Amazon US, Amazon UK, and Amazon AU**

Store Geolocation	Search Parameter 1: Search Terms	Search Parameter 2: Amazon Department	Does *Her Christmas Cookie* appear in the search results?
Amazon.com	Katrina Jackson	All Departments	No
Amazon.co.uk	Katrina Jackson	All Departments	No
Amazon.com.au	Katrina Jackson	All Departments	No
Amazon.com	Katrina Jackson Her Christmas Cookie	All Departments	No
Amazon.co.uk	Katrina Jackson Her Christmas Cookie	All Departments	No
Amazon.com.au	Katrina Jackson Her Christmas Cookie	All Departments	No
Amazon.com	Katrina Jackson	Books	No
Amazon.co.uk	Katrina Jackson	Books	Yes (third page, after titles by other authors)
Amazon.com.au	Katrina Jackson	Books	Yes (fourth page, after titles by other authors)
Amazon.com	Katrina Jackson Her Christmas Cookie	Books	Yes
Amazon.co.uk	Katrina Jackson Her Christmas Cookie	Books	Yes
Amazon.com.au	Katrina Jackson Her Christmas Cookie	Books	Yes
Amazon.com	Katrina Jackson	Kindle Store	Yes (last search result, after titles by other authors)
Amazon.co.uk	Katrina Jackson	Kindle Store	Yes (last search result, after titles by other authors)
Amazon.com.au	Katrina Jackson	Kindle Store	Yes (on last page of search results)

Amazon.com	Katrina Jackson Her Christmas Cookie	Kindle Store	Yes
Amazon.co.uk	Katrina Jackson Her Christmas Cookie	Kindle Store	Yes
Amazon.com.au	Katrina Jackson Her Christmas Cookie	Kindle Store	Yes

The table shows search results for the US, UK, and Australian Amazon stores, the three geolocational sites that Sales Rank Express provided metadata for. However, searches for the keyword combinations in the different departments on the French, German, Japanese, Canadian, and Mexican sites yield similar results. The title does not appear at all in All Departments regardless of keywords. It may show up in the Books department, but on one of the latter results pages, and it will show up in the Kindle Store, but its placement depends on the specificity of the keywords. The Japanese site has an age verification page that moderates access to adult content, including Jackson's novel, but is the only one to do so. The explicit intervention on the Japanese site further demonstrates that the search function is mediated based on adult content flags and the growing role of platforms in determining acceptable content in popular culture, including who is deemed acceptable and in what contexts.

The format of the book and thus the department through which the book is sold—print/Books or ebook/Kindle Store—also seem to impact whether it is flagged as adult. Melissa Blue, who also writes erotic romance under the pseudonym Dakota Gray, for example, has a few books where the same title has been flagged differently depending on the format. The print versions of *Perv*,[55] *Her Insatiable Scot*,[56] *Kilt Tease*,[57] *Kilted for Pleasure*,[58] *Scot Appeal*,[59] and *To One Hundred*[60] were all flagged as containing adult material, while the Kindle versions of each of these were marked as safe. A few print titles by Xio Axelrod, likewise, were flagged as containing adult materials: *Falling Stars*,[61] *Starlight*,[62] *La Promesse*,[63] *Camden*,[64] *The Warm Up*,[65] and *Fast Forward*.[66] The audio title for *La Promesse* was also flagged as containing adult material. None of these titles, however, have been hidden from the search results page. This does raise questions around why format might have an impact on the technological consequences of the adult flag. Do different departments have their own rules of organization and acceptable content? Even in the immensely data-rich sphere of Amazon, the rules guiding the organization of metadata and content online are not consistent. The discrepancy between format editions suggests that books may be subject to different processes depending on the Amazon department in which they belong. It is not clear how or why, given that KDP allows a streamlined process for authors to publish across formats with minimal, if any changes, except to file format.

The treatment of Jackson's novella demonstrates the technological capabilities Amazon has to suppress books and highlights a distinction between the explicit rejection of content and implicit suppression of content in its ecosystem. That is, there is a difference between actual removal from the site and being hidden behind technological mechanisms, including the search function. The implicit suppression of this title in the moderated search function is wholly based on the increased datafication of books in this sphere and enacted through opaque forms of governance. Given that most users on Amazon are unlikely to adjust their search parameters when searching for a product, this is likely to have major implications for the discoverability of these books by new readers and, consequently, the sales of romance by authors of color and LGBTQ+ authors. The impact of this socio-technical decision could be profound for self-published authors who are often excluded from brick-and-mortar bookstores and rely primarily on sales from Amazon and, even more so, self-published authors of color and queer authors who have been historically marginalized in and excluded from traditional publishing.

The effects of devoting time and energy to appealing decisions can be economic as well as emotional. As feminist scholar Sara Ahmed explains, complaint means "committing yourself, your time, your energy, your being", and the "embodied nature of the work of complaint" means "we can be worn down as well as worn out by what we have to do when we go through a complaint process."[67] Racially biased moderation is thus a literal barrier to entry—it can prevent works from being published and authors earning money from their creations—as well as a structural barrier to entry as it can wear down authors emotionally and steal time which could be spent on other creative and professional pursuits. The technical inability for authors to even see whether their books are flagged without testing across different geo-sites combined with the opacity with which publishing platforms like

Amazon define adult content presents significant challenges for authors writing and publishing romance fiction.

What Constitutes Adult Material on Amazon?
A Walkthrough of the ToS

The impact of having titles flagged as containing adult materials is clear, so what constitutes adult content for Amazon? How do authors know if they are creating content that will be flagged as adult material? In 1964, in lieu of a definition of obscene material, US Justice Potter Stewart famously wrote, "I know it when I see it."[68] How do Amazon's automated and human moderators know when they see it? Only very recently, Amazon added a section to its Metadata Guidelines for Books policy page that provides information on selecting yes or no to the question of sexually explicit images or title.[69] Historically though, and at the time when I spoke to authors, Amazon's governance and moderation structures have been as opaque in detail as they were imprecise in action. Platform ToS and EULA typically set out the parameters of acceptable content and behaviors online,[70] but often authors and publishers would discover content violations randomly through trial and error. Even now, the references to what constitutes sexually explicit images and titles are brief, vague and do not cover all of the violations authors report experiencing. As the following walkthrough of the site demonstrates, knowing what is and is not allowed on the site is not as simple as going to the ToS page on Amazon.[71] First, there is no single ToS page on Amazon. A simple Google search for "amazon terms of service" yields several results of Amazon-owned pages, including AWS, Prime, Services, Seller Central, Australia Seller Central, Kindle, and so on.

On Amazon.com, the conditions of use and privacy notice could be found in a footer menu at the bottom of the homepage alongside "Interest-Based Ads" and the copyright notice. The Conditions of Use page outlined intellectual property claims, liability, returns and refunds, and content guidelines. This included a statement that users may post reviews, comments, photos, videos, and other content

> so long as the content is not illegal, obscene, threatening, defamatory, invasive of privacy, infringing of intellectual property rights (including publicity rights), or otherwise injurious to third parties or objectionable, and does not consist of or

contain software viruses, political campaigning, commercial
solicitation, chain letters, mass mailings, or any form of "spam"
or unsolicited commercial electronic messages.[72]

Notably, it did not describe what constitutes obscene, threatening, or otherwise objectionable content, nor did it specify what "other content" falls
under this condition of use. Unfortunately, navigating to the conditions
of use on the Kindle Direct Publishing platform (amazon.kdp.com) did
not provide a straightforward answer either. Here, our adventure into the
spider-web of Amazon policy notifications truly begins.

Mirroring Amazon, in the footer at the bottom of the KDP homepage
were links to the terms and conditions, privacy notice, and conditions of
use. While the terms and conditions reference "Content Requirements,"
they did not provide any specific detail on what these are or link to a page
that does. The content requirements terms simply stated, "You must ensure
that all Book content is in compliance with our Program Policies for content
at the time you submit it to us" (section 5.1.2).[73] To find the KDP content
requirements or guidelines, I went back to the homepage and clicked on the
unlikely-to-be-helpful "help" link in the small header menu at the top right-
hand corner of the page. The KDP Help Center homepage contains a sidebar
menu of Help Topics including, among other things, "Legal & Content
Guidelines" and (under "User Guides") "Kindle Publishing Guidelines."[74]

Under Legal & Content Guidelines was a link to "Kindle Direct Publishing Terms and Conditions," which directed users to a page with a single
link that leads to the Conditions of Use page linked from the Amazon.com
homepage—the one that states users may post reviews, comments, photos,
videos, and other content so long as the content is not illegal, obscene, and
so on. A second link under the Legal & Content Guidelines menu option
led to "Program Policies," which noted that some content that may be considered objectionable was allowed on Amazon:

> As a bookseller, we believe that providing access to the written
> word is important, including content that may be considered
> objectionable. We carefully consider the types of content we
> make available in our stores and review our approach regu-
> larly, listening to feedback and investigating concerns from
> our customers. We reserve the right to remove content from
> sale if we determine it creates a poor customer experience.[75]

This page did reiterate that content deemed to be illegal or offensive was prohibited, and provided some detail on what constituted offensive content:

> We don't sell certain content including content that we determine is hate speech, promotes the abuse or sexual exploitation of children, contains pornography, glorifies rape or pedophilia, advocates terrorism, or other material we deem inappropriate or offensive.[76]

As can be seen thus far, Amazon employs a discursive strategy of ambiguity in its ToS regarding material it deems offensive. Ambiguity, as in the phrases "other material" and "may be considered objectionable" affords Amazon discretion and flexibility in enforcing guidelines through acts of moderation, while also minimizing its responsibility for hosting such material.

At the bottom of the Program Policies page was a list of hyperlinks for "Offensive and Controversial Materials" which led to a page housed within Amazon's Seller Central. Seller Central is the Amazon interface for brands and merchants to market and sell their products directly to Amazon's customers. This seemed like a useful page—self-publishers sell books on Amazon, after all—and it usefully included actual examples of infringing content. However, the first line of text on the page stated that "Amazon's Offensive Products policies apply to all products except books, music, video and DVD."[77]

Again, at the bottom of the page was a hyperlink to "Content Guidelines for Books." The information on the Content Guidelines for Books page was identical to the beginning of the KDP Program Policies page. Most of the available hyperlinks on this page led back to the Seller Central page. At this stage of the walkthrough, we are two hyperlinks deep into the KDP Program Policies subpages, with a slight detour to Amazon Seller Central, and now stuck in a loop of hyperlinks and subpages that either did not clearly delineate what constitutes objectionable material, or did not apply to books.

There was one more promising hyperlink on the Program Policies page for "Community Guidelines." This link led to a general Amazon.com page and was thus not specific to KDP. Rather, these guidelines

> apply to any content (including text, images, video, and links) you submit to Amazon and actions you take (such as voting

on helpfulness or smiling at a post) when using Community
features. These Guidelines also apply to your interactions with
other members of the Community.[78]

The results of violations were also described here but as they did not apply
to books published via KDP, it was not very helpful. However, this was
also the first page to state, under a section subtitled "Respect Others," that,
in addition to obscene or pornographic materials, content that is lewd or
contains nudity or sexually explicit images is prohibited. At the beginning
of this section was a statement that "something that may be disagreeable to
you may not violate our Guidelines," which reinforces ambiguity and serves
to reduce Amazon's liability around objectionable content. Further down
this page on Community Guidelines was a section on "Sexual Content"
that further rejects a definitive interpretation of sexually explicit material.
It stated:

> Some products containing sexual content and some sex and
> sensuality products are permitted to be sold on Amazon, and
> we encourage users to express their opinions about those
> products. Some sexual content such as nudity and sexually
> explicit images or descriptions is restricted because audiences
> within our Community may be sensitive to that content.[79]

The phrase "permitted to be sold on Amazon" was hyperlinked back to
Amazon Seller Central. This hyperlink led to a page that required a log in
to access the Seller Central platform, to a page entitled "Sex & Sensuality,"
which only included examples of permitted and prohibited listings and, at
the bottom, linked back to the KDP Content Guidelines for information
relevant to books. Again, I landed in the same ouroboros of webpages.
    At the top of the Sex & Sensuality Seller Central page, however, was
the breadcrumb menu schema that led to this destination page, each with
links to the parent page: Help / Program Policies / Restricted Products /
Sex & Sensuality. Navigating back to the Program Policies page for the
Seller Central platform this time (instead of the KDP Program Policies)
provided another list of hyperlinks under subheadings; under "Product
and Listing Requirements" was "Product Guidelines" which seemed to
be specific to the sexual wellness category on Amazon's marketplace and

explicitly distinguished these products from other "sexually explicit artistic or scientific products."[80] While this page specifically stated it does not apply to artistic products, which we may assume includes books, the "Adult Products Policies & Guidelines"[81] page usefully provides evidence that there is a flag for sexually explicit content: IS_ADULT_CONTENT.

The metadata on book titles collected from Sales Rank Express showed that some titles were flagged as adult content. Despite Amazon distinguishing adult products from sexually explicit artistic products, it seems the latter are still subject to some of the same rules that prohibit nudity and explicit language. With regards to inappropriate language, romance author Zoe York has stated on Twitter that her novel *Hate Fuck* was removed for offensive language while the re-uploaded book using the euphemistic misspelling *Hate F*@K* in the title was acceptable.[82] More recently, author Bree Bridges tweeted that when updating the product descriptions of her books, the word "erotica" was flagged alongside the flame emoji as keywords that violated community guidelines. Amazon's moderation systems explicitly target sexual content or adult material but make it nearly impossible for authors and publishers using KDP or the ecommerce platform to know what constitutes violations except through trial and error.

To find a definition of adult content in Amazon's ecosystem, without simply Googling keywords, is a confusing, tiresome, and, as evidenced by the walkthrough here, quite boring process, full of misdirection, loops, and nebulous terms. This is a purposeful strategy for Amazon as ambiguity helps the platform evade liability and make subjective decisions regarding the fate of content on its servers. As the KDP terms and conditions state, Amazon is "entitled to determine what content we accept and distribute through the Program in our sole discretion" (section 5.1.3).[83]

The Community Guidelines quote, which encourages "users to express their opinions" about sexually explicit content, suggests that the platform's subjective decisions are informed, at least in part, by the number and intensity of customer reports. This approach also forces authors to self-censor out of fear that they may be crossing the line. For Amazon, this means less work reviewing potentially objectionable content and allows greater opacity when passing down a judgment to authors who are deemed to violate the terms and conditions.

Amazon's moderation systems can also be biased against people with marginalized sexualities. There are recent anecdotal reports that terms like "bisexual" and "queer" in book descriptions have been flagged as adult content and blocked by Amazon's automatic detection software, but more research is needed on this. This discriminatory moderation is (possibly) an inadvertent side effect of broader governance structures that target sexually explicit content, with which marginalized sexualities and genders are sometimes associated due to their politicization. Striphas, for example, notes that Amazon alleged the 2009 incident was allegedly due to an employee mistakenly marking books classified as gay and lesbian as "adult" material.[84] Amazon's human and automated governance processes both mark and politicize content and keywords associated with marginalized people and communities in a cyclical way. People train the machine learning automatic detection software to recognize certain traits in content, the software flags associated content, and the human editorial review team makes final decisions, often in line with the automated decision.

Naming content for what it represents is expected, useful even. Treating content associated with marginalized people and communities differently to content associated with unnamed, hegemonic populations—cisgendered, heterosexual, White people—is a flaw in Amazon's moderation system that replicates systemic bias against BIPOC and LGBTQ+ people. Amazon's governance and moderation systems are an imprecise but impactful part of publishing via the platform, affecting how authors and publishers disseminate texts as well as how readers find them and thus the circulation and sales potential of books.

Publishing and the De-platformization of Sex

The reticence of digital publishing platforms towards adult content exists within a broader deplatforming of sex on social media in recent years that tends to relegate and push out LGBTQ+ and other marginalized users, as has been seen most visibly on Tumblr and OnlyFans. Bans to adult content online occur through updates to Community Guidelines and ToS that prohibit sexually explicit content. Marginalized groups, including LGBTQ+ and particularly queer people of color, gender nonconforming, and kink communities, who rely on digital networks for sexual self-expression, community, and knowledge are especially impacted by the deplatforming of sex and sexually explicit materials online.[85] These bans reinforce conservative, US-specific notions of appropriate content, despite the global impacts.

Tumblr's ban of adult content in 2018, including "photos, videos, or GIFs that show real-life human genitals or female-presenting nipples, and any content . . . that depicts sex acts,"[86] after the app was removed from the Apple app store particularly harmed sexually marginalized people and artistic communities.[87] The shift in policy on OnlyFans, which banned sex work on which the platform built its popularity, only to reverse this decision after public outrage, also harmed marginalized groups and precarious workers. Katrin Tiidenberg and Emily van der Nagel argue that by normalizing sex on social media "as is, as part of everyday life," users may be encouraged to question White, capitalist patriarchal norms, such as heteronormativity, body normativity, racism, ableism, and ageism both on and off social media.[88]

These content policy changes are informed by legal and technological frameworks. Bans of adult material became widespread on corporately owned US-based platforms after the US Senate passed the package bill of FOSTA-SESTA (Fight Online Sex Trafficking Act and Stop Enabling Sex Traffickers Act) in 2018.[89] Tumblr's changes also occurred in response to its removal from the Apple app store and in 2020, OnlyFans announced and later abandoned its decision to ban sexually explicit content after several banks refused to work with the platform as payment processors.[90] These cases highlight the way that interdependent platform ecosystems and technological and economic infrastructures also regulate what kind of content is acceptable on platform microsystems as well as the politicized nature of these decisions. While it must comply with the local laws in which it operates, Amazon operates its own digital infrastructure. KDP and the ecommerce site is based on its own web services and operates its own payment processor, meaning the company has more responsibility, and more scrutiny is required regarding Amazon's categorization processes and governance decisions as they affect other platforms hosted on its web services and/or built on its API and software infrastructure.

The way these socio-technical systems are impacting cultural production is evident from Jackson's experience with *Her Christmas Cookie* on Amazon. Simone Shirazi, an author published on Wattpad and Radish, has similarly had to compromise her creative expression due to platforms' governance systems. Shirazi retitled *Once Upon a One Night Stand* to *Once Upon a One Night Mistake* across platforms after Facebook temporarily banned her from advertising on the platform due to its automatic detection software interpreting the original title as mature content. What platforms allow and disallow, how they name cultural objects and position them in the marketplace affects the artwork and careers of authors dependent on their platforms, particularly historically marginalized authors who have been largely excluded from and are precariously placed in the cultural industries.

Conclusion

Categories, classifications, tags, and lists are practical tools for organizing content and cultural objects, particularly in the age of digital abundance. Categories are thus useful and necessary mechanisms in processes of reception, particularly to sort through large genres like romance fiction. Readers of romance fiction look to the romance categories on Amazon as they look to the romance shelves in bookstores and those looking specifically for romances written by Black authors and/or with Black protagonists will look to texts categorized as African American or Black romance. Category names are also situated historically, sociopolitically, and hierarchically in relation to other names. The hierarchization of classification codes and subject headings in traditional knowledge organization systems is not rendered flat online as algorithms work to program and order content for users based on popularity metrics and capitalist interests. These systems undermine the autonomy associated with self-publishing and can negatively affect authors' sales through rigid opportunities for discoverability.

These findings show that platform classification and governance systems that structure opportunities of discoverability are engrained with the same biases that pervade traditional publishing and can negatively impact authors from historically marginalized communities. Through a top-down classification system, genre categories on Amazon replicate and reinforce the subjugation of historically marginalized groups evident in traditional systems of knowledge organization including BISAC, LCC, and DDC. Moderation decisions are enacted through Amazon's automatic detection software Rekognition, which is biased against people of color and targets sexually suggestive imagery and language, a convention of many romance fiction covers and subgenres. More heterogeneous approaches to categorization, such as tagging on Wattpad, may offer a more inclusive and responsive way of classifying and sorting creative content. However, as Wattpad has expanded its commercialization of content on its platform, its categorization system has also changed from an open form based on popularity metrics to a mix of user-generated and curated, top-down forms that reinscribe the othering of stories by and about historically marginalized groups. Self-published authors on Amazon and Wattpad may be free from traditional gatekeepers, but they are not free from gatekeeping entirely as platforms continue the marginalization of authors from culturally diverse groups in the publishing industry as existing societal biases are encoded into platform technologies and processes.

Many of the authors I interviewed expressed feelings of frustration, anger, sadness, and resignation over the lack of human presence in Amazon's review processes, and constantly changing, opaque and inconsistent forms of governance. As Axelrod said, books get flagged by computers and Amazon "treat[s] your books like toothpaste. They don't care that it's creative work."[91] This apathy towards cultural production and depersonalization of creative producers in the interest of commercial dominance will have significant impacts on the future of the cultural industries as platforms become more and more central to the production and distribution of books and media. Changes to platform infrastructures, regimes of visibility and algorithms that relate to the way content is classified and moderated will drastically sway independent creators' ability to build sustainable careers. This is only exaggerated by the way neoliberal individualization is intensified on platforms, while platforms continue to evade responsibility for programming decisions by positioning themselves as intermediaries.

CHAPTER 4

From Platform to Print

How Pipelines Structure Exclusion

IN THE SECOND HALF of 2019, Wattpad published six inaugural titles under its newly established imprint Wattpad Books. These titles, as well as those published in years since were sourced directly from the authors and stories on the platform, chosen from what has been fashioned into a digital slush-pile of epic proportions. Wattpad is not the first platform to enter the trade publishing market. Amazon Publishing was launched in 2009 and now comprises seventeen imprints spanning a range of genres. Other user-generated content platforms such as Inkitt and Radish have also started publishing print and electronic titles, while Macmillan's Feiwel and Friends launched its own platform to feed its Swoon Reads imprint. And in 2023, Tik-Tok's parent company ByteDance began approaching self-published romance authors to re-publish their titles under its publishing imprint 8th Note Press. Since 2021, Wattpad has introduced a further three imprints under its publishing division Wattpad Webtoon Book Group—W by Wattpad Books, Frayed Pages x Wattpad Books, and Webtoon Unscrolled—each serving different markets and genres.

These enterprises represent a new model of publishing company in the early twenty-first century: the platform publisher. These publishing imprints source the manuscripts and authors they publish from the user-generated content on their proprietary social media platforms, and acquisition decisions are informed by engagement data. The integration of logics from conglomerate and platform capitalism is fundamental to how platform publishers operate. The phrase that Wattpad prefers, scattered throughout its marketing copy relating to Wattpad Books and its other imprints, is "the combination of art and science" but it points to the same logic of adopting extractive data-driven approaches with cultural evaluation and production. While Wattpad's publishing imprint certainly sits within a highly commercial pan-entertainment strategy, they also market the book as an ultimate end product; at the time of writing, the about page for Wattpad Webtoon Book Group reads "We strive to create objects that you will want to collect and keep!"[1]

This new publishing model thus obfuscates the distinction historically made between platforms and publishers that has predicated on different organizational structures, practices of use, and self-conceptualizations. Rhetorically and practically, publishers have historically taken creative and legal responsibility for the work they put into circulation while platforms attempt to evade liability by identifying as intermediaries for information, strategically positioning themselves "both to pursue current and future profits, to strike a regulatory sweet spot between legislative protections that benefit them and obligations that do not, and to lay out a cultural imaginary within which their service makes sense."[2] As Aarthi Vadde neatly summarizes, "publishers stand behind their authors. Platforms evanesce around their creators."[3] Of course, as we have seen already, platforms are not just intermediaries for information; they structure content and users in specific ways through visibility algorithms, interface design, governance, economic structures, and so on. And platform publishers explicitly complicate this established binary; they engage in and explicitly connect the processes of algorithmic amplification and data capitalism associated with platforms and the editorial and cultural production work of traditional publishers. The uneasy tension between platform and publishing processes is evident in the way stories travel from their serialized digital form on Wattpad to become a book that exists in digital and traditional spaces of book culture.

In 2015, Wattpad began fine-tuning the acquisition approach of its imprint, creating a pipeline of internal programs, including the Watty Awards, Paid Stories and Ambassadors Programs, that funnels authors into the Wattpad Creators Program (formerly Wattpad Stars). The Creators program is the pool from which Wattpad selects the stories published under the imprint, adapted into film or television series by Wattpad Studios, as well as several other commercial opportunities, including creating sponsored content and participating in brand partnerships. There is a bottleneck kind of structure to this pipeline that means not all authors who enter the pipeline will reach the commercial endpoints.

The pipeline comprises both human and non-human actants that work together to surface and value stories that shape publishing decisions. These actants include Wattpad staff, authors, readers (humans, though there may be some bots amongst the authors or readers) and machine learning software, algorithms, data, and programs (non-human, though there are certainly humans behind the design and oversight of these processes). Actor-network theory (ANT) is a useful frame for these dynamics, particularly in its insistence on flattening actants so that each is as important as the next as well as its emphasis on the performance of relationships between them in upholding the network.[4] Humans rely on non-human actants in decision-making, but non-human ones also rely on humans, and the pipeline ultimately works because the relationships between actants are constantly being operationalized—made and remade—to produce an apparently coherent system of valuation.

Wattpad's pipeline, where successive programs are used to discover and reaffirm success, is a highly concentrated, networked version of aspects of traditional publishing and media. It works to create a large pool of potentially marketable authors and stories that Wattpad may develop, diverging from approaches by traditional publishers that typically invest in the development of a small number of debut authors. In doing so, it adapts the so-called tried-and-trusted model of success theorized in adaptation studies where awards and sales influence which books are made into films and television series and, conversely, which films and television shows are novelized, and so on.[5] In Wattpad's system, the Watty Awards, StoryDNA machine learning algorithms, and Wattpad Creators Program adapt traditional markers of symbolic capital.

Despite the flattening of actants that make up this pipeline, the system it produces is not immune to unequal power structures. While popularity data is positioned as the primary logic directing content in this pipeline, there are other structures that determine inclusion, exclusion, and inequitable outcomes despite the global geographical, racial, and ethnic diversity of the authors on the platform and in the Creators program. The capitalist nature of Wattpad's system, with the ultimate end goal for the company to profit from these authors and their intellectual property, means that it is not always a safe space for culturally diverse authors whose historical exclusion in the publishing industry has been linked to understandings of marketability by industry professionals. Notwithstanding evidence of some improvement since Naver's acquisition, Wattpad tends to reinforce the cultural, linguistic, and Western geographical hegemony that has long plagued the traditional global publishing industry.

This chapter explores the contours of Wattpad's pipeline and publishing list of Wattpad Books and Wattpad Webtoon Book Group. As seems to be the case with internet-related research (indeed all contemporary research), the acquisition by Naver and subsequent merger of Wattpad and Webtoon in the publishing imprint occurred shortly after I had finished interviewing authors for this research. The analysis thus spans pre- and post-acquisition, referring to Wattpad Books and Wattpad Webtoon Book Group as appropriate.

Human and Algorithmic Tastemaking in the Watty Awards

There are several entry points to Wattpad's commercial pipeline, but the most visible is the Watty Awards, the platform's annual literary prize competition. The awards were first held in 2011 with three categories: popular, on the rise, and undiscovered. A year later, in collaboration with Margaret Atwood, Wattpad added two poetry categories: Enthusiast and Competitor. These early awards were fan-voted affairs and, as indicated by the titles of the categories, venerated an amateur form of creativity. Ivey Choi, an Asian American author of teen fiction, was shortlisted for the award in 2011 when popularity was the governing principle. According to Choi's memory, for every genre, there were four or five books listed under the different categories (popular, on the rise, undiscovered), and readers would vote for the winner so typically the story with the largest readership won.[6] Despite surface appearances, this kind of crowdsourced voting system is not always egalitarian, as evidenced by Authomony, a crowdsourced discoverability platform by HarperCollins, that was shut down in 2015 after users began to game the system through organized voting collectives.

The structure and judgment of the Watty awards changed around 2015, around the time Wattpad began investing more readily in its commercial entertainment ventures. Now, the awards are judged by Wattpad staff and Ambassadors, there are multiple genre categories, and they have become an important node in Wattpad's commercial programs as the winners and finalists of these annual awards are invited into the Wattpad Creators (Stars) program. Literary prizes have long been positioned as arbiters of and incubators for success in book culture. They simultaneously signify and bestow prestige, generate commercial success, and can propel venerated texts into a broader adaptation industry.[7] Before having the chance to benefit from this exchange of capital, though, several structures adjudicate access to this consecratory mechanism.

Before Wattpad stories can be evaluated, the eligibility requirements of the Watty Awards impact the titles and authors that may be considered for the prize. As contemporary publishing scholar Alexandra Dane points out, "entry guidelines for individual literary awards ensure that particular authors and titles will not, or cannot, be considered for the prize," which results in them being excluded from the symbolic and economic rewards of prizewinning status and influences "field-wide perceptions [of literary value] and the production of literary tastes."[8] The Watty Awards have an open submission process, meaning any author who has published a story on the platform can submit their story for consideration. To be *eligible* for consideration, however, the work must be original and at least 50,000 words in English or 40,000 words if written in another language. Authors must also be at least thirteen years old and have written permission from a parent or legal guardian to enter and claim any prizes if they are under eighteen years old, a point to which we'll return shortly.

Non-English language stories are only permitted in the category for completed works, and eligible languages include French, Italian, German, Spanish, Portuguese, Dutch, Turkish, Filipino, and Indonesian. These languages are reflective of some of the most popular territories for Wattpad (including the US, Philippines, Brazil, and Turkey), but for an author to become a Creator they must also write in one of these languages, indicating the commercial markets in which Wattpad is primarily interested. Authors from other countries with robust online writing industries, such as China, Japan, and Korea, are excluded from this entry point if they write in their national languages. At the time of writing, more than a year after Naver's acquisition and integration with Webtoon in the Studios and Books divisions, the exclusion of Korean is surprising, but it is possible Wattpad and Webtoon have determined that the Korean market is already served by Webtoon creative content or an update to the eligibility rules may occur in future years.

The language requirements to gain entrance to the Watty Awards and Creators program significantly affects the prospects of authors from countries and language groups not represented, including those who speak other languages or dialects in countries that are seemingly included. Wattpad author Sol Tuberosum, for instance, lives in the Philippines but is not fluent in Filipino.[9]

She resides in Iloilo City in the Western Visayas region and speaks/writes in Hiligaynon/Ilonggo and English languages, which means that while she can and has become a Creator (through writing in English), she is effectively excluded from the commercial partnerships that Wattpad has developed in the Filipino-based entertainment industry. As in the traditional industry then, language is a strong mediator in the landscape of platform publishing, contributing to the formation of literary audiences and in turn commercial opportunities. In Wattpad's pipeline, it is also mediated algorithmically.

After the changes to the awards around 2015, Wattpad began to use its machine-learning software, StoryDNA, to determine eligibility and produce a manageable shortlist. StoryDNA uses machine learning, deep learning and recurrent neural networks that analyze language, word use, sentence structure, and grammar of texts as well as narrative elements. This makes up part of the "science" of Wattpad's pipeline, which replicates and reproduces racial, cultural, and language biases that pervade the traditional creative and cultural industries.

Research into algorithms, large language models, and other automated decision-making technology more generally demonstrates how these tools can embed and replicate biases through input data, labeling, and training, which can result in the further marginalization of historically marginalized people.[10] In the case of StoryDNA, the analysis of language, word use, sentence structure, and grammar most negatively impacts people writing in their second languages and is thus unlikely to result in greater diversity in publishing. StoryDNA also compares Watty award entrants to popular titles on the site as well as classic literature, which became part of the Wattpad database in 2007 through a partnership with Project Gutenberg that saw the publication of thousands of classics on Wattpad, from Jane Austen to Charles Dickens. Both these samples largely privilege White, cisgendered, Western narrative elements, and language. The potential for StoryDNA or any other pattern-recognition machine learning software to promote greater inclusivity and diversity in the awards is severely limited as output is strongly influenced by input data. In other words, if Wattpad determines "good" stories—stories worthy of winning an award that are often in turn published in print or adapted to film or television—based on narratives that accord to a White taste logic, they are merely going to produce more of the same.[11]

After this algorithmic pre-selection and shortlisting process, the English Watty awards are judged by a committee of Wattpad staff. In 2020, Wattpad shared the list of judges of the Watty award for the first time to highlight the human side of the awards. The following job titles were represented on the judging committee: copyright team lead, content acquisitions lead, editorial specialist for Paid Stories, associate editor for Paid Stories, product manager for content discovery, user experience researcher, product designer, editorial manager, talent manager, community engagement specialist, talent operations specialist, senior account specialist in brand partnerships, story marketing manager, content development manager for Wattpad Stars, and head of Wattpad Studios in Asia. Evidently, the judges for the awards work in roles associated with the platform's commercial programs. It is perhaps one of the most obvious ways the governing logic of the prize has transformed from reflecting readerly popularity to indicating potential commercial success.

While the English awards are judged by Wattpad staff, the awards in languages other than English are judged by Wattpad Ambassadors from relevant national groups. Wattpad Ambassadors are selected users who perform free, digital labor for Wattpad, including organizing stories into categories, running community initiatives, content moderation, and judging prizes. Their work often impacts the visibility and discoverability of various Wattpad stories and authors. Content Ambassadors, for example, do some moderation work. Before the tagging system was introduced, they would change categories of stories that were deemed to have been categorized incorrectly on the site. As content Ambassadors become more senior, their moderation work expands to include deleting spam accounts or those that breach the content rules of Wattpad. Ambassadors that work on engagement, in contrast, tend to focus on a single genre category (e.g., romance, science fiction, fantasy, LGBTQ+ fiction) as well as curating lists and running contests to promote stories within the genre. Sol Tuberosum, a Filipino author I spoke to, is a Wattpad Ambassador in the Philippines, whose role consists of managing community profiles, participating in in-person Wattpad events, and engaging with other Wattpad readers.[12] Ambassadorships have a level of prestige associated with them and provide these users with a degree of proximity to platform operations, but constitute the kind of free, affective labor prevalent in fan communities.

Ambassadors nevertheless play an active part in the taste-making of stories and authors on Wattpad. Their work in curating, sorting, and classifying content and, in some instances, judging Watty Awards directly impacts which authors and stories readers interact with, and the associated engagement data that informs algorithmic systems such as StoryDNA.

Ambassadors are more closely connected to Wattpad staff, other Ambassadors, and active users, and are more likely to be invited to join the Creators program compared to the average user, regardless of whether they win a Watty award. As networked users with a high degree of influence, Ambassadors are an important node in Wattpad's commercial pipeline. While data plays a significant role in Wattpad's book publishing and pan-entertainment businesses, the human aspect of Wattpad, represented by Watty judges, Ambassadors, and readers, is paramount to the continued functioning of the commercial pipeline.

Precarity in the Creator Program

Writers who win a Watty award or are identified by Wattpad in some other way as producing popular and/or high-quality work are invited to the Creators Program, formerly the Stars Program, where they are provided opportunities to commercialize their writing. The prestige associated first with being a Star and subsequently a Creator obscures the precarity these authors experience. In addition to the long-term uncertainty of remuneration outlined in chapter 2, authors of color and queer authors in this program experience further destabilization by particular dynamics in their relationship with the platform and other authors in the partner program. While members of the Stars Program, the authors I spoke to face a double bind when it came to the organizational governance of the partner community; they were at once bound by specific rules of participation that enforce respectful behavior, and subject to exclusionary behavior by other Stars.

Writers who signed onto the Stars Program were bound by a Stars Behavior and Values Agreement, which outlined the offerings of the program, expectations of writers and termination terms. This contract included clauses relating to expectations of activity and engagement: Stars must continue to upload quality content to the platform with a new update or story at least every six months and must interact with readers and other communities at least every three months. The contract also stipulated respectful behavior—to each other, to Wattpad staff, and to partners—and embody company values of positivity, professionalism, respect, integrity, and sound judgment. Stars had to agree not to post false or inflammatory comments about Wattpad or its initiatives, any content on the platform, or other Stars or users, and they must not publicly share any comments regarding frustration, concerns, or complaints that they have with Wattpad.

The clauses in the agreement that delineate appropriate and respectful behaviors share similarities with morality clauses in traditional publishing and legacy media contracts. Such clauses enable employers to terminate a contract if a creator behaves in a way that reflects poorly on the hiring company, and while they have only increased in prominence since the #MeToo movement, these clauses were first introduced in 1921 by Universal Pictures in response to Fatty Arbuckle's manslaughter trial. The Behavior and Values Agreement, like morality clauses, outlined ideal behaviors by Wattpad Stars. Unlike morality clauses, though, the emphasis is less on being a morally decent person and more a desired embodiment of favorable brand associations. Through their ranking and activity, Stars ensured that Wattpad was seen to appear as a lively, dynamic, and socially involved platform where writers' dreams of "making it" were possible.

While the stipulations in the partner agreement are perhaps unsurprising from a commercial company, there is a deeply unequal relationship between Wattpad and much of its user base. Many writers that were invited to be part of the Stars Program, and now those that are invited to the Creators Program, are often young or have been on the platform from a young age, unfamiliar with what constitutes a fair publishing deal or may not realize the potential value of their work and are often highly aspirational. Invitations to the Stars/Creators Program are sometimes met with wariness but can also feel like a writer's first big break, entrance through a sought after gate that allows them to earn money from their writing.

The opening of this gate, though, does not guarantee authors compensation for their writing. When Wattpad introduced the Creators Program, it did so with tiered levels, each with different requirements and remuneration; the lowest level required writers to post at least five hundred words per week with no income in return. Wattpad invited authors to the program on a predetermined level and writers had to earn their way up the ladder through metrics such as increased engagement. Though Wattpad reportedly removed the levels in late 2023, it retains some form of what Robyn Caplan and Tarleton Gillespie term "tiered governance"—a strategy whereby platforms offer "different users different sets of rules, different material resources and opportunities, and different procedural protections"[13]—by offering some Creators stipends of up to $25,000 while others still perform the labor of a Creator for free.

Unlike traditional publishing contracts, in which authors license particular intellectual property rights to the publisher, contracts for the partner program stipulate that Wattpad receives exclusive rights to particular stories for a period of time (most of the initial Creator contracts seemed to be twenty-four months) and that the platform *may* do something with the IP. In this system, writers have little power to leverage or negotiate their position. The inequitable precarity experienced by Creators formalizes those experienced by Stars. Not all Stars were presented with equal opportunities or equitable compensation for the same opportunities.

A short time after our interview, Ivey Choi decided to leave the Stars Program and, shortly again after that, the platform. Her resignation came in mid-2020, a month or so after the murder of George Floyd by a Minnesota police officer and during the subsequent global Black Lives Matter protests that sparked reckonings with racism across social and cultural dimensions. Several blog posts, articles, Reddit threads, and Twitter posts were published that detailed the marginalization and inequitable treatment of BIPOC and LGBTQ+ people on Wattpad and in the Stars Program in particular. These accounts highlighted the inadequate promotion, visibility, and representation historically marginalized authors experienced across the platform and commercial programs. Accounts of microaggressions and tone-policing from other authors and Wattpad staff were detailed alongside accusations of the company's historic inaction around safety, reform, and support for affected authors.

In the public statement explaining her decision to leave, Choi expresses the culture of marginalization and exclusion in the Stars Program:

> BIPOC have been consistently demonized for speaking up about valid concerns regarding the marginalization of BIPOC (and other marginalized identities, but let's focus on BIPOC for now). This included on the platform as well as the environment of the Stars program. Some of you say the Stars community is no longer a "safe space for conversation." Any forum has **never** been a safe space for BIPOC to speak honestly. [...] Time and time again BIPOC are forced to use language that is dialed down and panders to White fragility. [...] I am writing this because I know I am not the only BIPOC who feels like we walk on eggshells while in the program. .... I will not apologize for being blunt about how exhausting being a BIPOC in the Stars program is. How can our writing and

content feel valued when we are constantly belittled by our
peers about our actual, lived experience as a BIPOC?[14]

Though a short excerpt from her resignation letter, this quote demonstrates the heavy impact the culture of Wattpad and the Stars Program had
on Choi. This is not a unique experience for Wattpad authors; excepting
for explicit references to the Stars Program, this statement could apply to
BIPOC, LGBTQ+, and authors from other marginalized communities in
traditional book publishing.

Another public resignation letter by Em Slough, another prominent
author and friend of Choi's who left the Stars Program at the same time,
further detailed the persistent nature of this dynamic. She wrote:

> For the past few years, I have struggled largely with feeling
> at home on Wattpad. As time progressed, I became tired of
> the uphill battle myself and so many other Black, Indigenous,
> and other Creators of color face. The constant marginaliza-
> tion of ourselves and our work in lieu of our White peers has
> never been easy, but it became more and more frustrating to
> watch our voices drown out by Wattpad's push for what was
> comfortable. Ultimately, the final straw was witnessing as,
> even after all of the feedback, and labor, and time, again and
> again our voices were overlooked for White authors trying to
> tell our stories. In 2020, I had hoped that we wouldn't still be
> having these conversations, trying to make our Own Voices
> and our own stories be heard, seen, valued.
>
> [. . .]
>
> Earlier this year, I had discussions with Wattpad about how
> they might operate as a site in order to provide better commu-
> nity, opportunity, and visibility to BIPOC. Myself and many
> other Stars who are BIPOC spent hours across days supplying
> the site with ideas, insight, and emotional labor for free. In
> return, we have found ourselves in a similar predicament once
> more . . . Through conversations between other creators, I
> only found myself more and more alienated, and more and

more tired. Over and over, I feel like creators of color find themselves in emotionally and mentally draining situations, where we are promised solutions, only to be faced with the same issues in a different form soon after, no solutions.

[. . .]

Today, I resigned from the Wattpad Stars program, as I no longer felt seen, heard or valued as a POC, not just as a writer with a platform. Myself and quite a few other Stars of color made this incredibly tough decision over the weekend. Our resignations were accepted with only an apology. It was my hope that while I had no more interest in being part of a program that further alienated me on the basis of my identity, that Wattpad as a company could find within itself the strength and the resource to offer solutions and alternatives, and to ultimately fight for its Stars of color before having to see us go. Instead, Wattpad went with the simplest solution: to let us leave.[15]

I replicate excerpts of these letters at length here for two reasons. First, because I believe it is important to convey these testimonials in full and, even more so, in their own words. And second, because they separately but significantly articulate the experiences and feelings of Choi, Slough, and other marginalized authors on Wattpad and in the Stars Program at the time, and go some way to detailing just how the culture of this platform community replicates harms against historically marginalized authors. Other authors I interviewed who were part of the Stars Program at the time noted similar experiences of inequitable treatment and marginalization. Their experiences reflect a commonplace pattern described by Lisa Nakamura, where women of color are punished and made to feel unwanted for the labor they perform to reduce and push back against discriminatory behavior online.[16]

Their experiences also show that the terms set out in the Stars Behavior and Values Agreement effectively served a select group, an outcome strengthened by the vague language in the agreement. Like the terms and conditions of platforms explored in the previous chapter, the clauses in this agreement tend to be written in hazy, imprecise terms, affording Wattpad discretion to determine how the agreement may be applied and terminate Stars from the program. Such statements as "Interactions that are deemed offensive or demoralizing will be dealt with at the discretion of the Wattpad Stars team" beg several questions. Offensive to whom? Demoralizing for whom?

Slough's reference to the "discussions" she had with Wattpad about how they might better support BIPOC authors shows that the company was aware of these issues and made attempts, if insufficient, to address them. One author I spoke to who wished for their comments on the matter to be anonymized reflected on how Wattpad's inaction to make the Stars Program more inclusive directly contradicted the company's marketing and mission statements, which has historically emphasized its commitment to diversity and inclusion. They stated:

> Their company mission is always to strive for inclusivity, but I feel like, or from what I've seen, the writers don't actually feel supported a lot of the time. They're just paraded out front, and when they're dealing with harassment, either from readers or from White writers who are also doing the parading like you've said, Wattpad typically does not engage. They just let the community figure it out, and that's maybe not the best approach. I think they've learned something happened and I don't want to really get into it, but something did happen [in 2020] where they realized that being inactive is no longer an option for them.

Most of the Wattpad authors I spoke to knew about the incident this author was referring to but did not want to go into details. At the time, there was little trace of what happened outside of the private Stars Discord channel, but the echoes of *something* was evident throughout the articles, blog posts, Reddit, and Twitter mentioned. What seems consistent between the media posts, public resignation statements, and limited information from my interviews is that the incident involved marginalized authors accusing White authors in the Stars Program of a lack of diversity in their works, racism, performative allyship, and/or microaggressions against BIPOC authors, and some of those authors responding in a negative way. There are obvious parallels between this event and the controversy surrounding

Courtney Milan and other BIPOC authors in more traditional spaces of publishing outlined in the introduction.[17] Both incidents spilled out of their closed community spaces (Discord for Wattpad, and RWA's Published Author Network forum) onto public platforms like Reddit and Twitter, and both are evidence of the systemic discrimination and racial inequality that pervades Western book publishing.

Wattpad initially deferred its responsibility for the negative experiences of the authors of color in its Stars Program, emphasizing its intermediary role as a platform. In mid-July 2020, though, after the resignations of Choi, Slough, and others, Wattpad emailed members of the Program, proclaiming its new position and approach moving forward: they would be hiring an external consultant as part its Community Wellness division "to help Wattpad move from a neutral platform to one that takes an anti-oppression stance."[18] While the effects of these efforts, if any, require future study, what is evident is that on Wattpad, where the some parts of the user base are reported to engage in targeted racialized harassment against people of color, the economic system of the pipeline is set up to favor authors who write stories that feature cisgendered, heteronormative, White characters and exclude non-hegemonic representations.

Published by Wattpad Books

Despite or perhaps in ignorance of the precarities of the program, many Wattpad writers aspire to become a Creator as much for its status marker as the commercial opportunities it presents. Indeed, the previous designation "Star" indicates the kind of prestige it confers; these are micro-celebrities on Wattpad. Star or Creator status lends credibility to titled authors in much the same way "bestselling" does in more traditional spaces of book culture, holding implicit promises about the quality of the authors' works. This platformed celebrification reflects a broader drive towards literary celebrity in contemporary book culture. Publishers invest in building authors' identities precisely because celebrity authors and other well-known or brand name authors—Junot Díaz or Danielle Steel, for example—are viewed as a more reliable economic investment in an industry where uncertainty is the norm. This is increasingly important in an industry where millions of books published each year compete with decreasing spaces for promotion in traditional media and a competitive attention economy online. The development of author brands, whereby authors themselves become marketable commodities, can aid in establishing both cultural and economic capital.

Rather than reproducing the same functions and strategies towards literary celebrity as in traditional publishing, Wattpad Stars have been, and Creators now are, a kind of funhouse mirror of literary celebrity. For most Wattpad authors that reach this status, this shorthand is legible only to in-members of the platform, though in territories where Wattpad has had a more significant impact on the national publishing and entertainment industries, this status symbol can extend far beyond the virtual realm. In our interview, for example, Filipino Wattpad author Demi Abilon stated that "in the Philippines, when you become a Wattpad Star, you reach that amount of followers, you're almost like a celebrity."[19] Regardless of their name recognition beyond the platform, their status functions as intended for the purpose of the pipeline: to supply Wattpad's commercial publishing and production lists.

Relatively few authors are published by Wattpad Webtoon Book Group, one of the most visible, prestigious, and financially lucrative endpoints of the pipeline. These final sections of the chapter explore what it means to be published by Wattpad's publishing division and the limitations of this data-informed approach to publishing. How does being published by the Wattpad Books imprint, the inaugural imprint, differ from traditional publishing models, and what potential is there for creating a more inclusive publishing model? These questions are examined here through the case profile of Daven McQueen, an Afro-Filipino American author whose debut novel *The Invincible Summer of Juniper Jones* was published by Wattpad Books in 2020,[20] as well as a content analysis of Wattpad Books' list from its launch in 2019 to the end of the data collection period in mid-2023.

When McQueen first joined Wattpad in her first year of high school in 2011, they did not anticipate the platform would set up its own publishing imprint. Indeed, any opportunities for writers to monetize their work directly through the platform were several years away. At the time they joined, Wattpad was very much a social writing community in both architecture and spirit. While many writers may have had aspirations of publishing and some traditionally published authors were using Wattpad—Margaret Atwood being one of the most famous examples—it was not seen as a pathway to the print publishing industry. This culture of use was reflected in the way writers used the platform and the kind of writing that appeared. For example, McQueen described their approach to using Wattpad was simply to

> write and write and write and just post and post and post, and I wasn't as concerned with [the idea that] this needs to be perfectly polished and edited because it felt like there was kind of an unspoken rule that anything we posted on Wattpad was in draft form and so there were no expectations that it would be of a particular quality or caliber.[21]

McQueen's writing ethos reflected the dominant amateur form of the platform in its early years. The culture and user demographic of Wattpad during its first eight or so years meant that enjoyable stories and characters were prized far above the quality of structure and written expression, which may still be the case for some users. However, this has shifted since the introduction of the Watty Awards and commercial programs that rely in part on StoryDNA, which assesses linguistic proficiency, written structure and grammatical accuracy, to inform the selection of writers and stories.

McQueen began posting the first draft of *Invincible Summer*, a young adult, historical coming of age novel set in the American South, in 2014 and completed it over the next year or so. During this time, there was what McQueen described as "a decent level of engagement" with the story.[22] The level of engagement was enough for McQueen to be invited to be part of the Stars Program in 2016, where they wrote some short stories for the platform but otherwise did not engage much with the platform during their college years. In 2019, though, they received an offer from Wattpad to publish *Invincible Summer* under the Wattpad Books imprint.

The offer of publication was first presented to McQueen by their talent manager at Wattpad, I-Yana Tucker, who went on to work as a writer for Shondaland. During the period of the Stars Program, Wattpad authors would only be connected with talent managers once they were in the program and their work was being considered for any of the platform's commercial programs (including the Studios and Paid Stories programs). Claire Kann, a Black author who was a Wattpad Star when we spoke and whose first three novels were published by Swoon Reads, explained that "if your work is actively being shopped, or if you were in the Paid Stories program, you are assigned a talent manager . . . otherwise you just stay in the [general Stars talent] pool."[23]

Talent managers were thus positioned as an intermediary between Stars and other Wattpad staff. According to McQueen, they worked to direct questions from authors to "whoever they need[ed] to go to" in Wattpad, and "also, ideally, [they were] your advocate" within Wattpad. They added, "So if you have concerns with the program, you'd go to them probably first and try to discuss solutions with them."[24] Talent managers also played an influential role in Wattpad's creative and commercial system, pitching authors and stories to Wattpad (a role now covered by "Scouts"), presenting authors with commercial opportunities within Wattpad or brokered by Wattpad with their partners, and supporting published authors with publicity events.

The role of talent managers highlights the confluence of different industry logics at play in Wattpad's organizational structure. Talent managers are an established profession in the traditional and social media entertainment industries.[25] At Wattpad, the role has crossovers with influencer managers in the way they would pitch commercial opportunities to Wattpad Stars, support their professional development, and mediate conflict. This link is not only theoretical: before joining Wattpad, Tucker worked in influencer management.

The talent manager role represents a greater convergence of two legacy publishing industry roles: literary agents and publicists, two professions that emerged in response to the conglomeration of the publishing industry and growth in the book and media markets in the second half of the twentieth century. McQueen likened the role of talent managers to agents in our interview, describing them as "kind of like your agent for Wattpad, except that they come from inside Wattpad."[26] In addition to representing authors to publishers and negotiating contracts and the licensing of rights, agents are increasingly involved in the double duty of managing and developing the long-term careers of their authors—a role that Tucker performed in small part for McQueen. During the publication of their debut novel, McQueen discussed their career trajectory with Tucker, telling me "at least with my talent manager, we talk about 'Okay, what do I want to do next? Where do I want to go from here?' Whether or not that involves Wattpad." This was not necessary standard for the role, with McQueen clarifying that "I don't know if that's because partly that I've expressed to I-Yana that I don't see myself with Wattpad forever and I want other opportunities, but even over the [s]ummer I had some agents reach out to me and she help[ed] me prep for the calls and stuff like that and we debrief them together."[27]

The internality of the talent manager role within Wattpad presents somewhat of a conflict of interest between Wattpad and the Star authors they
represented. While influencer managers may develop relationships with
brands and clients and agents develop relationships with certain editors
and publishers, they both operate independently from these organizations.
Their client is the creator, and they are often remunerated through a percentage of commissions or royalties. Wattpad talent managers, in contrast,
are employed by Wattpad, suggesting that their ultimate role is to ensure
success for Wattpad, however it may be measured. The double responsibility
talent managers have for authors and the company also means that, unlike
agents in traditional publishing, they are not involved in contract negotia-
tions. In McQueen's case, the similarity talent managers had with agents in
representing the author in some ways acted as a dissuasion to hire an agent
to represent them in negotiating their contract with Wattpad. They said:

> I dealt with [the contract] myself, with advice from my parents.
> So that is an interesting thing, because most writers going into
> a contract with a publishing company have an agent, and so
> I was lucky that I had I-Yana who was as transparent as she
> could be, but there was still a lot that I didn't know at the time.
> I think I would have been bolder about negotiating and stuff
> like that if I'd had an agent or a lawyer.[28]

Like Creators now, McQueen's experience suggests a significant power
imbalance between Wattpad and potential Wattpad Books authors, who
are positioned with little negotiating power. Given that Wattpad's user base
skews towards young women and other marginalized groups, and many
users sign up in their early to mid-teens as McQueen did and develop an
affinity and trust for the platform, puts them in an even more precarious
position.

After signing the contract with Wattpad Books, the publication story of
Invincible Summer follows that of the traditional publishing industry closely:
McQueen worked with an editor from Wattpad on structural and copy edits,
was paired with a publicist who worked with the marketing team to create
a promotional campaign, and the book was released the following year in
print and ebook formats. While the plot of the story did not change, the
editing process involved changes to the structure, transforming the style

from that of serialized online fiction to one that was more mainstream print. The changes included tightening up the plot and removing scenes that McQueen described as "fan service," or the material in a work of fiction or fictional series that is intentionally added to please their Wattpad readers. The inclusion of this material in the original Wattpad story demonstrates a primary way that social authorship seems to manifest on the platform. Therefore, while the Wattpad readership was central to *Invincible Summer* being published in the first place, as their reading data informed the initial acquisition decisions, the removal of fan service from the published book demonstrates the broader market Wattpad intended to target beyond the platform.

Wattpad Books demonstrates the way platform publishers adapt and imitate features of traditional publishing while integrating them with features of platform capitalism. In doing so, Wattpad Books leans into notions of impartiality and reliability of popularity data to set them and their acquisition decisions apart from legacy practices. The practicalities of Wattpad Books being part of the global book industry creates a more nuanced picture.

Indeed, Wattpad Books operates within a context of cooperative competition, or coopetition to use Maria Bengtsson and Sören Kock's term,[29] developing partnerships with traditional publishers through sub-rights deals. Wattpad Books titles are distributed by Macmillan in the US, Raincoast Books in Canada, and published by Penguin Random House in the UK and Australia. Wattpad also competes with distribution platforms for sales. *Invincible Summer*, as with all books published by Wattpad Webtoon Book Group, is available as a Wattpad Original (formerly Paid Stories), and sold via Amazon, Booktopia, Barnes and Noble, and other online and brick-and-mortar bookstores. Wattpad's co-opetition with traditional publishing conglomerates and other platforms highlights the messy interlinks between legacy institutions and platforms in the twenty-first century. The extent of this vast ecosystem is explored more in the next chapter.

The Limits of Data in Book Publishing

The factors that minimize diverse and inclusive representation in the different facets of the pipeline—from the Watty Awards to the Creators program—shape the output, or list, of Wattpad's publishing enterprise. As discussed already, eligibility in the Creators program is limited to authors who work in English and so Wattpad Webtoon Book Group unsurprisingly operates in the Anglophone book industry. However, the global geographical, racial, and ethnic diversity of the authors of the platform and partner program from which Wattpad sources the titles it publishes presents distinctive opportunities for greater diversity in its publishing list. This idea is emphasized in the marketing copy of the imprint, as the about page reads: "We publish the most popular and diverse voices—because inclusivity looks like all stories being told."[30] Based on a content analysis of authors' identities of the books published by the Wattpad Books imprint as detailed in their bios, Wattpad's data-driven approach to publishing does not seem to improve the geographical, racial and ethnic diversity of the authors it publishes.

Of books published under this list from 2019–2023, 33 percent were by BIPOC authors and 59 percent by White authors. The merger with Webtoon changed things slightly: Before the merger, 24 percent of titles were written by BIPOC authors and 74 percent by White authors compared to 48 percent by BIPOC authors and 37 percent by White authors after. The increase here in BIPOC authors in the time since the merger is due to eight graphic novels published by South Korean creators and sourced from Webtoon, rather than Wattpad. Prior to the merger, there was a stark decline: nine out of the ten BIPOC authors in the list were published in the first year of Wattpad Books (2019–2020), and only one published in the second year (2020–2021). While the racial and ethnic diversity of Wattpad Books authors replicates the same White taste logic that pervades traditional publishing, the geographic diversity of authors is slightly better.

Between 2019 and 2023, 61 percent of authors published by Wattpad Books were from North America and 39 percent from elsewhere. There are several problems with examining location of authors through a binary lens that condenses territories that are not North America as "the rest of the world," but doing so starkly shows how Wattpad Books replicates the hegemony of the North American market, particularly that of the US, in the traditional global publishing industry. The increase in South Korean authors after the acquisition of Wattpad by Naver impacted the geographical hegemony of North America to a lesser extent than it did the racial diversity of authors, partly because the initial disparity was less stark. Before the merger, 64 percent of Wattpad Books authors were based in North America and 36 percent somewhere in the rest of the world. After, 56 percent were based in North America and 44 percent somewhere else in the world. It is worth noting that while Filipino Wattpad authors are not represented in the Wattpad Books list, they are widely published in the Philippines where Wattpad has developed several partnerships with local publishers, as we'll explore in the next chapter. But for Wattpad Webtoon Book Group, North America is the primary market for Wattpad books, despite some of its largest user bases being in non-Western countries.

The lack of diversity in Wattpad Books may speak, at least in part, to the systemic marginalization and exclusion of diverse voices and stories that plagues the traditional global book industry, and an entrenchment of this White taste mainstreaming by Wattpad. It is possible that if Wattpad valued different kinds of reader metrics, they may be encouraged to publish the kinds of books that would achieve the anti-oppression stance they proclaimed in their response to the resignation of several Stars mentioned earlier. Discussing the limitations of Wattpad's diversity efforts, Simone Shirazi told me:

> I've found that I have a much bigger audience of people outside of North America when it comes to my non-White stories, essentially, which is really interesting to see . . . I've noticed that I have a lot more readers from Nigeria on those more diverse stories.[31]

Wattpad's apparent disinterest in developing non-US and non-English markets for their books except in particular cases and their adherence to the global capitalist structures of the traditional industry through Wattpad Webtoon Book Group means that it does not provide any meaningful alternative in terms of cultural and racial inclusivity.

This Anglophone, and more specifically North American, bias illustrates a fundamental flaw in using logics of popularity and programmability to source content from a platform where diverse stories and creators are not actively encouraged or even safeguarded. The kinds of popular stories that succeed on Wattpad are written in English, tend to feature mainstream hegemonic representations, namely White characters. As one author put it in our interview, "Wattpad has always been a predominantly White platform. Readers are from all over, but the stories that have gotten popular have been White, straight romance novels."[32] This bias that is evident in the output of Wattpad Books is intensified through the pipeline where the authors of these stories face fewer barriers. Wattpad cannot rely on platform reader data to ensure diversity and inclusion in its publishing list and, as with traditional publishers, must actively work to acquire culturally inclusive works if they want to publish a diverse range of authors and stories. The same author articulated this flawed cycle: "Because Wattpad's whole deal is that they work through data, the way that they find Stars is like, 'okay who's popular?' Well it tends to be these White writers writing these [White] romances."

This is not to say that diverse works are not popular or commercial. A decade ago, before Wattpad began offering monetization to authors, Melanie Ramdarshan Bold observed that many of the 150 most popular Wattpad authors by follower count wrote about inclusive themes, such as gender identity, pansexuality, and intersectional feminist themes. These authors and their stories, she argued, pointed to the way that "Wattpad, and self-publishing in general, can be a vehicle for expressing otherness and offering a response to the underrepresented in traditional publishing."[33] However, the commercial media that Wattpad has produced since proves that popularity data does not reliably improve diversity, equity, and inclusion. Another author described how editorial bias of Wattpad staff contributed to the lack of diversity in their list, saying,

> I think Wattpad has a type of book that it knows does well and at the end of the day in trying to be profitable and make money, that's what is going to be promoted the most. I mean, I get it to some degree that you want to put out content that you know people will like, but I think there is some level of, "We're only going to put out content that we know people like, even though it's probably true that if we put out other content, people would also like that."

It is possible then that Wattpad uses data in much the same way Claire Squires describes editors in traditional publishing houses using data to confirm their acquisition decisions.[34] Regardless, the assumption that drawing content from a global platform, created and read by a global user base will result in greater diversity, an idea that has been promoted by Wattpad's own marketing, is a false equivalency. In addition to Shirazi's assertion that much of her audience for her more inclusive stories are located outside of North America, she and other authors recounted experiences that suggests the user base that Wattpad relies on for sourcing popular content is not wholly receptive to representations of diversity and inclusion.

As explored in chapter 2, several BIPOC authors have experienced targeted harassment, negative comments and sometimes death threats over the cultural and racial representation and politically progressive themes in their Wattpad stories. While it would be remiss of me to flatten the entirety of the Wattpad reader-base based on any one subgroup, the experiences these authors faced of racially motivated harassment and trolling at the very least indicate that the reader data Wattpad uses to inform its acquisition decisions includes bias. Moreover, Wattpad furthers the marginalization and exclusion of BIPOC authors and queer authors through their editorial practices.

Practices of editorial bias that have long plagued the traditional publishing industry, often disguised as pragmatism and market orientation, are replicated by Wattpad Books through its editorial decisions and remuneration packages. One author I spoke to drew attention to the fact that the first title published by Wattpad Books with an Asian American main character was written by a White author, Natalie Walton. She added, "I love her, she's a wonderful writer and I trust her fully but from an editorial accountability standpoint I think they could have done better." The author I spoke to continued by pointing out that the stories that Wattpad was publishing by Asian American authors since Walton's novel tended to feature White characters, so, she said, "there's this kind of disconnect between what they're trying to do versus what they're actually doing" in terms of diversity and inclusion.

Wattpad further strengthens the privilege afforded to White authors through their remuneration of intellectual property. One author interviewed spoke about how reliance on popularity metrics also resulted in inequitable advances and royalty deals. They shared that "some books like *The QB Bad Boy, Bro Code*, [and] some other books that came out that had a larger following got higher advances, not necessarily because the team believed in the quality of the work or the importance of the story, but because they were more popular." Paying different advances to different authors is a practice in traditional publishing as well, determined by different kinds of popularity indicators such as brand name or celebrity authors, previous sales records, and auctions. However, this information shows that Wattpad seems to be replicating the racialized disparities in advances of traditional publishing, as evidenced by the viral 2020 Twitter hashtag #PublishingPaidMe. This grassroots data collection showed how the advances given by traditional publishers, and particularly the opacity around this information, is used to disadvantage authors from marginalized backgrounds, who often receive less even when they meet popularity metrics that indicate potential commercial success.[35]

Conclusion

When Wattpad launched, it was seen to fulfill promises of egalitarian participation. Adopting an ethos from active online fanfiction communities and the kind of unfettered writing that would be found on platforms like LiveJournal. The formalization of writing on Wattpad through its commercial pipeline and as a platform publisher now owned by a major tech conglomerate highlights the shrinking space online for non-commercial creative production that inspired ideas of a more equitable, participatory culture. As a result, Wattpad Books—and the platform publisher model more generally—does not radically alter the landscape for traditionally marginalized authors, merely shifting the exclusionary gates imposed by traditional publishers further along the path of production and obscuring editorial biases under the guise of a data-driven publishing.

The commercialization of writing across Wattpad renders its community of users into creators and audiences, and online creativity into market-oriented production. Platform publishers like Wattpad Books seem to replicate the White taste logic that pervades traditional publishing, which reproduces syllogistic ideas of White, middle-class readers as the "core audience"[36] and White authors as the bearers of quality and authority.[37] As Anamik Saha argues:

> it is the very process of industrial cultural production—that is, its techniques and systems of rationalization—that contain racializing tendencies or, put another way, is the means through which racist ideologies manifest and foster. Moreover, the increasing adoption of new media technologies and big data in cultural production allows this to happen in a more insidious and severe fashion.[38]

These techniques and systems are replicated by Wattpad Books, where the professionalization, aestheticization, and institutionalization of platformed creativity through Wattpad's formal and formalizing structures creates a system in which platform power is entrenched and hegemonic market conditions are reinforced and results in the continued marginalization and exclusion of BIPOC, LGBTQ+, and other politically minoritized groups.

The marginalization of these authors and imagined readers by Wattpad is made even more troublesome by Wattpad's historic branding, which depicts the company as one that cares about and actively improves the diversity of global storytelling. Its emphasis on using reader data and supposedly objective metrics as rationalizing measurements to inform acquisition decisions—the "combination of art and science"—works to minimize the responsibility of the human parts of its taste-making system and renders its publishing outcomes as something that is neutral rather than what is actually is: the outcome of exclusionary structures and biased input data.

Since the release of ChatGPT in November 2022, much of the discussion around books and AI has focused on the risks generative AI poses to the industry; *if* ChatGPT can produce legible (or dare I say, quality) text and Dall-e acceptable cover artwork, what does this mean for authors and cover designers? But the reliance on machine learning and artificial intelligence technologies in the acquisition process and decision-making by Wattpad serves as a warning sign for the publishing industry more broadly. What would the literary landscape look like if algorithms and AI were responsible for which books were published?

Several years ago, Jodie Archer and Matthew Jockers used text-mining, topic modeling and stylometrics to develop a model that could identify bestselling novels with the hopes that it would be able to predict future bestsellers.[39] And while the model naively excludes any other factors that contribute to the production of bestsellers—marketing and publicity efforts, to name but one[40]—and any such model is yet to be taken up by publishers, their study hints at the tendency for predictive models to replicate White racial hegemony in publishing when they are trained to identify success or quality based on a dataset of books that accord to a White taste logic (i.e., bestsellers and literary prize winners).

Similarly, StoryDNA, which is trained on literary classics and popular Wattpad stories and privileges authors writing in their first language by examining language, word use, sentence structure, and grammar of texts, is designed (intentionally or not) to uphold hegemonic White, Western narratives as quality. The imagined reader for which this system of cultural production works is not only a White, middle-class person, but an algorithm that stands in for that White, middle-class reader. The result is an algorithmic aesthetic that produces a hegemonic sameness (to what was successful before). The inability for data and technical systems to produce a very diverse book list emphasizes the importance of humans in creating a more diverse, inclusive publishing sector and book culture. However, the human parts of Wattpad's pipeline demonstrates the urgent need for human involvement to be explicitly anti-racist and push back against the dominant rationalizing/racializing logic that structures contemporary book culture.

In this model of publishing, authors are almost entirely dependent on platforms, relying on opaque platform determined metrics of success and rigid frameworks of remuneration. The piecemeal commercial opportunities afforded to authors in Wattpad's pipeline mirrors kinds of post-Fordist insecure work that treats labor like "water," or "a resource to be turned on and off at will."[41] While the majority of authors in traditional publishing spaces are also afforded little economic or occupational security (a 2015 survey, for instance, found that the average income derived from writing for Australian authors amounted to AU$12,900),[42] platform publishing introduces platform-specific precarities for authors akin to those experienced by other kinds of social media content creators; a precarity that is amplified for people of color in platform publishing models as racial inequality is reinforced through algorithmic and human taste-making functions.

Wattpad's creative economy is powered by a neoliberal ethos of self-commodification, where creative involvement is heavily mediated by inequitable computational and human structures. The platformization of publishing results in an industry where authors are increasingly dependent on platforms to create, publish, distribute, and earn money from their creative works. However, these authors are not wholly bound by individual platforms. Circumventing the logic of capture that underpins these platforms' capitalist business models, authors often fashion their writing careers across platforms and traditional institutions in a broad entertainment ecosystem that spans both online and offline spaces.

CHAPTER 5

The Entertainment Ecosystem

Creative and Productive Networks
Beyond the Platform

WE STARTED THIS BOOK with an introduction to Simone Shirazi, who came to Wattpad in her teens and over the next decade or so became a successful writer by many measures. Several of her stories earned millions (sometimes tens of millions) of reads, which propelled her to become a Wattpad Star and part of the short-lived Wattpad Futures program where she earned a share of ad-revenue from the platform. Her popularity also led to Radish, one of Wattpad's closest competitor platforms, reaching out and persuading her to publish her stories on their platform for a better deal. Shortly after, she was offered a job as a full-time writer for Radish, creating Radish Originals with a team of writers. In 2023, she realized her dream of being traditionally published, securing a deal with Pan Macmillan for *Cross the Line*, a contemporary sports romance novel that had never been published online before. Simone's journey is indicative of the broader ecosystem in which platform publishing operates, across a broad array of digital platforms and traditional institutions.

So far, this book has focused on platform microsystems, how their remuneration structures, classification algorithms and moderation systems, and organizational operations shape the activities and careers of platform-dependent self-published authors. But these platforms do not exist in isolation, nor do the authors working on them always limit themselves to a single platform. Rather, publishing platforms and the authors using them are part of a constellation of media: building on José van Dijck's conceptualization of the connective social media ecosystem, which theorizes social media platforms as operating relationally to each other, whether through interdependence, interoperability, competition, and/or collaboration.[1] Examining the platformization of publishing, though, highlights how publishing platforms and platform authors are positioned within and alongside other digital and traditional creative, cultural, and entertainment media sectors in a global entertainment ecosystem. This hybrid entertainment ecosystem comprises other cultural and entertainment websites, apps, and platforms (e.g., Netflix, Tumblr, and TikTok); as well as legacy institutions in the cultural and entertainment industries (e.g., Simon & Schuster, Penguin Random House, the Frankfurt Book Fair); and individual producers, intermediaries, and consumers.

Drawing on interviews with authors and a review of gray literature, this chapter explores how the entertainment ecosystem takes shape through networks forged from two concurrent directions: by platform companies and individual producers. First, it tracks Amazon and Wattpad's attempts to build multinational, multi-platform media organizations through the commercialization and adaptation of intellectual property. It focuses particularly on Wattpad's impact on the Filipino publishing and entertainment media industries as a synecdoche of its global pan-entertainment business model. Second, it charts how authors circumvent platforms' monopolistic imperatives by developing their own platformed approach to self-publishing through their connective and creative networks.

Importantly, the presentation of the entertainment ecosystem here is relational as any mapping of the networks and relationships embedded in the ecosystem necessarily changes depending on the platform, author, or text that is positioned as the starting point. This chapter, therefore, does not offer a definitive cartography of the entertainment ecosystem, but rather offers a heuristic framework for examining the growing interconnectedness of the media, publishing, and cultural industries driven by processes of platformization by exploring the networks forged by Amazon, Wattpad, and some of the authors who use these platforms to publish romance fiction.

Regardless of the central node used to map networks (author or platform), the entertainment ecosystem is defined by hybridity, between digital and physical spaces, commercial and non-commercial activities, and the complex interplay between platform preferences and authorial or creator agency.

Un-siloing Platform Publishing

The entertainment ecosystem has been formalized in large part by the development of platform companies' multi-platform approaches to the production and distribution of creative content. A "thorny" term, multi-platform refers to "a strategic approach where media companies are focused on making or putting together products and services with a view towards delivery and distribution of that content proposition on not just one but across multiple platforms."[2] Media theorists informed by political economy have proposed numerous terms to describe the corporate or managerial structures from which multi-platform media products emerge as well as the products themselves, including synergy,[3] cross-promotion,[4] brand extension,[5] entertainment supertexts,[6] content recycling and streaming,[7] and a 360-degree approach[8] to content. These strategies have emerged from conglomerate media companies' push to gain maximum mileage out of single cultural products and in response to—and in some cases driving—the increasing technological, economic, and cultural convergence of the past few decades.

Wattpad and Amazon have become multi-platform media companies through the strategic development of networks and data resources within and across media sectors. These networks and data support the companies' business models and act "as strategic instruments to carve out a niche vis-à-vis competing platforms."[9] The specific business models adopted by Wattpad and Amazon are vastly different but are both underpinned by logics of platform capitalism and contribute to their expanding influence in the entertainment ecosystem.

Wattpad has adopted a pan-entertainment business model in which it commercializes the intellectual property posted to its social media platform as well as data generated by its users through in-house multimedia programs and partnerships with other producers and publishers. Some Amazon divisions, such as its book publishing and production ventures, also focus on the commercialization of media (i.e., through Amazon Publishing and Prime Studios). However, Amazon's dominance in the publishing and media industries (and consumer culture and society, more broadly) result from its technological and organizational infrastructure, including KDP, Amazon Web Services, and its warehousing and delivery systems. Amazon and Wattpad have not only built technology infrastructures that collect data from customers and readers but specifically design services and programs for the purpose of collecting more data, which informs their content strategies in the entertainment ecosystem. Though their impacts on contemporary media industries are distinctive, both Amazon and Wattpad demonstrate the increasing prominence of digital publishing platforms in the contemporary entertainment ecosystem.

By the third decade of the twenty-first century, Amazon seems to have a stake in nearly every commercial and media sector. It has stakes in virtual assistance and smart home technology (launching Alexa in 2013 and acquiring Ring in 2018), the video game world (acquiring Twitch in 2014), health and insurance (launching Amazon Protect in 2016), and groceries (purchasing Whole Foods in 2017). Most prominently, perhaps, is its Amazon Web Services, which was made available to developers in 2002 and for public usage in 2004, and which now provides the foundation for approximately one-third of the internet.[10] Amazon's dominance in the contemporary product and service economy and media landscape is due to anti-competitive business practices as well aggressive horizontal and vertical integration that have built the company's extensive infrastructure and product inventory.

Since its origins as an ecommerce bookstore in the mid-1990s, Amazon has attempted to capture every aspect of production, distribution and reception across the publishing sector. Amazon has invested in the development and sale of ebooks with the launch of the Kindle ereader and Kindle Direct Publishing platform in 2007, book reception through its acquisitions of Goodreads in 2013 and Shelfari (now defunct), audiobook format with its acquisition of Audible in 2008 and launched of its Audiobook Creation Exchange marketplace, and publishing through its Amazon Publishing imprints in 2012. It has developed innovative ecommerce technologies, including one-click purchasing, and acquired competitor online book marketplaces, including Book Depository and AbeBooks. Each venture has further cemented Amazon's dominance in contemporary book culture. This walled garden approach in which Amazon attempts to incorporate and control all levels of production, distribution, and reception is mirrored in other media sectors in which Amazon has a stake, notably in film and television. Amazon acquired IMDb in 1998 for its data and began selling DVDs and videos in its marketplace alongside books. It launched Amazon Studios to develop original TV shows, movies, and comics in 2010 and acquired MGM studios in 2022 to become Amazon-MGM Studios. It divested Amazon Prime Video from Amazon Prime in 2011, and released the Amazon FireTV in 2014, which first enabled customers to add streaming services to their televisions.

Amazon has achieved its dominance in part by attempting to control every point of activity in the book and media sectors through an extreme logic of capture that has involved acquisitions of competing companies (e.g., Audible and Goodreads). Once under the Amazon umbrella, though, the entertainment sectors of its business ecosystem remain relatively discrete. Books acquired by Amazon Publishing imprints are not sourced with the goal of adapting them for film or television by Amazon Studios or for Amazon Prime Video, for example. The role of each of Amazon's media enterprises is not based on an interdependent approach to commercialization of intellectual property across its business ecosystem, as is the case with Wattpad, but as a product that contributes to the development of lucrative customer profiles for advertising and sales across Amazon's various departments.

Amazon uses data, resources, and property from different corporate ventures within its umbrella media organization. The books division, for example, uses the extensive data resources, such as customer reviews and sales data, from the ecommerce platform to find commercially promising books and compete as a publisher in the contemporary publishing industry. This method essentially follows the same kind of crowdsourced discoverability logic used by Wattpad Books. A number of the books first acquired by Amazon were originally self-published. For example, Zetta Elliot's YA novel *A Wish After Midnight* was originally published through CreateSpace, a self-publishing platform that was folded into Kindle Direct Publishing, and Maria Murnane's romance novel *Perfect on Paper* was originally published via BookSurge in 2007, a print-on-demand subsidiary of Amazon. According to Aubrey Rose, a self-published author who turned down a publishing deal with Amazon in 2013, Amazon offered a small advance (US$5,000 to Rose) with 35 percent royalties and demanded exclusivity in sales. Amazon seems to have targeted self-published authors during this phase to establish the imprint for as little financial risk as possible.[11]

As Amazon Publishing grew in resources, it began acquiring authors who had been traditionally published and were big names in their respective genres. In 2019, Amazon Publishing's romance fiction imprint Montlake Romance acquired bestselling author Sylvia Day's novella *Butterfly in Frost* with a seven-figure deal.[12] Day, although originally a self-published erotica author, has been published by many US publishers including HarperCollins, Kensington, Macmillan, Harlequin, and Penguin Random House, and is a number one New York Times bestselling author whose work has appeared on dozens of bestseller lists worldwide. Colleen Hoover, another author who originally self-published and was quickly picked up by Simon & Schuster's Atria Books, has since signed with Montlake.

This approach by Amazon Publishing and Prime Video feeds into the company's overarching Prime strategy. Described by Bezos at a technology conference in 2016, Amazon invests heavily in exclusive and (likely) popular video content on its Prime platform to encourage customers to sign up to the Prime program. In turn, this theoretically converts viewers into shoppers as Amazon bundles other offers into the Prime program, such as fast shipping. As Bezos summarized, "When we win a Golden Globe, it helps us to sell more shoes" because Prime members tend to buy more on Amazon than non-Prime members.[13]

This substantial shift in strategy indicates that while self-publishing has proven to be a successful entry point into the contemporary publishing field for some authors, Amazon is now more focused on authors with already established status and proven sales success. These previously successful authors can be self-publishing authors from historically marginalized backgrounds, as is the case with Alyssa Cole, who began her career self-publishing, has since signed with traditional romance publishers such as Avon and Kensington and had an Audible Original audiobook produced by Amazon. The strategies of Amazon Publishing and Audible Originals are indicative of the practices that Amazon has engaged in to build its dominance and power across product sectors, which some argue verges on, if not crosses into the territory of, anticompetitiveness. Amazon owns the technologies of book production, the marketplace in which these products are sold, and participates in these markets.

In contrast to Amazon, Wattpad's business model focuses primarily on the commercialization of user data and intellectual property. Once self-described as the YouTube for books, Wattpad now promotes itself as a multi-platform entertainment company by implementing a pan-entertainment business model. Wattpad's pan-entertainment model adopts and adapts that seen in China's technology companies and web literature industry. First proposed by Tencent Vice President Cheng Wu, a pan-entertainment model describes a business ecosystem of connected entertainment industries centered on the production and professionalization of intellectual property across multiple media formats.[14]

It is a strategy that has been matured by Tencent and other Chinese technology companies such as Baidu and Alibaba, the development of which is tied to the favorable national policy Internet Plus, which was designed to promote the integration of advanced technologies with traditional culture industries to promote economic growth and advance China's soft cultural power globally. The pan-entertainment model has underpinned the massive growth of China's online literature industry through "redistributing, remixing and re-bundling intellectual property (IP) in transmedia platforms, and crossing traditional industrial boundaries."[15]

Wattpad's pan-entertainment model is based on the integration and commercialization of intellectual property posted to its creative writing and reading platform through partnerships and in-house projects across global markets. As explored in the previous chapter, Wattpad integrates the user-generated content posted to its site into its commercial programs. In addition to venture capital investments, the company generates revenue through Wattpad Premium (a freemium model where users can pay for an ad free experience); Wattpad Insights (monetizing user and usage data) sold at international rights fairs like the Frankfurt Book Fair; brand partnerships; and Wattpad Next (its Paid Stories Program).

Stories also have the potential to travel beyond the site through partnership schemes, intellectual property deals brokered by the platform, and on-selling of trend data. Wattpad has developed partnerships with several traditional publishers—including Sourcebooks, Hachette Audio and Hachette Romans, and Summit Media in the Philippines—to republish Wattpad stories from the site into print books. The platform has also partnered with production companies to co-produce stories for film and television across the globe including with iFlix in Indonesia, Huayi Brothers in South Korea, and Syfy and Sony in the United States. The diversification of Wattpad's multi-platform pan-entertainment business model leverages the interconnectedness of media industries in an increasingly convergent and globalized media landscape.

The adaptation of Wattpad texts from their serialized form online to print books and films reflects the emerging role of digital publishing platforms in the adaptation and entertainment industries in the early twenty-first century. Books have long been popular sources for films; they were the basis for approximately thirty percent of narrative films made in Hollywood's classic period and books that have been commercially successful or award-winners have long been prioritized for adaptation.[16] These logics are reinforced on Wattpad but strategically combined with insights generated through the extensive data the platform gathers on users and content that indicate popularity and potential success.

Wattpad uses social media logics of programmability, datafication, popularity, and connectivity[17] to inform decisions around which texts may travel across media sectors in their pan-entertainment business. Authors and stories that accrue markers of high status and popularity, such as high follower or read counts—primarily brand name and microcelebrity authors as well as authors who win Watty Awards on the platform, become Wattpad Creators (formerly Stars) and travel through the Wattpad pipeline mapped in the previous chapter—are more likely to benefit from Wattpad's pan-entertainment model. However, the movement of high performing authors and texts on Wattpad in the entertainment ecosystem predates the establishment of the platform's award and Stars Program.

The Kissing Booth by Beth Reekles is one of the most prominent examples of the power of Wattpad in the adaptation of intellectual property in the entertainment ecosystem.[18] Reekles originally published the story in 2011 on Wattpad, where the story won the Most Popular Teen Fiction Watty award and amassed more than 19 million reads and 40,000 comments over the following two years. In 2012, an editor at Random House Children's Publishers (RHCP) reached out to Reekles via direct message on Wattpad and acquired the rights to *The Kissing Booth* in a three-book deal, releasing it as an ebook in 2012 and a paperback in 2013. In 2013, Reekles sold the film rights to Komixx, a UK-based production company, and three years later Netflix ordered the film. RHCP released a movie tie-in print edition to coincide with the film release in 2018, which featured the Netflix thumbnail image for the film on the cover. In 2018, Netflix reported that its Netflix Original adaptation of *The Kissing Booth* was the most re-watched film on the platform globally.[19]

The adaptation journey of *The Kissing Booth* is indicative of the new possibilities for book publishing and media adaptation that re-work traditional processes but does not break from them completely. This story, which originated as a serialized platform story on Wattpad and was adapted for a streaming video on demand (SVOD) platform, illustrates the growing centrality, in some cases dominance, of digital companies and platforms in the contemporary entertainment ecosystem. *The Kissing Booth* is also representative of most of the texts that move between sectors and forms in the Wattpad's entertainment ecosystem in the West; narratives that are for young adults, romantic, White, and heteronormative. There are exceptions to this on local levels, particularly in the Philippines and other Southeast Asian countries, where Wattpad and online writing platforms have invested in stories with local characters and content.

Wattpad has had a substantial impact on the publishing and media industries in the Philippines in particular, where it has partnered with local publishing houses to create imprints and television networks to create series from Wattpad content. Wattpad's position in the Philippines is a prime example of the way Wattpad, as a globalized platform, enters and adapts to localized cultural industries using a pan-entertainment model and provides insight into the impact that Wattpad and other platforms like it may have on the creative industries more globally. The focus on this territory as a case study also serves to de-Westernize research and hegemonic discourses of diversity and inclusion in book culture, which have primarily been explored through Western, particularly American, contexts.

Wattpad's Blueprint in the Philippines

Wattpad has had a substantial impact on the publishing and entertainment media industries in the Philippines, where it has embedded itself in the local entertainment ecosystem by partnering with local publishing houses and television networks to publish and produce stories from the platform. While such partnerships exist globally—in the US, the UK, Germany, and France, for example—Wattpad's influence on the Filipino publishing and media culture is particularly acute. Wattpad's position in the Philippines illustrates the way Wattpad as a globalized platform enters and adapts to localized cultural industries. While Wattpad is creating some opportunities for greater diversity and inclusion in Filipino book and media culture, post-colonial tensions play out in the dominant languages of both traditional and platformed cultural production. Media products developed from Wattpad also benefit from distinctly Filipino modes of reception. Exploring Wattpad's position in the Filipino publishing and media industries thus provides insight into the platform's goals more globally as well as its impacts on diversity and inclusion in the local book and media culture, outside hegemonic Western territories.

Despite the professionalization of Filipino Wattpad writers through the platform's formal partnerships and more informal networks in the Philippines, it proved difficult to get in contact with possible case profile authors. This was due, I think, in large part to the timing of my data collection for this stage of the research, which unluckily fell during the first year of the COVID-19 pandemic when lockdowns affected so many people's ability to do more than was necessary to get through their daily lives. This section is therefore based on interviews with only three authors, but whose publishing experiences proved very rich.

The first author, Mina V. Esguerra, writes contemporary romance, young adult and new adult fiction and began her career with a traditional publisher. In 2013, she began #RomanceClass, an online romance writing class that evolved into a robust and active self-publishing community.[20] She also began experimenting with Wattpad around this time, primarily as a marketing tactic, and now also works as an agent, working with LA-based Bold MP to develop romance media by Filipino creatives for an international audience. The second is Sol Tuberosum, a Watty Award winner, Wattpad Star and Outreach and Content Ambassador for Wattpad, who writes queer romance fiction. And the third, Demi Abilon, is a Wattpad Star who writes across genres and has been traditionally published and secured a TV deal for her Wattpad stories. These three authors all joined Wattpad between 2011 and 2013 and have used the platform in different ways, for different purposes over the years. Abilon's career in particular has been almost entirely shaped by Wattpad's pan-entertainment business model, but all three authors' experiences highlight the close connections Wattpad has forged in the Filipino publishing and entertainment media industries and, in particular, how the platform is adapting to the local book and media cultures.

Wattpad has had a significant impact on the publishing and entertainment industries in the Philippines, generating a new way intellectual property and creative content is sourced and produced. Many large Filipino publishers began to acquire popular authors and stories from Wattpad in the early 2010s mostly by reaching out to authors directly on the platform. Demi Abilon, for example, signed a three-book deal for *The Peculiars' Tale*, a sci-fi YA trilogy originally published on Wattpad after an editor at Psicom reached out to her through the direct messaging function on the platform.[21] In 2014, Wattpad established its first formal partnership in the Philippines with Pop Fiction, an imprint of Summit Media. The same year, major national production companies including Viva Films, TV5, and ABS-CBN began adapting Wattpad stories into films and television series, mostly as Filipino teleseryes or P-dramas.

In some cases, Wattpad authors and texts move through both legacy industries in the Filipino entertainment ecosystem. An early and important example is *She's Dating the Gangster* by Bianca B. Bernardino, which began as serialized fiction on CandyMag.com's Teen Talk section and became popular on Wattpad after being cross-posted there.[22] In 2013 *She's Dating the Gangster* was republished by Summit Media's Pop Fiction imprint, prior to the official partnership, and the following year it was released as a film by ABS-CBN Film Productions Inc. The relationship between Wattpad and traditional publishers and entertainment media producers in the Philippines represents a level of integration not previously seen with the platform's global partnerships and may be considered as a kind of testing ground or blueprint for Wattpad's pan-entertainment aims globally.

For half a decade, these partnerships tended to play out as an informal network, with Wattpad sharing data insights about popular authors and stories and brokering IP deals. In 2019, Wattpad further infiltrated the Filipino book publishing industry by formally partnering with Anvil Publishing to create Bliss Books, an imprint dedicated to publishing Wattpad fiction. Abilon benefited from this partnership, publishing another novel *Wake Up, Dreamers!* with Bliss Books in 2019. Like *The Peculiars' Tale, Wake Up Dreamers!*[23] won a Watty Award—in 2015 and 2019 respectively—propelling Abilon into the Wattpad Stars program and through the commercial pipeline described in the previous chapter. While the romance and teen fiction lists of many large Filipino publishing houses feature Wattpad authors and stories, this partnership furthers the platform's ability to shape local publishing and book culture.

The brand power of Wattpad in the local publishing landscape is emphasized through the paratextual alignment of Bliss Books covers with the platform. Authors' Wattpad usernames feature prominently on the covers of these novels, often to the exclusion of their real names. The Bliss Books logo, positioned in the top right-hand corner of the front covers, features the distinct Wattpad brand orange, titled Hero Orange, which also appears as a border around the cover image. These paratextual elements indicate the importance of the authors' Wattpad audiences and the way in which status is transferable between the platform and traditional book spaces such as

bookstores and promotional events in the Philippines. Wattpad's relationship
to Filipino publishers is one of coopetition; the platform operates collaboratively and competitively with publishers through its pan-entertainment
strategy by sharing data insights and brokering deals through partnerships
with several publishers as well as being directly involved in the curation of
the Bliss Books publishing list.

While Wattpad occupies a less central position in the Filipino television
and film industry, its impact on local productions is still striking relative
to the rest of the world. In addition to publishing her novels, Albion has
worked with the broadcaster TV5 as part of their Wattpad Presents productions. Airing from 2014–2017, Wattpad Presents was a weekly series
with a thirty-minute runtime that was produced by a partnership between
Wattpad and TV5 and adapted stories from the platform. In the beginning, Wattpad stories were broken into installments, spanning four to five
episodes, but eventually stories from the platform were produced to be
standalone thirty-minute episodes. Wattpad has since brokered deals and
developed partnerships with production companies globally, including,
for example, with Netflix, Hulu, Sony, Huayi Brothers in South Korea,
iFlix in Indonesia, and eOne in Canada. Wattpad's partnership with TV5
to produce Wattpad Presents films represents their first and most closely
integrated partnership in this sphere. Several factors make the Philippines
such a receptive territory for Wattpad's pan-entertainment forays into local
film and television industries.

The entertainment media landscape of the Philippines has a long history
of innovation and development. The Philippines has a very well-developed
national television industry that has been a national "conveyor of popular
culture and entertainment" and has not experienced the same disruptions
or audience fragmentation presented by digital technologies as in other
markets.[24] Rather, digital and mobile technologies have largely supported
the industry as Filipino "television producers have been very successful in
reintegrating successful content from new media platforms into traditionally broadcast programmes."[25] Television, including free-to-air television,
remains a dominant and influential medium in the Philippines, reported
as the most used and trusted media format.[26]

The power of the television industry in the Philippines is augmented
by the inclusion of state-run media as well as acute concentration of media
ownership in this sector. At the beginning of the twenty-first century, three

of the top five television stations in the Philippines were state-owned, though these three stations accounted for only 17.5 percent of the market share of viewing.[27] As of 2019, the two biggest television conglomerates, ABS-CBN and GMA, had an audience share of around 80 percent, though these conglomerates further their reach by also operating regional stations or relaying their programs to independent regional stations.[28] The government still influences these networks as all television franchises must be approved by the government, particularly the House of Representatives and are regulated by the National Telecommunications Commission government agency. The concentration of television media was further consolidated in 2020 when the Duterte government did not renew the broadcast license of ABS-CBN, one of the largest networks in the Philippines.[29] With few independent competitors, the high media concentration meant that once Wattpad was successfully integrated in the media cycle, its influence proliferated across the nation.

As in the publishing industry, much of the television programming has been characterized by profitable national popular content. However, Filipino audiences are also very receptive to transcultural popular media. Filipino creators have adapted the Japanese and Thai Boys Love genre to create their own Pinoy Boys Love videos on YouTube and writing on creative writing platforms, for example.[30] Alongside the regular importation of influential US entertainment media and romance fiction in the publishing industry, Filipino audiences have imported and adapted many Asian popular culture entities to their entertainment production and consumption. Filipino fans have actively engaged in transcultural spaces online such as Japanese anime and manga and Korean drama communities.[31] As a global platform, Wattpad is a useful source of local and transcultural content for the dynamic media landscape of the Philippines.

Media products developed from Wattpad benefit from distinctly Filipino modes of reception and fan practices that have resulted in a dedication to Wattpad stories and authors not seen to the same degree in other markets. The first mode is *kilig*, a Filipino term that refers to an affective feeling of romantic excitement, which typifies the relationship between Wattpad authors, readers, actors, and story characters. Kilig is an important and highly unique feature of the Filipino romance and teen fiction genre worlds, especially among young fan communities, and key to the affective nature of relationships between writers, actors, and readers associated with Wattpad media. This is particularly evident in highly attended annual Wattpadder meetups at malls and book fairs around the country where Wattpad authors who have been traditionally published or had their stories adapted reach a kind of literary celebrity that is similar only to the major blockbuster young adult fiction writers in the West. In our interview, Abilon noted that "in the Philippines, when you become a Wattpad Star, you reach that amount of followers, you're almost like a celebrity."[32] Wattpad authors like Abilon who have had their stories published by a Filipino publishing house often visit bookstores and attend events around the country for book tours. These and Wattpad-run author signing events typically have large turnouts of readers, which contribute to the continuation of Wattpad literary celebrity in the Philippines.

The second mode of reception is the development and investment in love teams. Love teams are pairs of celebrities launched by mainstream Filipino studios to appear in a succession of films, TV series, advertisements, and other media together, and who are often interpreted as (and sometimes become) a romantic couple in real life. They have become a feature of the romance stories Wattpad has adapted and republished in the Philippines as well as how Filipino Wattpad users navigate the platform. While Filipino love teams date back to the silent film era of the 1920–1930s, contemporary love teams are heavily mediated and social media is a key mechanism in their creation and proliferation.[33] Love teams like that of Kathryn Bernardo and Daniel Padilla, who starred in the Wattpad Presents film *She's Dating the Gangster*, have become integral to the user experience on Wattpad in a kind of feedback loop. Ashleigh Gardner, the Deputy General Manager, Wattpad Studios, Publishing, has stated that #KathNiel (a portmanteau of Kathryn Bernardo and Daniel Padilla from *She's Dating the Gangster* and other films) was the most-searched term on the platform in the Philippines in 2016.[34] This in part drives the successful reception of Wattpad media, which in turn feeds into the continued popularity of and engagement with the platform in the country.

Both kilig and love teams are key to the affective nature of relationships between writers, actors, and readers associated with Wattpad media and feeds the successful adaptation of media in Wattpad's pan-entertainment ecosystem of the Philippines. The fact that nearly all Wattpad-originated texts that are adapted in the Filipino entertainment ecosystem are teen fiction and/or romance make these fan practices especially common. The prominence of kilig and use of love teams in Wattpad-produced texts, which feeds back into users' behaviors on the platform, also highlight some of the localized ways platformization unfolds in nationally structured cultural industries. This is especially true when considering if and how Wattpad encourages more diverse representation in the books and media produced, which are nationally, historically, and culturally situated. The Filipino Wattpad authors interviewed for this research, who write queer-friendly, sex-positive romance fiction within the Filipino context, demonstrate the potential of the platform to enhance diversity within local book cultures but highlight the complex ways this plays out in practice.

Localized Platformization

The Filipino romance fiction produced on and republished from Wattpad exists within a complex sociopolitical and biblio-history that has been marked by the dominance of certain languages and the marginalization of queer love. Situating Wattpad's participation in the Filipino publishing and media industries thus highlights the sociopolitical contexts that shape and (hyper)localized tensions that arise through processes of platformization. In the context of the Philippines, romance fiction has been strongly influenced by the country's colonial history and historically socially conservative politics.

There is a complex interplay between language, class, and taste at play in the Filipino cultural industries, with language being a key site in which post-colonial tensions play out. This dynamic has been shaped by America's colonization of the Philippines in the first half of the twentieth century and impacts of Marcos's presidency (1965–1986) and the implementation of Martial Law (formally 1972–1981). English was the primary language of instruction in formal educational settings between 1901 and 1974, which resulted in English-language titles dominating the industries until the late twentieth century and historically produced for and marketed to middle- and upper-class audiences who could afford this kind of education. Several factors in the late twentieth century shifted dynamics to the Filipino language. First of all, Filipino was developed from several local dialects (most prominently Tagalog, the dialect around the Manila region) and established as a national language in 1972. Second, the dwindling value of the peso alongside importation restrictions implemented under Marcos forced several local book traders and media companies to change business models, with many turning to producing books and media in Filipino and local dialects.[35]

Now, the Filipino publishing industry is dominated by the national languages of Filipino and English, sometimes appearing as Taglish (the lingua franca that code-mixes Filipino/Tagalog and English and serves as a kind of meeting point for Filipinos coming from different social classes). Tagalog/Taglish romance fiction has been a local powerhouse since it was first introduced in the 1980s when restricted importation laws and rising inflation under the Marcos dictatorship prompted local distributors of Mills & Boon fiction to start publishing local authors. While Tagalog romances remain a dominant and bestselling part of the Filipino romance industry, several new competitors have worked to carve out their own segments of the market in the twenty-first century. In the early 2000s, the development of English-language romance fiction by conglomerate publishers (beginning with editor Tara F. Sering at Summit Media) sought to capture middle and upper-class readers (Class A-C in the Philippines).

In a country with over 120 local languages, Wattpad presents opportunities for a greater diversity of languages in Filipino fiction by allowing creators to publish on the platform in any language they wish. However, most Filipinos on the site read and/or write in Filipino, Taglish, or English. Further to this, Wattpad is, above all, a commercial company and interested in the types of IP that are likely to do well in established national markets and so most Wattpad stories published by local publishers or adapted for film and television are also typically written in Filipino or Taglish. Therefore, while creators can publish in whatever language they wish, if they want to leverage their writing for commercial ends then they must adhere to established market languages. Wattpad thus replicates the language conventions of traditional publishing and media industry in the Philippines and reinforces the limited professional opportunities for authors of English and other languages in this entertainment ecosystem.

In both systems of production, the commercial opportunities for media by creators working in regional Philippine languages are even more limited. For Sol Tuberosum, who is from Iloilo City in the Western Visayas region of the Philippines where the local language is Hiligaynon/Ilonggo, the ability to write in English contributed to her initial decision to publish on Wattpad and find an audience. She described how the language barrier of not speaking Filipino/Tagalog impacted her publishing opportunities, including in regard to finding readers on Wattpad:

> Aside from English, I really have no other choice, because in Wattpad there are Filipino stories, but most of them are Tagalog, which is a local language, and I live in a different region, so I speak and write in a different language. Essentially, there's also regional differences in languages, so it's English or my other local language, so I got into English because of that.[36]

Even so, English is still relatively marginal in the Filipino entertainment ecosystem. Stories published by Bliss Books are written in Filipino or Taglish, replicating the language conventions of romance fiction published by traditional houses, and most Wattpad-produced films and television series are produced in Filipino. As Tuberosum described, "Filipinos are very fluent in English, but then it's not widely accepted in the publishing industry because Filipino stories are a priority," which she suggests results in Filipino authors being "sort of contained in our own publishing world."[37] By privileging creators working in dominant national languages in their lucrative IP partnership deals, Wattpad reinforces Western colonial power dynamics that structure the global publishing industry.

To give an idea of how traditional market conventions influence publishing activity on the Wattpad platform, at the time of writing, there were just under 6,000 stories tagged #Filipino, 7,600 tagged #Tagalog, and 7,000 tagged #Taglish, compared with only seventeen stories tagged #Hiligaynon and eight tagged #Ilonggo. While the colonial hegemony of the English language on the internet and in the global cultural industries means that most writers wouldn't use an #English tag, there are still more than 33,000 stories that do. This does not mean that there are not more stories written in these languages but does give an indication as to their relative use on the platform.

While writing in English does not provide Tuberosum with a clear path to being traditionally published in the Philippines, it does generate more publishing opportunities for authors more globally, particularly in North America and the UK, which are the largest markets for romance and teen fiction (the other category in which she writes). The ability to participate in a wider, more global romance genre world was an important factor for

Tuberosum, who also writes romance fiction featuring LGBTQ+ characters. When we spoke, one of her professional goals was to reach as wide an audience as possible to maximize her impact in diversifying LGBTQ+ Filipino representation both locally and internationally. In her words:

> There are a lot of Filipino authors, right, but not a lot of them write in English that can be read globally and appreciated globally, and I think a very small percentage of them are part of the LGBT community itself. That's kind of my inspiration [for writing on Wattpad], too.[38]

By writing in English and reaching a more global audience, she hopes to enhance queer Filipino representation beyond the Philippines.

Tuberosum is among a small number of authors writing LGBTQ+ Filipino romance fiction on Wattpad. There are only a couple of hundred stories on Wattpad with both a tag indicating the story is Filipino (e.g., #Philippines, #Filipino, #Tagalog) and one indicating it features LGBTQ+ characters or themes (e.g., #LGBT, #LGBTQIA, #Queer). The combination with the highest result is #Filipino and #LGBT with 207 results. The dearth of queer Filipino stories is perhaps a symptom of the broader sociopolitical landscape of the Philippines regarding LGBTQ+ rights, and is certainly reflected in the traditional publishing space. Tagalog pocketbook romance books, for example, tend to be highly attuned to this political context; according to Precious Hearts publisher Segundo Matias, the inexpensive local Tagalog romances became more popular than their Mills & Boon equivalents because the "novels' morality codes reflected values embraced by many in the Philippines," where divorce, abortion, and marriage equality are not currently legally recognized.[39]

For the authors I spoke to, the marginalization of LGBTQ+ authors and stories in the Philippines was an ongoing issue they considered as part of their creative practice. For Tuberosum, it has been another reason to write in English and shaped how she wants her work to be published. She said:

> The reason that I'm a bit hesitant and a bit apprehensive of publishing locally is because the Philippines is not a very gay-friendly nation. And we are getting better, but there is this

> stigma. I think I only have to mention that we are a Roman
> Catholic country. . . . So I thought that was a big barrier,
> because I know a lot of authors who initially wanted to write
> queer stories and are queer themselves, but they chose to
> pursue more, can I say, commercialized stories. Stories that
> they know will be more accepted by our community here in
> the Philippines.[40]

Here, Tuberosum highlights the sociopolitical and cultural context that
mediates diversity and inclusion Filipino publishing, including nationally
specific understandings of what constitutes diverse and inclusive representation for this market.

Demi Abilon's *Wake Up, Dreamers!*, which features a gay character and
was published by Bliss Books in 2021, demonstrates how Wattpad's involvement in the Filipino publishing industry could contribute to positive change.
Wake Up, Dreamers! had accumulated more than 1.4 million reads by the
time of its print publication and it's this proven success on Wattpad that
can be leveraged by writers and editors wanting to publish more diverse
fiction. Put differently, Wattpad can use popularity metrics to demonstrate
a local market for inclusive fiction through the tried-and-trusted success
of inclusive stories.

For Esguerra, a shared ideology is at the heart of the self-publishing
#RomanceClass community of which she founded and continues to be a
part. It has made the community so productive over the years and what
made it a safe space for so many of the writers. This shared vision includes
the relatively smaller, genre-specific things (for example everyone "had
to be behind the idea that the happy ending was required because in the
beginning some people were fighting us on that") as well as broader social
issues, such as the use of contraceptives or kind of political affiliation that
was acceptable. This has created a kind of self-selecting effect:

> It's not the entire group but I notice that some [were] actually
> were in support of authoritarian regime and I'm sure they don't
> feel comfortable any more in the group because of how we
> started writing about politics or started writing about certain
> rights or like just being able to sell condoms and pills here has
> been such a debate and then we're writing condom jokes and

banana-scented jokes . . . so now we're more vocal about our advocacies because I guess it's easier if it's more upfront and an author or reader is not into that, then they maybe don't join.[41]

The progressive ethos of the group has meant that for many writing inclusive narratives is something in which they have actively invested. As Esguerra described:

> The other thing that we're doing is I guess acknowledging what we were doing not enough of. So, like very specifically in LGBT, in queer romance, so it's mostly straight women in the group and so last year we had a lecture led by [two queer members] telling us how to write our books better because we didn't have to write queer romance, but they said they wanted to see themselves as characters in the books and not the stereotypical like the friend and like this.[42]

From this lecture, several members of the community published an anthology of queer romance together. In this way, #RomanceClass has evolved through them directly addressing what they see as the gaps in Filipino romance fiction, a genre that has historically been politically conservative, sexually demure, and with strong religious overtones.

Thus, it is not only processes of platformization that play out in response to national cultural industries, but also what meaningful diversity and inclusion looks like. In this latter issue, Wattpad's impact is not straightforward. While the platform seems to support queer representation in the books and media it has a hand in publishing and producing, it maintains the same colonial dynamics of the traditional, global publishing and media industries.

Platformed Author Careers

Networks in the entertainment ecosystem are not only created in response to the business interests of platforms. Shifting the focus from platforms to authors reveals other pathways that establish the entertainment ecosystem, which often go against platform-driven imperatives. Authors create connections between platforms, institutions, and media environments through their creative and professional praxis and, in doing so, work to minimize and circumvent attempts at control and capture by platforms. While some authors work exclusively on individual platforms—Katrina Jackson, for instance, only publishes on Amazon using its KDP platform to format and publish her works—many others build careers across a variety of competitive and complementary platforms, software, and institutions.

Authors may circumvent Amazon's integrated production, dissemination, and reception platforms by using support software to create and disseminate their titles more widely or cross-post their stories on Wattpad and other creative writing and reading platforms. Many Wattpad authors work across multiple platforms as well, such as Shirazi, who moved to Radish and is now traditionally published. And nearly all the authors interviewed use social media platforms for branding and marketing or were part of writing communities on LiveJournal or Tumblr. Many of the authors interviewed for this research have also graced fan fiction sites at some point in their writing histories, where they discovered their love of writing or honed their craft. Most authors' work also spans traditional spaces of book culture. Some have previously been published by multinational presses, others had recently signed traditional publishing contracts when I spoke to them, and Mina V. Esguerra is part of a self-publishing collective. Some authors have been or were part of the Romance Writers of America, the genre's largest industry organization, and some have their self-published titles stocked in brick-and-mortar bookstores such as The Ripped Bodice in Los Angeles and Brooklyn. Together, these elements make up a rough sketch of the entertainment ecosystem from the perspective of self-published romance authors.

For self-published romance authors—indeed for many publishers across markets—Amazon is the largest market for ebook sales but despite its dominance, few authors rely solely on Amazon to self-publish. In its relative shadow are several other platforms that self-published romance authors may use to as part of their creative and professional practice, including other self-publishing production and ecommerce platforms; service platforms and software for word-processing, formatting, and distribution; and social media platforms with creative writing communities that contribute to authors' creative development and marketing activities. Mapping author networks in the entertainment ecosystem demonstrates how self-published authors forge careers across digital, physical, and institutional spaces and negotiate their creative and professional relationships to digital publishing platforms and the power these platforms wield.

Throughout this research, I used the case profile identifiers of "Amazon author" or "Wattpad author" to flesh out the two case study publishing platforms. And while these identifiers were only ever meant as a heuristic to delineate which platforms these authors' experiences would primarily illustrate, they do imply a restrictive praxis on behalf of these authors that is often far from the reality of their experiences. In her research exploring how Amazon incentives shape the creation and production of novels, Laura Dietz clarifies that the authors she profiles "describe writing novels and choosing a platform on which to share them, not the other way around."[43] This process is a familiar one; the authors profiled in this book identify as writers rather than by the platforms on which they rely to publish their works. With few exceptions, they do not feel much loyalty to particular platforms but will use the ones that make the most sense at the time they need to publish.

Most of the Amazon self-published romance authors interviewed for this research, for example, also publish and disseminate their titles through Apple Books, Google Play, Kobo, Barnes and Noble, and Smashwords as well as Amazon. When publishing to Amazon, they tend to bypass elements of the KDP integrated production process, and instead turn to third-party software platforms to prepare their files as well as alternative dissemination platforms. Scrivener, a word-processing application, is commonly used by authors at the writing stage and while it can export texts into ebook formats such as EPUB and Kindle, it is not optimized for this production work. The authors I spoke to use software like Vellum and Draft2Digital, which are software programs that specifically cater to formatting ebooks and print books for various platform reading software (Amazon, Apple, Google Play and Smashwords) and operate as a distribution platform that delivers ebook files to these distribution platforms.

Draft2Digital and Vellum act as aggregators that enable authors to "go wide" from one platform dashboard. Distributing books via multiple platforms—or wide distribution—is especially important for self-publishers in the contemporary market to increase sales. Individualized formatting, which involves creating optimized files for different vendors, improves reader experiences and thus reduces the likelihood that customers will return books for poor formatting. Draft2Digital also allows self-publishers to disseminate their ebooks through digital library catalogs like Overdrive and Bibliotheca, which have historically been inaccessible to self-published authors, which opens distribution channels into several territories, including Denmark, Norway, Sweden, Germany, the Netherlands, Australia, New Zealand, and Malta.

While there is no integrated software to publish to Wattpad—at most, authors may draft chapters in Word or Google Docs and then upload chapter-by-chapter to the platform—many Wattpad authors use other platforms to write and publish their works. Shirazi, for example, migrated to Radish after they approached her and offered a more transparent way for her to earn money from her writing. At the time, Shirazi's stories had earned tens of millions of reads on Wattpad and while she was part of the Futures program, in which we earned a percentage of ad revenue, the platform was yet to establish more stable monetization programs. Radish, which was marketing itself by quality assurance as the "Netflix for books" (rather than Wattpad's original positioning as the "YouTube for books"), offered authors a way to earn money through its freemium micropayments model, through which users can read several free chapters or "episodes" before making payments of about twenty to thirty cents to unlock new episodes (users also have the option of waiting an hour to unlock episodes for free).

Radish competes with Wattpad in more implicit ways too. For example, its differing interface affordances also made Radish a competitive alternative for Shirazi, who liked that it did not include a comment function in its interface when she first joined (though it introduced commenting in 2020). After the targeted racial harassment Shirazi experienced on Wattpad by readers described in chapter 2, she "really enjoyed the quiet of Radish" in its early days.[44] These differences in payment structures and technical affordances demonstrates the competitive nature of the entertainment ecosystem, particularly with social media publishing platforms such as Radish and Wattpad, which are relatively newer sites and still establishing themselves as fixtures in the broader global cultural industries. The entertainment ecosystem is therefore a space of ongoing co-opetition as platforms work strategically with and against other platforms as well as traditional media institutions and authors negotiate their own professional practice within and across these organizational environments.

In 2020, Radish hired Shirazi as a story lead for their Radish Originals, the platform's short form serialized fiction developed in-house. In this role, Shirazi "help[ed] come up with and edit [Radish] Originals," working collaboratively "with a team of Emmy Award-winning soap opera writers."[45]

Radish Originals are published on the platform alongside user-generated content, including Shirazi's sole-authored titles. Radish's decision to hire soap opera writers is not wholly surprising as serialized online fiction and soap operas share distinctive conventions—they can both tend toward the dramatic and are potentially never ending. As Shirazi notes, "They're two very different things, but our model [at Radish] is to make sure that people want to keep coming back. We want to have fun with it. We want to be creative."[46] While this is not an example of the adaptation of creative content, it demonstrates how media forms are increasingly influencing and adopting conventions of one another in the entertainment ecosystem.

During her initial move to Radish, Shirazi saw the marketing potential of working across two competing platforms. Posting on both Wattpad and Radish provided an opportunity to expand the number of readers and earn money through multiple platform monetization systems. She posted the first two stories in a series on Radish for free and charged for the third book in the series, a similar strategy used by some Amazon authors who lower the price of the first book in a series to encourage readers to buy in. As Shirazi describes it, once you "have people hooked on the series, if they're really interested in reading, they'll come and pay for it."[47]

Publishing across multiple social media publishing platforms is a common marketing strategy for authors to build readerships, engage in readerly communities and promote their books. Claire Kann, for instance, initially posted her creative works on Swoon Reads, who published her first three novels through its affiliated print imprint. Kann used Wattpad and its in-built readership to market her books, uploading a couple of her novels to Wattpad as part of a marketing plan to expand her audience. Once Swoon Reads publishes a novel from the platform as a book, the original draft is removed from the platform except for an excerpt, but earlier drafts of Kann's Swoon Reads-published novels remained available on Wattpad until late 2020 as she built her author brand and readership across platforms.

The marketing potential of social media writing platforms such as Wattpad was highlighted by Esguerra as well, who publishes samples of her novels to Wattpad as a marketing tactic.[48] Indeed, the members of #RomanceClass, the self-publishing community Esguerra founded, use several platforms and digital genres to market their books and build and reinforce community ties. Since its beginnings as an online romance writing class using email as its pedagogical channel, #RomanceClass has since evolved into a post-digital, multimedia biblio-community. Together they have produced a fiction podcast, are developing film adaptations, and hold biannual events in which local actors are hired to perform live readings of community-published texts.[49]

In-person live readings held prior to the COVID-19 pandemic were highly mediated events; the readings are recorded and posted to YouTube and Twitch, and reception occurs both in-person and on social media platforms like Instagram and Twitter where moments from the readings circulate as photos and gifs. In 2020 and 2021, the community hosted these and other events wholly online due to the COVID-19 quarantine measures in the Philippines. The annual April Feels Day event was streamed online, members from the community hosted Mukbang Nights videos in which a few members of #RomanceClass would eat food and discuss their books, and the community developed a web series called *Hello, Ever After* that featured actors from the live reading events reading new epilogue-style scenes from already published community titles.[50] The latter two online events drew on the growing popularity of born-digital genres in Southeast Asia and other virtual performances around the globe. Esguerra's use of Wattpad in conjunction with the other multimedia and multi-platformed activities of #RomanceClass demonstrates how authorial praxis through platform publishing is typically highly dynamic, dispersed, and global.

Conversely, Wattpad authors also use social media platforms to promote their works, build readerships and commercialize their author brand. Despite the in-built audience on Wattpad, marketing outside the platform has become essential in building a larger readership as it is for Amazon authors. Shirazi described how the difficulty in gaining visibility and new readers on Wattpad has meant authors act increasingly like traditional and self-published authors who must "promote [themselves and their work] on other social media on Twitter, on Facebook, on TikTok of all things."[51]

Social media presents a relatively cheap and effective avenue for marketing but may also be instrumental in the creative and professional development of self-published authors. Katrina Jackson and Xio Axelrod, two self-published Amazon authors, described how fan fiction sites served as an important entry point to writing and publishing for them, demonstrating the increasingly blurry distinction between amateur, recreational, non-commercial writing, and publishing and professional (or professionalized), commercial writing on publishing platforms in the entertainment ecosystem.

Jackson began reading and writing fan fiction and romance short stories on the site Valent Chamber while she was completing her graduate
degree.[52] Valent Chamber is an archive of fan fiction and original stories
by women of color. The site was launched in 2008 as a part of the Valent
message board dedicated to celebrating the talent of actress, singer, and
songwriter, Renee Elise Goldsberry. In addition to shaping her writing
practice, the non-commercial sharing economy logics of fan fiction platforms have influenced Jackson's publishing practice. While Amazon does
not allow authors to permanently distribute their books for free, Jackson
said she would if she could.[53] Instead, she has made her stories available in
Kindle Unlimited, Amazon's ebook subscription library, which she views
as a more cost-effective way for readers to read several ebooks per month.

For Axelrod, active fan fiction and writing communities on social media
platforms were instrumental in her early development as a writer. Axelrod
started writing *Buffy the Vampire Slayer* fan fiction on LiveJournal, a popular
writing platform in the 1990s and early 2000s on which online blogs, jour-
nals, and diaries proliferated. When the show ended in 2003, Axelrod said
that "we all kind of disbanded and a lot of those writers became real writers.
Quote-unquote real writers."[54] Without the active community encouraging
her engagement, she stopped writing for a time. In 2013, she returned to
posting creative writing online when she set up a Tumblr blog. Tumblr is a
customizable microblogging platform that was launched in 2007 and has been
incredibly popular among writers, photographers, artists, and fandoms.[55]

Axelrod was encouraged by her followers—"like 30 [of them] maybe"—to
write more and so she published an early, serialized version of her first book,
Falling Stars, on the platform. As she describes it:

> So I wrote some more and wrote some more and people kept
> asking for more and more and more and I went away again to
> Europe, came home and a friend of mine was tweeting about a
> story that she was reading and I was like "what are you talking
> about" and she was like "yeah this woman, she puts up a chapter
> like every other day and blah blah blah" and I was like "that's
> mine!" and she said "no it's not." I was like "yes," and sent her
> the nextchapter and she said "oh my god, you have no idea
> how many people are reading this . . ." and I found that I had
> thousands of readers, it was crazy and I had no idea.[56]

While Axelrod could easily track her metrics on Tumblr, including follower count as well as how many users reblogged and liked her posts, she did not see when her story initially traveled beyond the digital walls of Tumblr as readers began discussing her story on Twitter.

By this point, Axelrod had around 20,000 words of what would become *Falling Stars* and a friend of hers suggested she attend the national Romance Writers of America conference to see if she could "do anything with it." It was this move into the traditional space of the romance industry's largest association that prompted Axelrod to consider how to commercially publish her work and she decided to self-publish.[57]

After proving her marketability as an author self-publishing her work, Axelrod was approached by traditional publisher Sourcebooks and in 2021 they published Axelrod's *The Girl with Stars in Her Eyes*. This novel became a Target Diverse Book Club Pick, Amazon Editors Pick for Romance in May 2021, and listed as a Goodreads Romance Readers Most Anticipated Books for May 2021. Being traditionally published thus expanded Axelrod's reach in the entertainment ecosystem through new avenues of reception typically unavailable to self-published authors, including, importantly, discount department stores. As this and the commercialization of IP through Wattpad's programs described in the previous chapter demonstrates, while platforms open many opportunities for writers, proximity to traditional institutions and codified platform activities remains a central component in authors finding success in the twenty-first century.

Conclusion

The entertainment ecosystem is complex and multifaceted. It is an environment where platforms, authors, and traditional institutions are increasingly connected through strategic partnerships, informal alliances, and uneasy competition. In the cultural industries of publishing and entertainment media, the entertainment ecosystem is underpinned by the commercialization and movement of intellectual property and data. Platforms increasingly finesse this trade through multi-platformed, pan-entertainment business strategies, where they are reliant on large and active user bases to determine the value of each bit of IP and then attempt to maximize the mileage of each piece in which they invest.

Where platforms forge centralized networks in the entertainment eco-system, driven entirely by economic imperatives and attempts at capture, authors create relational networks through their creative and professional practices. These author-driven networks include connections to symbiotic third-party platforms; competing digital publishing platforms; and other spaces dedicated to creative writing, reading, and publishing as authors work across platforms and traditional book-related spaces to market their work and develop their craft. Authors' creative and productive networks illustrate the myriad practices of self-publishing that do not fit neatly into platform-driven structures. These perspectives jointly considered point to the contradictions of power embedded within the platform publishing and the broader entertainment ecosystem.

At the outset of this chapter, I warned that the entertainment ecosystem was a heuristic framework, one that changed depending on the vantage point of the observer and what was positioned as the starting point on which to focus. Situated fairly squarely between the disciplines of publishing and platform studies, this research positions books and book publishing as a central node in the entertainment complex of the twenty-first century but much can be said about other media objects and industries. This chapter begins to map the networks forged by Amazon, Wattpad, and some of the authors who use these platforms to publish romance fiction. And yet it only captures a moment in time and there is a lot it leaves out.

Wattpad's pan-entertainment ventures have only expanded since the platform was acquired by Naver and ostensibly merged with Webtoon (at least for the purposes of commercializing IP) in 2021. Further, if we were to extend the focus beyond production to the reception of books (a compo-nent mostly outside the scope of this research but that certainly influences creation and production processes), we could extend the picture of the ecosystem presented here to include numerous other platforms and spaces such as Goodreads, Storygraph, Instagram, TikTok, private WhatsApp group chats, brick-and-mortar bookstores, book clubs, and libraries. These additional spaces would undoubtedly provide further evidence as to the movement, hybridity, and dynamism of the entertainment ecosystem as it traverses platformed and institutional networks as well as digital and physical spaces.

For both platform companies and authors, building networks across the entertainment ecosystem is an attempt at minimizing risk. The coordinated distribution of connected media assets across delivery formats is driven by an economic imperative to achieve economies of scale among increasingly fragmented audiences. This strategy works for platform companies and authors in contradictory ways: companies develop the technological and organizational infrastructure of the ecosystem to enhance their capture of users (both creators and audiences); and authors often disperse their production activities across platforms in the ecosystem to avoid the precarity of capture and their (over)reliance on individual platforms that may change or disappear at any moment.

While authors negotiate and, in some ways, undermine aspects of platform control, circumventing efforts of capture by engaging in dispersed publishing practices, power remains primarily concentrated in and wielded by platforms, traditional conglomerate publishers, and legacy institutions. These entities determine the mechanisms, rules, and conditions for access, remuneration, and overall experience.

FROM THE EARLY DAYS of ARPANET to the emergence of the internet and platform era, digital networks have held implicit promises that they would bring about a democratization of society, politics, and cultural production. These promises are deeply entangled with technological determinist ideas that the affordances of platforms inherently enable users to participate in community. But platforms do not just exist as technical infrastructures. People animate platforms and determine whether ideals of equitable participation are realized, from the users who create and circulate content, to the executives, managers, and staff who determine and enforce policies of engagement. The experiences of BIPOC and LGBTQ+ authors on Amazon and Wattpad demonstrate that the racial and cultural biases perpetuated by the legacy book industry are being built into digital book publishing spaces, and that publishing platforms have failed to live up to early promises that they would herald in a democratization of cultural production. While old gatekeepers of publishing may be circumvented through the platformization of publishing, new but similarly opaque barriers have emerged in their place.

Inequalities of Platform Publishing brings together publishing and platform studies to investigate how technological and industrial imperatives interlock on platforms to simultaneously empower and marginalize authors of color and queer authors. Through extensive case studies and profiles, original interviews with authors, digital walkthroughs of platforms, metadata analysis, and review of gray literature, this book shows how embedded systems of discrimination play out across platforms' commercial structures, recommender and classification algorithms, governance systems, and organizational cultures. Ultimately, this book contends with the contradictions and realities at the heart of platform publishing: namely, that platforms both enable and constrain self-publishing authors in various ways.

The platformization of publishing, which is occurring in tandem with other media and cultural industries, has resulted in seismic shifts within and between sectors. I model platform publishing in a broader entertainment ecosystem that comprises platforms; legacy cultural institutions; and individual producers, intermediaries, and consumers, and is animated by networks forged between these constituents. While platformed publishing represents a new form of book production, it is deeply informed by the broader cultural and economic rules of the book and media industries as well as the specific platform microsystems in which it occurs. The entertainment ecosystem builds on José van Dijck's connective ecosystem framework to explore the dynamic relationship between these two constituent forces.[1] Van Dijck theorizes social media platforms as operating in two configurations: as individual microsystems, comprising a range of constitutive components including technology, users/usage, governance, ownership, business model, and content; and a larger connective ecosystem, in which platforms interact with each other in distinctive and formative ways. In this way, the entertainment ecosystem framework has heuristic value for investigating the technological, economic, and sociocultural contexts in which books and authors circulate online and a consideration of cooperative intermedia relationships and emerging media forms that exist within this dynamic sphere of creative production.

Drawing on media ecology, the entertainment ecosystem framework usefully contextualizes platform publishing in longer histories of media production, articulated by the fields of book history and media archeology, and acknowledges how relationships, logics, and practices extend within and across industry sectors. While platforms may implement their own systems for producing books, the logics of the traditional publishing industry are evident in a myriad of ways—from how books are categorized on platforms, as seen in chapter 3, to the editorial processes of platform publishers detailed in chapter 4. Like ecosystems of the natural environment, media ecosystems are dynamic entities, subject to periodic disturbances and containing potential for resilience. The entertainment ecosystem framework thus allows for platformed cultural practices that are mutable to change over time and by centering different platforms or participants. Platformed publishing is also located in and responsive to broader temporal, cultural, and sociopolitical contexts.

Rematerializing and relocating the social and political context of platform publishing further highlights the ecosystem in which platformed cultural production exists and the power structures within. The view of the ecosystem presented in this book spans both digital and physical, platformed and traditional, public and private spaces. For instance, many of the interviews I conducted with authors who use Amazon were done at the

Romance Writers of America Conference at the Marriott Marquis in New York. Other interviews were done via Zoom during COVID lockdowns where authors were often located at their desks in their homes, often the same places where they wrote and published their novels. The ecosystem in which platform publishing is embedded is not only vast and very much material, but also relational and embodied. It is not separate to these broader realities but built through them.

Platformed publishing may be further contextualized by what Kate Crawford and Vladan Joler refer to as a "vast planetary network," that is "fueled by the extraction of non-renewable materials, labor, and data."[2] The full ecosystem of platformed publishing spans sites like Salar de Uyuni in southwest Bolivia where the lithium for Kindle batteries is extracted; the Amazon warehouses across the globe where workers pack print books as fast as they can for minimum wage; and the highways, trucks, and cars that delivery drivers occupy to meet Amazon's promise of one-day shipping for Prime members. It encompasses office buildings in Nairobi, New Delhi, and Manila where content moderation of book text and covers is often outsourced, as well as those like Seattle, Toronto, and Seoul where Amazon, Wattpad, and Webtoon were respectively launched.

To many, most of these feel far away and almost abstract in their existence; to others, the material realities of these locations and spaces are immediate. The Amazon warehouse employees who are responsible for the distribution of a good proportion of print books do this work in appalling conditions; reports from employees reveal that workers are timed to complete tasks, fear taking bathroom breaks so sometimes resort to relieving themselves in bottles, and are generally "treated like robots."[3] Their unsafe working conditions are compounded by job insecurity and poor remuneration, with many only earning the US minimum wage of $15 per hour and employed on a casual basis. At the same time, Jeff Bezos, the company's founder, executive chairperson and former CEO, is estimated to be one of the richest people in the world. His personal fortune increased during the COVID-19 pandemic when many people across the globe faced job losses and increased financial insecurity, including authors. Wattpad provides a different, yet equally stark picture of the economic conditions of platform publishing; since launching in 2007, it has raised over US$100 million in venture funding and was sold to Naver for more than US$600 million in 2021 while most of its user base generate content and reader data for free.

Like authors in the traditional publishing industry, BIPOC authors often earn less compared to White authors when it comes to advances. This absurd wealth disparity, emblematic of the epoch of late capitalism and propelled by logics of platform capitalism, will only perpetuate existing inequalities in book culture.

Digital technologies have been transforming book publishing for more than half a century, during which they have inspired experimentation with forms and formats, made processes more efficient and cost-effective, and transformed modes of reading. The ingress of Big Tech into book culture in the early twenty-first century relationship requires a reconceptualization of how we define self-publishing as the practice becomes increasingly dependent on platforms and platform companies. As argued in chapter 1, self-publishing is now almost entirely synonymous with platformed publishing. These publishing platforms transform established power dynamics within the contemporary publishing industry and use these changes to reinforce the idea that they herald in a democratization of cultural production. But although they do provide access to BIPOC and LGBTQ+ authors who have been underrepresented and underserved by traditional publishers, publishing platforms are yet to fully empower these authors and offer radical alternatives to legacy systems that result in their marginalization.

The promises associated with platforms and internet technologies become handy rhetorical devices to elide this fact. Both Amazon and Wattpad implicitly and explicitly promote ideas that they improve access to publishing despite their enforcement of systems that structure inequitable participation. Chapter 2 shows how Amazon emphasizes the power authors retain in publishing through Kindle Direct Publishing through their promotional and educational resources. Phrases such as "everything from content to price is totally up to you" and "after all, *you're* the author" stresses the creative freedom afforded to authors through this mode of publishing.[4] Wattpad, on the other hand, actively leans into promises that their platform improves the diversity and inclusion of voices and stories in publishing. Over the last few years, Wattpad's about page has promised variations on hosting the diverse voices and stories from around the globe. At the time of writing, it reads:

> We're setting stories free. . . . The walls that kept storytelling in film, TV, and publishing something reserved for an elite few?

They're crumbling. People from around the world are picking up their phones and laptops, and creating their own narratives. And tens of millions of them are doing it on Wattpad.[5]

But as the authors' stories in this book shows, we need to push back against this particular style of branding that revives the false promises of a democratization of cultural production online and elides the inequitable experiences of users on their platforms. Simone Shirazi articulated the discrepancies between Wattpad's branding and her experiences on the platform, stating

> They do talk big, and I think when they do have those marginalized voices, they push them to the forefront and it's just like, "Oh, look, guys. Look at how good of a job we're doing," when in the background, you know you're publishing books that are exclusively White. I won't name titles, but you see they're examples of them trying to be woke and yet, they're still pushing these stories that really aren't very progressive. They end up being pretty problematic and not good representation and all of this stuff while still trying to claim like, "Oh, guys. Look at what a good job we're doing. Look at who we're focusing on. Look at who we're featuring," but Wattpad has this issue where they continuously say they're driven by data. That's how they know who to publish . . . [and] it's just like, "Well, what kind of data and is the data inherently biased?" because these really popular stories tend to be almost all about White people, like cis, White, straight people and able-bodied at that. You can try as much as you want to have your token diverse books, but if you're still going to push those traditional White stories and champion those more than anything else, and if those are your real money makers here, it's just like, "Are we really making a change or are we just sitting back and patting ourselves on the shoulder for a tiny bit of work?"[6]

In this way, publishing platforms like Amazon and Wattpad draw on the ideals of freedom and openness promised by the internet for their own commercial interests. On an individual level, this greater accessibility is true; anyone can set up accounts and publish almost whatever they want on their platforms as long as it is in line with the terms of service. But what equitable access exists beyond the ability to publish? Platforms may use the discourse of inclusivity to signal a progressive ethos in their marketing copy but not necessarily implement structures that facilitate an equitable culture in their workplace, on their platform, or in the cultural objects they produce. On a systemic level, then, platforms do not offer a radically different alternative from traditional publishing.

Processes of datafication at the heart of platformed publishing further limit efforts towards greater diversity and inclusion. The classification, moderation, and ranking of authors and books are increasingly left to automated systems that often replicate existing biases and uphold hegemonic taxonomies. Amazon's inclusion of authors' profile data in its classification system reproduces biases from traditional knowledge organization systems such as BISAC and Dewey Decimal that order books by and about BIPOC and LGBTQ+ people lower in the hierarchical structure. Chapter 3 further shows how automated moderation systems, which treat the cover image, paratext, and text of books as data points to determine their acceptability for publication, disproportionately and unfairly treat people of color and LGBTQ+ identities as "adult material" and either suppress or remove it from the platform. This kind of datafication will increasingly impact how books are written and designed, as algorithms like Amazon's A9 (its search results ranking algorithm) and also-bought categories determine the visibility and potential sales value of books. In an industry where profit margins are reportedly slim, this will likely lead to further homogenization of books. We are already seeing this with the current illustrated cover design trend in romance fiction—epitomized by Leni Kauffman's cutely stylized designs— which easily circumvent negative content moderation outcomes, but also fit nicely with the so-called Instagram aesthetic.[7]

Chapter 4 explores the implications of datafication on the actual texts that are published too, demonstrating how Wattpad's reliance on reader data from the platform to inform its acquisition decisions first for Wattpad Books and now for Wattpad Webtoon Book Group does not ensure diversity and inclusion in its publishing list. The potential harms of data are magnified by platforms using it as a discursive foil to evade responsibility for the actions of their algorithms and staff. Wattpad's emphasis on using reader data and supposedly objective metrics as rationalizing measurements to inform acquisition decisions works to minimize the responsibility of the human parts of its taste-making system and renders its publishing outcomes as something that is neutral rather than what it actually is; that is, the outcome of exclusionary structures and biased input data. As with traditional publishers, if Wattpad truly wants to publish diversely, the human staff must actively work to acquire culturally inclusive works and not rely solely on data to do this work for them.

The dominance of these platforms in the contemporary publishing and media industries pose further risks to culture and cultural production as they become increasingly dependent on and controlled by platforms. These risks have been considered by cultural studies scholar Ted Striphas, who argues that "human beings have been delegating the work of culture—the sorting, classifying and hierarchizing of people, places, objects and ideas—to data-intensive computational processes." This rise in algorithmic culture, he continues, risks "the gradual abandonment of culture's publicness" and results in "the emergence of a strange new breed of elite culture purporting to be its opposite."[8] We are yet to see the full abandonment of book culture's publicness, despite the inroads platforms such as Amazon have made. In film and television, the proprietary and competitive snapping up of culture is felt through the streaming wars, as platforms such as Netflix, Prime, and Disney Plus seek to hold the rights to and produce popular content to encourage more subscribers. The exclusivity of original productions to these platforms, for example, highlights how so much of our access to beloved film and television are dependent on platforms. While many texts from Wattpad and especially Amazon would survive if these sites were to go down for whatever reason, just as many may be lost forever. While we may wonder at the literary value of these platform-dependent texts, it is the power that these platforms wield in the creation of, hosting of, and access to culture that should be of concern to anyone interested in book culture and literary history.

In these and many other ways, platforms have seemed to gain unilateral power by providing alternative avenues for publishing and providing what has become essential infrastructure for the dissemination and consumption of books by traditional institutions and independent producers alike. Digital publishing platforms wield tremendous power in contemporary book culture and mediate every stage of the publishing cycle for self-published authors. Amazon and Wattpad control the conditions of entry for authors on their sites, dictate publishing possibilities through their interface designs and commercial structures and configure the mechanisms of discoverability of authors and their titles. Working against this backdrop of fluctuating institutional dominance are authors, who also gain power and greater agency in the context of the platformization of publishing. Authors engage with platforms in strategic ways to suit their creative and professional goals, forging their own networks across the entertainment ecosystem, as shown in chapter 5. Despite their limitations, platforms such as Amazon and Wattpad enable BIPOC and LGBTQ+ authors who have historically been excluded and marginalized within the traditional publishing and media industries to publish their works with minimal gatekeeping and greater creative control. In this way, self-publishing on platforms is an important, valid and impactful mode of publishing, particularly in popular fiction genres, which allow authors working within non-hegemonic publishing territories to participate in the global contemporary book culture to a greater degree than ever before.

But this power is relational, wielded over different actors in different ways at different times and the power of platform-dependent authors is not uniform either. Authors who experience greater success through high sales, readerships, or traditional publishing deals are more likely to form direct links to platform personnel—bigger-name authors on Amazon are connected with author representatives and Wattpad Stars are connected to talent managers at Wattpad through whom they can more readily resolve their problems on the platform and make the process of publishing more efficient and profitable. To make the nuances of these relational power dynamics visible, we need big and small data accounts of what is happening on platforms just as we need more information on how traditional institutions in book culture perpetuate exclusion and marginalization. We need to focus on people's situated experiences and stories, including those from non-Western (non-hegemonic) publishing territories and localized writing and publishing communities, further removed from Ameri-centric ideologies of platforms and publishing.

The unmet promises of platforms to deliver a more equitable, democratized publishing culture underscore the importance of better diversity and inclusion at traditional publishing entry points too. Traditional publishers are not acquitted of the role they continue to play in the systemic marginalization and exclusion of BIPOC and LGBTQ+ authors and books. More needs to be done across the board, including within traditional publishing houses and literary organizations as well as by platform companies, to create more space and dismantle structural barriers for authors of color and queer authors. This is even more pressing in the current entertainment landscape, as traditional publishing and other media sectors are increasingly connected to and reliant on platforms, as explored in chapter 5. As Anamik Saha and Sandra van Lente argue, the voguish action of implementing in-house diversity policies has little impact on racial and social inequalities because "the dominant culture treats it as a mere add-on to existing structures."[9] Likewise, Richard Jean So's examination of Toni Morrison's tenure at Random House in the early 1980s demonstrates the desperate need for structures that support and encourage diversity that are not dependent on well-meaning individuals, but are multilayered, intentional, and lasting.[10] What is needed is a radical transformation of the structures of the publishing industry, across platforms and traditional institutions, that combines diversity policies with positive action initiatives, intentional equitable design, and governmental regulation. This action must be led by people and cannot be dependent on automated systems.

Appendix 1: Case Profile Authors

Demi Abilon is a Filipino author who publishes contemporary romance and young adult fiction. Her Wattpad fiction has been published in the Philippines by Psicom and Bliss Books, including *Wake Up, Dreamers!* (2021).

Xio Axelrod is a Black American author who is self-published across Amazon, Kobo, Google, Apple Books, and other platforms. She writes contemporary romance. In 2021, her title *The Girl with Stars in Her Eyes* was published by Sourcebooks.

Melissa Blue is a Black American author of contemporary romance who is self-published across Amazon, Kobo, Google, Apple Books, and other platforms. She also writes erotic romance under the pseudonym Dakota Gray.

Ivey Choi is a Korean American author and former Wattpad Star. She writes diverse new adult fiction and romantic comedy novels. She left Wattpad in 2020 and has published on Radish.

Mina V. Esguerra is a Filipino author, previously traditionally published by Summit Books, and founder of #RomanceClass, a self-publishing collective in the Philippines. She writes romance, young adult fiction, and chick-lit. She joined Wattpad in August 2012 where she publishes some fiction and writing advice.

Katrina Jackson is a Black American author, self-published on Amazon and sold via Kindle Unlimited. She writes queer contemporary romance and erotica.

Claire Kann is a Black American author, Watty Award winner, and Wattpad Star, and publishes young adult and contemporary and queer romance. She also published fiction on Swoon Reads and has been published by Swoon Reads and Berkley.

Jackie Lau is an Asian Canadian author who is self-published across Amazon, Kobo, Google, Apple Books, and other platforms. She has published on Wattpad under Jackie Lau and another pseudonym. She writes romantic comedy novels featuring Asian Canadian characters.

Daven McQueen is a queer Afro-Filipino American author, Watty Award winner, and Wattpad Star. They joined Wattpad in January 2015 and publish young adult and romance. Their Wattpad fiction story *The Invincible Summer of Juniper Jones* was published by Wattpad Books in 2020.

Courtney Milan is an Asian American author who is self-published across Amazon, Kobo, Google, Apple Books, and other platforms. She writes historical and contemporary romance. She has previously been traditionally published by Harlequin and is a former board member of the Romance Writers of America.

Farrah Rochon is a Black American author who is self-published across Amazon, Kobo, Google, Apple Books, and other platforms. She has been a two-time finalist for RWA's RITA Award and has been a Romantic Times Book Reviews Reviewer's Choice Award nominee. She writes diverse contemporary and sports romance. She has previously been traditionally published by Harlequin's Kimani Romance imprint and was a director-at-large for RWA. Her series, beginning with *The Boyfriend Project* (2020), is published by Hachette's Forever imprint.

Simone Shirazi is a Black and Persian American author, Watty Award winner, and former Wattpad Star who publishes contemporary diverse romance and joined Wattpad in December 2013. Shirazi has published and been a content writer for Radish. Her title *Once Upon a One Night Mistake* was published by Radish in 2021, and *Cross the Line* was published by Macmillan in 2024 under the name Simone Soltani.

Suleikha Snyder is an Indian American author who is self-published across Amazon, Kobo, Google, Apple Books, and other platforms. She writes contemporary and Bollywood-inspired romance.

Sol Tuberosum is a Filipino author who publishes queer, f/f romance on Wattpad, Wattpad Star, and Wattpad Ambassador. Sol joined Wattpad in April 2013.

Appendix 2: Methodology

This book primarily takes a qualitative multi-method case study approach informed by relational ontology. Data were collected from fourteen semi-structured in-depth interviews with self-published romance authors who are BIPOC and/or LGBTQ+; classification and moderation metadata collected through Amazon's API; a walkthrough of platform terms of service, and gray literature including platform blogs and reportage. While each of these methods have been summarized briefly in the preceding chapters, this appendix provides greater detail on their implementation. I acknowledge the strengths of qualitative research and interviews in emphasizing individuals' experiences within particular contexts, an approach that draws on an epistemology of standpoint feminism and its acknowledgement of the impact of social position impacts on how we know and interpret the world.

Case Studies and Case Profiles

Overall, this book uses a case study approach to analyze two significant publishing platforms: Amazon and Wattpad. Case studies allow in-depth exploration from multiple perspectives of a particular context, in which evidence is collected using different methods. Using a variety of methods offers different angles for comprehending the complexity and uniqueness of each case as well as multiple points of discovery for the multitudinous experiences of BIPOC and LGBTQ+ authors on these platforms while the qualitative approach emphasizes experience and subjective ways of knowing. As these platforms and the authors who use them exist in situ and relationally in the broader entertainment ecosystem, other platforms and institutions also come into the frame as they become important to the participant authors. These case studies are animated by what Helen Simons terms "case profiles." Simons defines case profiles as "shorter cameos of individuals" who "may be quite prominent" within the context of the case study whose perceptions, interpretations, and interactions provide more nuanced information regarding the actual experience within and meaning of the case study.[1] The case profiles in this book are the interview participants, who use or have used Amazon and/or Wattpad to publish their creative works.

Interviews

Between 2019 and 2022, I conducted fourteen semi-structured in-depth interviews with self-published BIPOC and LGBTQ+ authors. Participants comprised women and non-binary individuals from the United States, Canada, and the Philippines (detailed in appendix 1), and were selected using a purposive sampling method. They were deemed to be information-rich cases, based on their prominence, activity, and popularity on each platform, a sampling methodology that undoubtedly relies on my own positionality as a reader of romance fiction and user of these platforms. Half of the interviews were conducted in-person at different locations in the US, including the 2019 Romance Writers of America conference in New York. The other half were conducted on Zoom after the COVID-19 pandemic and lockdowns restricted travel in 2020–2021. On average, interviews lasted an hour and while the conversations did not follow a rigid set of questions, a similar interview protocol was used to guide every conversation. This protocol included questions in three main groupings: authors' writing and publishing practice on platforms, their views on inclusive romance fiction, and their experience with the romance publishing community. Semi-structured interviews allow for greater agency than structured inter-views as participants can direct the conversation to topics and angles that they deem important. Another important aspect of semi-structured inter-views is their constructivist nature; both the researcher and participant work to co-create the knowledge produced through dialogue. Transcripts of the interviews were produced and shared with participants, who were provided an opportunity to amend, clarify, and approve parts of their own transcripts. Interview transcripts were then coded and analyzed using a thematic analysis approach.

Metadata Analysis

The metadata analysis focused on the case profile authors and their titles. The methods employed for collecting and analyzing metadata related to platform categorization and governance systems necessarily differed for

Amazon and Wattpad as access to key metadata and information varied across the two platforms and over the research period. When I began collecting metadata of book categories from Amazon in 2019, I used a platform called Sales Rank Express, which collected and collated book metadata from Amazon through its API, including price, filter statuses, categories, (linked) paired titles, and so on for its US and UK stores. At this time, Amazon also showed the categories of books in the left-hand column on books' marketplace pages, which enabled a comparison between how a book was categorized on the backend and where it appeared on the front end. Likewise, I could compare the status of any flags or filters (i.e., for adult content) through Sales Rank Express and compare the impact it had on books in the marketplace. In mid-2020, Amazon changed the conditions of its API, rendering Sales Rank Express useless and sometime the same year, the left-hand list of categories and departments in which a book sat in the marketplace also disappeared, rendering my method for mapping categories useless too. By this stage, I had fortuitously collected the data for all my Amazon case studies. Unfortunately, without access to Amazon's API or affiliate program, through which access to the API is still available, reproducibility of this data collection method is not possible. Any further category metadata for books was collected using the Book Category Hunter tool on the website Nerdy Book Girl that uses the Amazon API, but no similar tool is available for adult filter flags.

Wattpad data is more publicly accessible. On Wattpad, categories were collected by scraping tags listed publicly on story homepages in line with the allowances of the platform at the time. When posting stories to Wattpad, authors choose from genre categories, such as romance and teen fiction, but can also enter free-text tags to boost keyword discoverability through the platform's search engine. Tags may still follow traditional subgenre descriptions or tropes, such as paranormal or enemies-to-lovers, but tend to be more idiosyncratic because they do not have to follow established categories. Wattpad tags were analyzed using a thematic analysis. A comparative analysis between Amazon and Wattpad categories presented an opportunity to consider the way digital classification systems work to position and present books by historically marginalized author groups, and whether user-generated categories radically reinvent or subvert classification systems that subjugate historically marginalized authors. Categories for Amazon titles were analyzed against the information on book classification provided by authors in interviews. Categories in Wattpad tags were open coded for common topics and themes.

Walkthrough and Website Analysis

The case study platforms, Amazon and Wattpad, were further analyzed using the walkthrough method and website analysis. These combined methods enabled an analysis of the interface, affordances, algorithms, terms of service, content, and architecture of platforms, as well as how these features are presented to the user. The walkthrough method is a way of systematically engaging with an app's interface to "examine its technological mechanisms and embedded cultural references to understand how it guides users and shapes their expectations."[2] This method is grounded in a combination of science and technology studies with cultural studies to perform a critical analysis of a given app. It involves the "step-by-step observation and documentation of an app's screens, features and flows of activity" that is contextualized within a review of the app's vision, operating model, and governance system. This sociocultural approach emphasizes an app or platform's symbolic elements and users' social interpretations, which would be overlooked with "big" data methods. It establishes a user-centered approach to analyzing a platform's intended purpose, embedded cultural meanings, and implied ideal users and uses as well as a foundation for further research that identifies how users resist these arrangements.

    The investigation of each digital publishing platforms' interface is complemented by a website analysis. Website analyses have been used primarily in business studies as a method for usability and prototype testing.[3] This method positions the medium and text of websites as analytical objects and analyses the website's media environment (the internet and application ecosystem), its textual environment (hardware and software), and its textuality (written elements, static image elements, moving image elements, sound elements, and the coherence and formal relations between them). In this book, I focus primarily on the content and design of websites, including information, navigation structure, search function, protected content, and presentation style or interface. My use of this method is informed by Johanna Drucker's theorization of interface as a "boundary space" that can be read as an object and a space that constitutes activity.[4] In this way, a website analysis positions the platform as a "field of possibilities" that shapes users' interactions and presents multiple semantic and interpretive potentialities.

Review of Gray Literature

Finally, gray literature was examined to ascertain supplementary information related to the operations of the platforms. Drawing on different modes of writing can productively contribute to scholarly knowledge production. The gray literature examined in this thesis was sourced from news outlets, platform blogs and reports, and industry reportage. The information sourced through this method is useful for corroborating and providing greater context regarding the experiences of authors as well as providing new information on platform histories and company strategy. Gray literature published by the platform companies will also present information regarding how platforms talk about themselves, which was compared to the primary data collected through the other methods to uncover disjoints in what a platform believes it is doing—or wants users to believe it is doing—and the actual experiences of users.

Notes

Preface

1 Anne Helmond, "The Platformization of the Web: Making Web Data Platform Ready," *Social Media + Society* 1, no. 2 (2015).

Introduction

1 Simone Shirazi, "Once Upon a One Night Mistake—the Webcomic," *Simone Shirazi* (blog), January 25, 2023, https://simoneshirazi.com/the-fairytale-series/.
2 Simon Peter Rowberry, *Four Shades of Gray* (Cambridge, MA: MIT Press, 2022).
3 Beth Driscoll, *What Readers Do* (London: Bloomsbury Publishing, 2024); Jessica Pressman, *Bookishness*, (New York: Columbia University Press, 2021).
4 Simone Murray, *The Digital Literary Sphere* (Baltimore, MD: Johns Hopkins University Press, 2018).
5 Wattpad and Webtoon merged in 2021, about halfway through this research project.
6 Karl Bergund, "Introducing the Beststreamer: Mapping Nuances in Digital Book Consumption at Scale," *Publishing Research Quarterly* 37 (April 2021): 135–51; Millicent Weber, "'Reading' the Public Domain: Narrating and Listening to Librivox Audiobooks," *Book History* 24 no. 1 (Spring 2021): 209–43.
7 Melanie Ramdarshan Bold, "The Return of the Social Author: Negotiating Authority and Influence on Wattpad," *Convergence* 24 no. 2 (June 2016): 117–36; Rowberry, *Four Shades of Gray.*
8 Robert Darnton, "What is the History of Books?," *Daedalus* 111, no. 3 (1982): 65–83.
9 Karl Berglund and Sara Tanderup Linkis, "Modelling Subscription-Based Streaming Services for Books," *Mémoires du livre: Studies in Book Culture* 13, no. 1 (2022): 1–30.
10 Padmini Ray Murray and Claire Squires, "The Digital Publishing Communications Circuit," *Book 2.0* 3, no. 1 (2013): 4.
11 Thomas Poell, David B. Nieborg, and Brooke Erin Duffy, *Platforms and Cultural Production* (New York: Polity Press, 2021), 4.
12 Nick Montfort and Ian Bogost, *Racing the Beam: The Atari Video Computer System* (Cambridge, MA: MIT Press, 2020).
13 Poell, Nieborg, Duffy, *Platforms and Cultural Production*, 4.
14 Tarleton Gillespie, "The Politics of 'Platforms,'" *New Media & Society* 12, no. 3 (2010): 347–64.
15 Aarhti Vadde, "Platform or Publisher," *PMLA/Publications of the Modern Language Association of America* 136, no. 3 (2021): 455–62.
16 Vadde, "Platform or Publisher," 456.
17 Anne Helmond, "The Platformization of the Web: Making Web Data Platform Ready," *Social Media + Society* 1, no. 2 (September 2015): 1–11.
18 Poell, Nieborg, Duffy, *Platforms and Cultural Production*, 4.
19 Poell, Nieborg, Duffy, *Platforms and Cultural Production*, 4

20 José van Dijck, *The Culture of Connectivity* (Oxford, UK: Oxford University Press, 2013).

21 See, for example: Rowberry, *Four Shades of Gray*; Simone Murray, *The Digital Literary Sphere*; Matthew Kirschenbaum, *Bitstreams: The Future of Digital Literary Heritage* (Philadelphia: University of Pennsylvania Press, 2021); Vilde Sundet & Terje Colbjørnsen "Streaming Across Industries: Streaming Logics and Streaming Lore Across the Music, Film, Television and Book Industries," *MedieKultur: Journal of Media and Communications Research* 37, no. 70 (2021): 12–31.

22 Amazon [@amazon], "The Inequitable and Brutal Treatment of Black People in Our Country Must Stop. Together We Stand in Solidarity with the Black Community—Our Employees, Customers, and Partners—in the Fight against Systemic Racism and Injustice," Tweet, *Twitter*, June 1, 2020, https://twitter.com/amazon/status/1267140211861073927.

23 Harlequin [@HarlequinBooks], "We Stand with Our Black Authors, Readers and Colleagues. We See You and Hear You. Black Stories Matter. Black Lives Matter," Instagram post, June 2, 2020, https://www.instagram.com/p/CA5-200l9ax/.

24 Amazon, "Our Workforce Data," US About Amazon, May 31, 2023, https://www.aboutamazon.com/news/workplace/our-workforce-data.

25 Karen Weise, "Amazon Workers Urge Bezos to Match His Words on Race With Actions," *New York Times*, June 24, 2020, sec. Technology, https://www.nytimes.com/2020/06/24/technology/amazon-racial-inequality.html.

26 Jodi Kantor, Karen Weise, and Grace Ashford, "Inside Amazon's Worst Human Resources Problem," *New York Times*, October 24, 2021, sec. Technology, https://www.nytimes.com/2021/10/24/technology/amazon-employee-leave-errors.html; Michael Sainato, "'I'm Not a Robot': Amazon Workers Condemn Unsafe, Grueling Conditions at Warehouse," *Guardian*, February 5, 2020, sec. Technology, https://www.theguardian.com/technology/2020/feb/05/amazon-workers-protest-unsafe-grueling-conditions-warehouse; Jay Greene, "Amazon's Employee Surveillance Fuels Unionization Efforts: 'It's Not Prison, It's Work,'" *Washington Post*, December 14, 2021, https://www.washingtonpost.com/technology/2021/12/02/amazon-workplace-monitoring-unions/.

27 David Streitfeld, "How Amazon Crushes Unions," *New York Times*, March 16, 2021, sec. Technology, https://www.nytimes.com/2021/03/16/technology/amazon-unions-virginia.html; Rachel Metz, "Amazon Will Block Police Indefinitely from Using Its Facial-Recognition Software," *CNN*, May 18, 2021, sec. Business, https://www.cnn.com/2021/05/18/tech/amazon-police-facial-recognition-ban/index.html.

28 Meredith Broussard, *Artificial Unintelligence* (Cambridge, MA: MIT Press, 2018).

29 Fred Turner, "Where the Counterculture Met the New Economy: The WELL and the Origins of Virtual Community," *Technology and Culture* 46, no. 3 (2005): 485–512.

30 Henry Jenkins, *Fans, Bloggers, and Gamers: Exploring Participatory Culture* (New York: NYU Press, 2006), 26.

31 Charlton D. McIlwain, *Black Software: The Internet & Racial Justice, from the AfroNet to Black Lives Matter* (Oxford, UK: Oxford University Press, 2019).

32 See, for example: Cathy O'Neil, *Weapons of Math Destruction* (London: Penguin, 2016); Ruha Benjamin, *Race After Technology: Abolitionist Tools for the New Jim Code* (Hoboken, NJ: Wiley, 2019).

33 John Battelle, "The Birth of Google," *WIRED*, August 1, 2005, https://www.wired.com/2005/08/battelle/.

34 Safiya Umoja Noble, *Algorithms of Oppression* (New York: NYU Press, 2018), 48.

35 André Brock Jr, *Distributed Blackness* (New York: NYU Press, 2020); Catherine Knight Steele, *Digital Black Feminism,* (New York: NYU Press, 2021); Sarah Florini, *Beyond Hashtags: Racial Politics and Black Digital Networks* (New York: NYU Press, 2019).

36 Poell, Nieborg, Duffy, *Platforms and Cultural Production,* 17.

37 "Where is the Diversity in Publishing? The 2019 Diversity Baseline Survey Results," Lee and Low Books, January 28, 2020, https://blog.leeandlow.com/2020/01/28 /2019diversitybaselinesurvey/.

38 Susannah Bowen and Beth Driscoll, *Australian Publishing Industry Workforce Survey on Diversity and Inclusion,* (Melbourne: University of Melbourne and Australian Publishers Association, 2022), 1–22, https://publishers.asn.au/Web/Web/Member -Resources/ResearchReports/Workforce_Survey_2022.aspx; Radhiah Chowdhury, "It's Hard to Be What You Can't See: Diversity within Australian Publishing: Lessons in Diverse and Inclusive Publishing from the United Kingdom," (2019–2020 Beatrice Davis Editorial Fellowship Report, 2020).

39 Laura B. McGrath, "'Books About Race': Commercial Publishing and Racial Formation in the 21st Century," *New Literary History* 54, no. 1 (2023): 771–94.

40 Anamik Saha and Sandra van Lente, *Rethinking 'Diversity' in Publishing,* (London: Goldsmiths Press, 2020), https://research.gold.ac.uk/id/eprint/28692/.

41 Melanie Ramdarshan Bold, *Inclusive Young Adult Fiction: Authors of Colour in the United Kingdom* (London: Palgrave Macmillan, 2019).

42 Alexandra Dane, *White Literary Taste Production in Contemporary Book Culture,* (Cambridge, UK: Cambridge University Press, 2023).

43 Richard Jean So, *Redlining Culture: A Data History of Racial Inequality and Postwar Fiction,* (New York: Columbia University Press, 2021), 20, emphasis in original.

44 Alexandra Dane, *Gender and Prestige in Literature: Contemporary Australian Book Culture* (London: Springer Nature, 2020).

45 Saha and Van Lente, *Rethinking 'Diversity' in Publishing.*

46 So, *Redlining Culture,* 183.

47 Catherine Knight Steele, *Digital Black Feminism* (New York: NYU Press, 2021), 1, 15.

48 Pascale Casanova, *The World Republic of Letters* (Cambridge, MA: Harvard University Press, 2004); Gisèle Sapiro, "Globalization and Cultural Diversity in the Book Market: The Case of Literary Translations in the US and in France," *Poetics* 38, no. 4 (2010): 419–39.

49 Carole Boyce-Davies, *Black Women, Writing and Identity: Migrations of the Subject* (Abingdon, UK: Routledge, 1994).

50 See, for example Mark Davis and Jian Xiao, "De-westernizing Platform Studies: History and Logics of Chinese and US platforms," *International Journal of Communication* 15, (2021): 1–20; Jodi McAlister, Claire Parnell and Andrea Anne Trinidad, *Publishing Romance Fiction in the Philippines,* (Cambridge, UK: Cambridge University Press, 2023).

51 Kim Wilkins, Beth Driscoll, and Lisa Fletcher, *Genre Worlds: Popular Fiction and Twenty-First-Century Book Culture* (Amherst: University of Massachusetts Press, 2022), 22.

52 Helen Simons, "Case Study Research: In-Depth Understanding in Context," in *The Oxford Handbook of Qualitative Research,* ed. Patricia Leavy, 2nd ed., Oxford Handbooks (New York: Oxford University Press, 2020), 680.

53 For a list of these case profile authors, see appendix 1.

54 See appendix 2 for more detail on methodology.

55 Patricia Hill Collins, "Learning from the Outsider Within: The Sociological Significance of Black Feminist Thought," *Social problems* 33, no. 6 (1986): 14–32.

56 Aja Romano and Constance Grady, "Romance Is Publishing's Most Lucrative Genre. Its Biggest Community of Writers Is Imploding," *Vox*, January 10, 2020, https://www .vox.com/2020/1/10/21055125/rwa-what-happened-resignations-courtney-milan -damon-suede-backstory-2020-ritas-conference.

57 bell hooks, *Talking Back: Thinking Feminist, Thinking Black*, (Boston: South End Press, 1989), 26.

Chapter 1: Digital Promise and the Platformization of Publishing

1 Megan Garber, "The First Characters Sent Through the Internet Were L-O-L," *The Atlantic*, published October 29, 2014, https://www.theatlantic.com/technology /archive/2014/10/the-first-characters-sent-through-the-internet-were-l-o-l/382074/.

2 Christine Larson, *Love in the Time of Self-Publishing* (Princeton, NJ: Princeton University Press, 2024).

3 Beth Driscoll, Lisa Fletcher, Kim Wilkins, and David Carter, "The Publishing Ecosystem of Contemporary Australian Genre Fiction," *Creative Industries Journal* 11, no. 2 (2018): 203–21, https://doi.org/10.1080/17510694.2018.1480851.

4 Michael Bhaskar, *The Content Machine* (London: Anthem Press, 2013), 54.

5 Richard Barbrook and Andy Cameron, "The Californian Ideology," *Science as Culture* 6, no. 1 (1996): 50.

6 See, for example, Manuel Castells, *The Internet Galaxy* (New York: Oxford University Press, 2001); John Naughton, "The Evolution of the Internet: From Military Experiment to General Purpose Technology," *Journal of Cyber Policy* 1, no. 1 (2016): 5–28, https://doi.org/10.1080/23738871.2016.1157619.

7 Castells, *The Internet Galaxy*, 16.

8 Castells, *The Internet Galaxy*, 29, 30–31.

9 Castells, *The Internet Galaxy*, 25.

10 Richard Barbrook and Andy Cameron, "The Californian Ideology," *Mute*, published September 1, 1995, https://www.metamute.org/editorial/articles/californian-ideology.

11 Barbrook and Cameron, "The Californian Ideology," 44.

12 Marshall McLuhan, *Understanding Media* (New York: McGraw-Hill, 1964); Alvin Toffler, *The Third Wave* (New York: Bantam Books, 1980).

13 Henry Jenkins, *Convergence Culture* (New York: NYU Press, 2006), 18.

14 Simon Peter Rowberry, *The Early Development of Project Gutenberg c.1970–2000* (Cambridge, UK: Cambridge University Press, 2023).

15 Padmini Ray Murray and Claire Squires, "The Digital Communications Circuit," *Book 2.0* 3, no. 1 (2013): 3–23, https://doi.org/10.1386/btwo.3.1.3_1.

16 Astrid Ensslin, *Pre-web Digital Publishing and the Lore of Electronic Literature* (Cambridge, UK: Cambridge University Press, 2022), 2.

17 Barbrook and Cameron, "The Californian Ideology," 50.

18 ABC 7 Chicago, "From the Archive: Jeff Bezos in 1999, Discussing His New Website Amazon.Com" Uploaded February 2, 2021, YouTube Video, 11:37, https://www .youtube.com/watch?v=VyeDiC2PcYo.

19 Millicent Weber, "'Reading' the Public Domain: Narrating and Listening to Librivox Audiobooks," *Book History* 24, no. 1 (2021): 209–43.

20 See, for example, Farhad Manjoo, "The iPad of Babel," *Slate*, published June 02, 2012, https://slate.com/culture/2012/06/childrens-books-as-ipad-apps-tablet-versions-of -kids-books-reviewed.html.

21 Al Gore, *Our Choice* (Push Pop Press, 2012), https://pushpoppress.com/ourchoice/.

22 Simon Peter Rowberry, *Four Shades of Gray* (Cambridge, MA: MIT Press, 2022).

23 Beth Driscoll, Lisa Fletcher, and Kim Wilkins, "Women, Akubras and Ereaders: Romance Fiction and Australian Publishing," in *The Return of Print? Contemporary Australian Publishing*, ed. Aaron Mannion and Emmett Stinson (Melbourne: Monash University Publishing, 2016), 74.

24 Andrea Ballatore and Simone Natale, "E-Readers and the Death of the Book: Or, New Media and the Myth of the Disappearing Medium," *New Media & Society* 18, no. 10 (November 1, 2016): 2380.

25 Timothy Laquintano, *Mass Authorship and the Rise of Self-Publishing* (Iowa: University of Iowa Press, 2013).

26 Ballatore and Natale, "E-readers and the Death of the Book."

27 Judith Stoop, Paulien Kreutzer, and Joost Kircz, "Reading and Learning from Screens versus Print: A Study in Changing Habits: Part 1–Reading Long Information Rich Texts," *New Library World* 114, no. 7/8 (2013): 284–300.

28 Ray Murray and Squires, "The Digital Communications Circuit," 19.

29 Simone Murray, *The Digital Literary Sphere* (Baltimore, MD: Johns Hopkins University Press, 2018).

30 Robert Darnton, "What Is the History of Books?," *Daedalus* 111, no. 3 (1982): 65–83.

31 Ray Murray and Squires, "The Digital Communications Circuit," 4.

32 Nick Levey, "Post-Press Literature: Self-Published Authors in the Literary Field," *Post45*, published March 2, 2016, https://post45.org/2016/02/post-press-literature -self-published-authors-in-the-literary-field-3/.

33 Laquintano, *Mass Authorship*, 23.

34 Kim Wilkins, Beth Driscoll, and Lisa Fletcher, *Genre Worlds: Popular Fiction and Twenty-First-Century Book Culture* (Amherst: University of Massachusetts Press, 2022).

35 Driscoll et al., "The Publishing Ecosystems of Contemporary Australian Genre Fiction."

36 Laquintano, *Mass Authorship*, 7–8.

37 Mark McGurl, "Everything and Less: Fiction in the Age of Amazon," *Modern Language Quarterly* 77, no. 3 (2016): 456, emphasis in original.

38 Larson, *Love in the Time of Self-Publishing*, 143.

39 Alison Baverstock and Jackie Steinitz, "Who Are the Self-Publishers?," *Learned Publishing* 26, no. 3 (2013): 211–23, https://doi.org/10.1087/20130310.

40 Bhaskar, *The Content Machine*, 105.

41 Interview with Farrah Rochon, July 24, 2019.

42 Interview with Suleikha Snyder, July 10, 2019.

43 Interview with Courtney Milan, July 27, 2019.

44 Interview with Milan.

45 Courtney Milan, *Hold Me* (Courtney Milan, 2016).

46 Ruby Dixon, *Ice Planet Barbarians* (Ruby Dixon, 2015).

47 Interview with Katrina Jackson, July 8, 2019.

48 Interview with Jackson.

49 Interview with Ivey Choi, October 9, 2020.

50 Melanie Ramdarshan Bold, "The Return of the Social Author: Negotiating Authority and Influence on Wattpad," *Convergence* 24, no. 2 (2018): 117–38.

51 Alexandra Dane, *White Literary Taste Production in Contemporary Book Culture* (Cambridge, UK: Cambridge University Press, 2023).

52 Interview with Sol Tuberosum, February 25, 2021.

53 Interview with Rochon.

54 Interview with Milan.

55 Interview with Milan.

56 Interview with Jackie Lau, July 25, 2019.

57 Interview with Lau.

58 Anamik Saha, "The Rationalizing/Racializing Logic of Capital in Cultural Production," *Media Industries* 3, no. 1 (2016): 1–16.

59 Interview with Lau.

60 Interview with Lau.

61 Simone Murray, *The Adaptation Industry* (New York: Routledge, 2005).

62 See, for example, Simon Peter Rowberry, "Ebookness," *Convergence* 23, no. 3 (2017): 289–305; Simone Murray, "Charting the Digital Literary Sphere," *Contemporary Literature* 56, no. 2 (2015): 311–39; Jessica Pressman, *Bookishness: Loving Books in a Digital Age* (New York: Columbia University Press, 2021); Matthew G. Kirschenbaum, *Bitstreams: The Future of Digital Literary Heritage* (Philadelphia: University of Pennsylvania Press, 2021).

63 See, for example, David Craig and Stuart Cunningham, *Social Media Entertainment: The New Intersection of Hollywood and Silicon Valley* (New York: NYU Press, 2019); Blake Hallinan and Ted Striphas, "Recommended for You: The Netflix Prize and the Production of Algorithmic Culture," *New Media & Society* 18, no. 1 (2016): 117–37; Thomas Poell, David B. Nieborg, and Brooke Erin Duffy, *Platforms and Cultural Production* (New York: Polity Press, 2021); Fatima Gaw, "Algorithmic Logics and the Construction of Cultural Taste of the Netflix Recommender System," *Media, Culture & Society* 44, no. 4 (2022): 706–25.

64 See, for example, Tully Barnett, "Read in Browser: Reading Platforms, Frames, Interfaces, and Infrastructure," *Participations* 16, no. 1 (2019): 306–19; Matthew Kirschenbaum, *Mechanisms: New Media and Forensic Imagination* (Cambridge, MA: MIT Press, 2008); Lisa Nakamura, "'Words with Friends': Socially Networked Reading on Goodreads," *PMLA/Publications of the Modern Language Association of America* 128, no. 1 (2013): 238–43; Simon Peter Rowberry, "Ebookness."

65 Anne Helmond, "The Platformization of the Web: Making Web Data Platform Ready," *Social Media + Society* 1, no. 2 (2015).

66 Carlos A. Scolari, "Media Ecology: Exploring the Metaphor to Expand the Theory," *Communication Theory* 22, no. 2 (2012): 204–25.

67 José van Dijck, *The Culture of Connectivity: A Critical History of Social Media* (New York: Oxford University Press, 2013), 25, emphasis in original.

68 Interview with Simone Shirazi, November 23, 2021.

69 Interview with Shirazi.

Chapter 2: Platformed Book Markets

1 Daniel Schiller, *Digital Capitalism* (Cambridge, MA: MIT Press, 1999).

2 José van Dijck, Thomas Poell, and Martijn de Waal, *The Platform Society: Public Values in a Connective World* (New York: Oxford University Press, 2018).

3 Nick Srnicek, *Platform Capitalism* (Hoboken, NJ: Wiley, 2016).

4 Claire Parnell and Beth Driscoll, "Institutions, Platforms and the Production of Debut Success in Contemporary Book Culture," *Media International Australia* 187, no. 1 (May 1, 2023): 123–38.

5 Shoshana Zuboff, "The Age of Surveillance Capitalism," in *Social Theory Re-Wired*, ed. Wesley Longhofer and Daniel Winchester, 3rd ed. (New York: Routledge, 2023), 203–13.

6 David S. Evans and Richard Schmalensee, *Matchmakers: The New Economics of Multisided Platforms* (Cambridge, MA: Harvard Business Review Press, 2016), 1.

7 Thomas Poell, David Nieborg, and Brooke Erin Duffy, *Platforms and Cultural Production* (New York: Polity Press, 2022): 3.

8 Simon Peter Rowberry, "Ebookness," *Convergence: The International Journal of Research into New Media Technologies* 23, no. 3 (2017): 294.

9 "Self Publishing," Amazon Kindle Direct Publishing, https://kdp.amazon.com/en_US/.

10 "Digital Book Pricing Page," Amazon Kindle Direct Publishing, https://kdp.amazon.com/en_US/help/topic/G200634500.

11 Interview with Xio Axelrod, July 24, 2019.

12 Clayton Noblit, "Up to Date List of KDP Global Fund Payouts," Written Word Media, April 16, 2024, https://www.writtenwordmedia.com/kdp-global-fund-payouts/.

13 Interview with Katrina Jackson, July 8, 2019.

14 Shannon Maughan, "The Audiobook Market, and Its Revenue, Keep Growing," *Publishers Weekly*, June 1, 2023, https://www.publishersweekly.com/pw/by-topic/industry-news/audio-books/article/92444-the-audiobook-market-and-revenue-keeps-growing.html.

15 Karl Berglund, *Reading Audio Readers* (London: Bloomsbury Publishing, 2024); Vilde Schanke Sundet and Terje Colbjørnsen. "Streaming Across Industries: Streaming Logics and Streaming Lore across the Music, Film, Television, and Book Industries," *Mediekultur* 37, no. 70 (2021).

16 Millicent Weber, "'Reading' the Public Domain: Narrating and Listening to Librivox Audiobooks," *Book History* 24, no. 1 (2021): 209–43.

17 Matthew Rubery, *The Untold Story of the Talking Book* (Cambridge, MA: Harvard University Press, 2016).

18 "Audible.Com Announces a Tenfold Increase in Audiobooks Produced Through the Audiobook Creation Exchange (ACX)," *Business Wire*, January 30, 2013, https://www.businesswire.com/news/home/20130130005427/en/Audible.com-Announces-a-Tenfold-Increase-in-Audiobooks-Produced-Through-the-Audiobook-Creation-Exchange-ACX.

19 Boris Kachka, "Audiobooks Are the New E-Books, Except They Might Keep Growing," *Vulture*, September 20, 2018, https://www.vulture.com/2018/09/audiobooks-are-booming-but-how-long-will-that-last.html.

20 Interview with Axelrod.

21 Interview with Axelrod.

22 Interview with Courtney Milan, July 27, 2019.

23 Interview with Axelrod.

24 Michael Kozlowski, "Audible is Focused on Audiobook Education," *GoodEReader*, July 21, 2016. https://goodereader.com/blog/audiobooks/audible-is-focused-on-audiobook-education; Heloise Wood, "Audible Strikes £150k Partnership with LAMDA," *The Bookseller*, July 19, 2018. https://www.thebookseller.com/news/audible-uk-and-lamda-join-forces-150k-partnership-833331.

25 Alyssa Cole, *The AI Who Loved Me* (Newark: Audible, 2020).

26 "Wattpad Creators Program," *Wattpad Creators*, https://creators.wattpad.com/programs-and-opportunities/wattpad-creators-program/.

27 David Graver, "Interview: Radish Fiction Founder, Seung Yoon Lee," *Cool Hunting*, April 25, 2017, https://coolhunting.com/culture/interview-radish-fiction-sy-lee/.

28 Lena Abou El-Komboz, Anna Kerkhof, and Johannes Loh, "Platform Partnership Programs and Content Supply: Evidence from the YouTube 'Adpocalypse,'" Working Paper (CESifo Working Paper, 2023), 3, https://hdl.handle.net/10419/272007.

29 Interview with Simone Shirazi, November 23, 2020.

30 Wattpad now pays Creators in their local currency but I neglected to ask at the time if the dollar amount Shirazi mentioned was in her local currency of USD or CAD, where Wattpad HQ is based.

31 Interview with Shirazi.

32 Interview with Shirazi.

33 Brooke Erin Duffy, Annika Pinch, and Megan Sawey, "The Nested Precarities of Creative Labor on Social Media," *Social Media + Society* 7, no. 2 (2021): 2.

34 Interview with Shirazi.

35 Interview with Shirazi.

36 "Writing Resources," Wattpad Creators, https://creators.wattpad.com/writing-resources/.

37 Interview with Shirazi.

38 Interview with Ivey Choi, October 9, 2020.

39 Aarthi Vadde, "Amateur Creativity: Contemporary Literature and the Digital Publishing Scene," *New Literary History* 48, no. 1 (2017): 37.

40 Melanie Ramdarshan Bold, "The Return of the Social Author: Negotiating Authority and Influence on Wattpad," *Convergence* 24, no. 2 (2018): 117–36.

41 Ramdarshan Bold, "Return of the Social Author," 16.

42 Interview with Claire Kann, April 2, 2021.

43 Vadde, "Amateur Creativity," 37.

44 Claire Parnell, "Reading and Writing Muslim Romance on Wattpad," in *The Routledge Companion to Romantic Love*, ed. Ann Brooks (New York: Routledge, 2022), 334–44.

45 Interview with Shirazi.

46 Interview with Choi.

47 Interview with Shirazi.

48 Interview with Shirazi.

49 Gerard Genette, *Paratexts: Thresholds of Interpretation* (Cambridge, UK: Cambridge University Press, 1997), 1.

50 Gérard Genette and Marie Maclean, "Introduction to the Paratext," *New Literary History* 22, no. 2 (1991): 261, emphasis in original, https://doi.org/10.2307/469037.

51 Genette, *Paratexts*, 2.
52 Ellen McCracken, "Expanding Genette's Epitext/Peritext Model for Transitional Electronic Literature: Centrifugal and Centripetal Vectors on Kindles and iPads," *Narrative* 21, no. 1 (2013): 105–24, https://doi.org/10.1353/nar.2013.0005.
53 Simon Peter Rowberry, *Four Shades of Gray: The Amazon Kindle Platform* (Cambridge, MA: MIT Press, 2022), 103.
54 Rowberry, *Four Shades of Gray*, 109.
55 J. Hillis Miller quoted in Genette, *Paratexts*, 1.
56 Karl Berglund and Sara Tanderup Linkis, "Modelling Subscription-Based Streaming Services for Books," *Mémoires Du Livre / Studies in Book Culture* 13, no. 1 (2022): 4, 17, https://doi.org/10.7202/1094131ar.
57 Sukhpuneet Kaur, Kulwant Kaur, and Parminder Kaur, "Analysis of Website Usability Evaluation Methods," in *2016 3rd International Conference on Computing for Sustainable Global Development* (New Delhi: INDIACom, 2016), 1043–46.
58 Niels Brügger, "Website History and the Website as an Object of Study," *New Media & Society* 11, no. 1–2 (February 1, 2009): 115–32.
59 Johanna Drucker, "Reading Interface," *PMLA/Publications of the Modern Language Association of America* 128, no. 1 (January 2013): 216.
60 Interview with Mina V. Esguerra, October 6, 2019.
61 Jodi McAlister, Claire Parnell, and Andrea Anne Trinidad, *Publishing Romance Fiction in the Philippines* (Cambridge, UK: Cambridge University Press, 2023).
62 Courtney Milan, *The Duchess War* (Courtney Milan, 2012).
63 Farrah Rochon, *The Dating Playbook: A Fake-Date Rom-Com to Steal Your Heart! "A Total Knockout: Funny, Sexy, and Full of Heart"* (Headline Eternal, 2021).
64 Jonathan Zittrain, *The Future of the Internet—And How to Stop It* (New Haven, CT: Yale University Press, 2008).
65 Jaci Burton, *The Perfect Play* (New York: Berkley Books, 2011).
66 Matthew G. Kirschenbaum, *Bitstreams: The Future of Digital Literary Heritage* (Philadelphia: University of Pennsylvania Press, 2021).
67 "#PUBLISHINGPAIDME," Google Spreadsheet, https://docs.google.com/spreadsheets/d/1Xsx6rKJtafa8f_prlYYD3zRxaXYVDaPXbasvt_iA2vA/edit#gid=1798364047.
68 Interview with Jackson.
69 Emily West, *Buy Now: How Amazon Branded Convenience and Normalized Monopoly* (Cambridge, MA: MIT Press, 2022).

Chapter 3: Sorting and Moderating Books

1 Ted Striphas, "Algorithmic Culture," *European Journal of Cultural Studies* 18, no. 4–5 (2015): 395–412.
2 Hope A. Olson, *The Power to Name: Locating the Limits of Subject Representation in Libraries* (Dordrecht: Springer, 2013).
3 Janice A. Radway, *Reading the Romance: Women, Patriarchy, and Popular Literature* (Durham, NC: University of North Carolina Press, 2009), 12.
4 Ben Light, Jean Burgess, and Stefanie Duguay, "The Walkthrough Method: An Approach to the Study of Apps," *New Media & Society* 20, no. 3 (March 1, 2018): 881–900.

5   https://nerdybookgirl.com/book-category-hunter/.

6   Data was scraped in line with the allowances of the platform at the time.

7   Hope A. Olson, "How We Construct Subjects: A Feminist Analysis," *Library Trends* 56, no. 2 (2007): 509–41.

8   Melissa Adler and Lindsey M. Harper, "Race and Ethnicity in Classification Systems: Teaching Knowledge Organization from a Social Justice Perspective," *Library Trends* 67, 1 (2018): 52–73.; Isabel Espinal, Tonia Sutherland, and Charlotte Roh, "A Holistic Approach for Inclusive Librarianship: Decentering Whiteness in Our Profession," *Library Trends* 67, no. 1 (2018): 147–62.

9   Olson, *The Power to Name*, 2.

10 Daniel Martínez-Ávila, "BISAC: Book Industry Standards and Communications," *KO Knowledge Organization* 43, no. 8 (2016): 655–62.

11 See for example, Catherine Knight-Steele, *Digital Black Feminism* (New York: NYU Press, 2021); Lisa Nakamura, *Cybertypes: Race, Ethnicity, and Identity on the Internet* (Oxfordshire: Routledge, 2002); Ruha Benjamin, *Race After Technology: Abolitionist Tools for the New Jim Code* (Hoboken, NJ: John Wiley & Sons, 2019).

12 Interview with Xio Axelrod, July 24, 2019.

13 Interview with Axelrod.

14 Interview with Axelrod.

15 Interview with Axelrod.

16 "KDP Categories," Amazon Kindle Direct Publishing, https://kdp.amazon.com/en _US/help/topic/G200652170.

17 Safiya Umoja Noble, *Algorithms of Oppression* (New York: NYU Press, 2018).

18 Richard Jean So, *Redlining Culture: A Data History of Racial Inequality and Postwar Fiction* (New York: Columbia University Press, 2020).

19 Larry Hardesty, "The History of Amazon's Recommendation Algorithm," *Amazon Science*, November 22, 2019, https://www.amazon.science/the-history-of-amazons -recommendation-algorithm.

20 Interview with Axelrod.

21 Ed Finn, *What Algorithms Want: Imagination in the Age of Computing* (Cambridge, MA: MIT Press, 2017).

22 Olson, *The Power to Name*.

23 Dakota Gray, *Adonis Line* (Dakota Gray, 2019).

24 Courtney Milan, Rose Lerner, and Alyssa Cole, *Hamilton's Battalion: A Trio of Romances* (Courtney Milan, 2017).

25 Courtney Milan, *Mrs. Martin's Incomparable Adventure* (Courtney Milan, 2019).

26 Xio Axelrod, *When Frankie Meets Johnny* (Xio Axelrod LLC, 2019).

27 Xio Axelrod et al., *Love Is All: Volume 3* (Xio Axelrod LLC, 2020).

28 Katrina Jackson, *Small Town Secrets* (Katrina Jackson, 2018).

29 Katrina Jackson, *Bang & Burn* (Katrina Jackson, 2019).

30 Xio Axelrod, *The Girl with Stars in Her Eyes: A Story of Love, Loss, and Rock-and-Roll* (Sourcebooks Casablanca, 2021).

31 Zakiya Dalila Harris, *The Other Black Girl* (New York: Atria, 2022).

32 Sally Thorne, *The Hating Game* (New York: Avon, 2016).

33 Beth Driscoll, "The Rise of the Microgenre," *Pursuit*, May 13, 2019, https://pursuit .unimelb.edu.au/articles/the-rise-of-the-microgenre.

34 Hope A. Olson, "The Power to Name: Representation in Library Catalogues," *Signs: Journal of Women in Culture & Society* 26, no. 1 (2001): 640.

35 David Weinberger, "Taxonomies to Tags: From Trees to Piles of Leaves," Hyper Org, modified January 20, 2006, https://hyperorg.com/blogger/misc/taxonomies_and _tags.html.

36 Maria Lindgren Leavenworth, "The Paratext of Fan Fiction," *Narrative* 23, no. 1 (2015): 47, emphasis in original.

37 Ludi Price and Lyn Robinson, "Tag Analysis as a Tool for Investigating Information Behaviour: Comparing Fan-Tagging on Tumblr, Archive of Our Own and Etsy," *Journal of Documentation* 77, 2 (2021): 320–58.

38 Sol Tuberosum, *Wish Granted* (Wattpad, 2020), https://www.wattpad.com/story /219675533-wish-granted.

39 Interview with Ivey Choi, October 9, 2020.

40 Interview with Simone Shirazi, November 23, 2020.

41 "Press and Announcements," *Wattpad*, https://company.wattpad.com/press.

42 Tarleton Gillespie, *Custodians of the Internet: Platforms, Content Moderation, and the Hidden Decisions that Shape Social Media.* (New Haven, CT: Yale University Press, 2018), 5.

43 Sarah Roberts, *Behind the Screen* (New Haven, CT: Yale University Press, 2019).

44 Interview with Katrina Jackson, July 8, 2019.

45 Katrina Jackson, *Her Christmas Cookie* (Katrina Jackson, 2018).

46 Katrina Jackson, *Private Eye* (Katrina Jackson, 2019).

47 Benjamin Sutton, "Facebook Censored a Stone Age Nude Sculpture, Venus of Willendorf," Hyperallergic, February 28, 2018, http://hyperallergic.com/429553/facebook -censors-venus-of-willendorf/.

48 Interview with Jackson.

49 Elia Winters, *Three-Way Split* (Entangled: Scorched, 2018).

50 Joy Buolamwini and Timnit Gebru, "Gender Shades: Intersectional Accuracy Disparities in Commercial Gender Classification," *Proceedings of Machine Learning Research* 81, no. 1 (2018): 15.

51 Reuben Binns et al., "Like Trainer, Like Bot? Inheritance of Bias in Algorithmic Content Moderation," in *Social Informatics*, ed. Giovanni Luca Ciampaglia, Afra Mashhadi, and Taha Yasseri (Cham, CH: Springer, 2017), 405–15.

52 Emily Dreyfuss, "Twitter Abuse Toward Women is Rampant, Amnesty Report Says," *Wired*, December 18 (2018), https://www.wired.com/story/amnesty-report-twitter -abuse-women/; Ysabel Gerrard and Helen Thornham, "Content Moderation: Social Media's Sexist Assemblages," *New Media & Society* 22, 7 (2020): 1266–86.; Susanna Paasonen, Kylie Jarrett, and Ben Light, *NSFW: Sex, Humor, and Risk in Social Media* (Cambridge, MA: MIT Press, 2019).

53 Interview with Jackson.

54 Interview with Jackson.

55 Dakota Gray, *Perv* (Amazon Digital Services, 2016).

56 Melissa Blue, *Her Insatiable Scot: Contemporary Scottish Romance* (Melissa Blue, 2014).

57 Melissa Blue, *Kilt Tease* (Melissa Blue, 2015).

58 Melissa Blue, *Kilted For Pleasure* (Melissa Blue, 2015).

59 Melissa Blue, *Scot Appeal* (Melissa Blue, 2016).

60 Melissa Blue, *To One Hundred* (Melissa Blue, 2016).

61 Xio Axelrod, *Falling Stars* (Xio Axelrod LLC, 2015).

62 Xio Axelrod, *Starlight* (Xio Axelrod LLC, 2016).

63 Xio Axelrod, *La Promesse* (Xio Axelrod LLC, 2016).

64 Xio Axelrod, *Camden* (Xio Axelrod LLC, 2017).

65 Xio Axelrod, *The Warm Up* (Xio Axelrod LLC, 2017).

66 Xio Axelrod, *Fast Forward: An Alt Er Love Novella* (Xio Axelrod LLC, 2017).

67 Sara Ahmed, *Complaint!* (Durham, NC: Duke University Press, 2021).

68 Paul Gewirtz, "On 'I Know It When I See It,'" *The Yale Law Journal* 105, no. 4 (1996): 1023–47, https://doi.org/10.2307/797245.

69 "Metadata Guidelines for Books," Kindle Direct Publishing, accessed March 3, 2025, https://kdp.amazon.com/en_US/help/topic/G201097560.

70 José van Dijck, *The Culture of Connectivity* (New York: Oxford University Press, 2013).

71 This walkthrough was conducted between 2022–2024 and I acknowledge that Amazon is likely to have changed some of the pages since then. As a snapshot in time, it is intended to demonstrate the opaque, ever-changing and sometimes circuitous system in which self-published authors work.

72 "Conditions of Use," Amazon, accessed January 25, 2022, https://www.amazon.com /gp/help/customer/display.html?nodeId=508088&ref_=footer_cou.

73 "Terms and Conditions," Kindle Direct Publishing, https://kdp-eu.amazon.com /agreement?token=eyJjbGllbnRJZCI6ImtpbmRsZV9kaXJlY3RfcHVibGlzaGluZ yIsImRvY3VtZW50SWQiOiJrZHAiLCJjYW5jZWxVcmwiOiJodHRwczovL2tccC 5hbWF6b24uY29tIiwiY2xpZW50TG9jYWxlIjoiTkEiLCJkaXNwbGF5UGFyYW1 zIjpudWxsfQ%7CeyJtYXRlcmlhbFNlcmlhbCI6MSwiaG1hYyI6IjNVTU9oejdYTE NWY1dsMUZFWWQwYnRRZN3FNR1FxOEJxVHpyaWhYS2dGVWM9IiwianNv bkhtYWMiOnRydWUsInR5cGUiOiJSRUFFX09OTFkiLCJhY2NlcHQiOmZhbH NlfQ&language=en_US.

74 "KDP Help Center Home," Kindle Direct Publishing, https://kdp.amazon.com/en _US/help?ref_=TN_help.

75 "Content Guidelines," Kindle Direct Publishing, https://kdp.amazon.com/en_US /help/topic/G200672390.

76 "Content Guidelines," Kindle Direct Publishing.

77 "Offensive and Controversial Materials," Amazon Seller Central, https://sellercentral .amazon.com/gp/help/external/200164670.

78 "Community Guidelines," Amazon, https://www.amazon.com.au/gp/help/customer /display.html?nodeId=201929730.

79 "Community Guidelines," Amazon.

80 "Adult Products Policies & Guidelines," Amazon Seller Central, https://sellercentral .amazon.com.au/gp/help/external/200339940?language=en_AU&ref=efph_200339940 _cont_202134820.

81 Headings on Amazon's ToS pages sporadically shift from title case to sentence case, which I have reflected in the walkthrough in this chapter. The inconsistency in terms of capitalization in headings on the ToS pages indicates that these pages have been written at different times and likely by different people, without a clear and consistent style guide. Given the polished and user-friendly interface for much of its services, making them as easy as possible to navigate and use, this inconsistency suggests that Amazon does not expect its users to pay close attention to the ToS.

82 Zoe York, "I Only Share That to Point out That I Never Sent Them Cease & Desist Letters for Having an Opinion over My Title. And It's a Really Awesome Title,

Even Better as Hate F*@k, and Not What I Originally Published It as: Hate Fuck. It Turns out, You Can't Do That.," Tweet, *@ZoeYorkWrites* (Twitter), December 11, 2019, https://twitter.com/ZoeYorkWrites/status/1204601612620247041 (Tweet deleted).

83 "Terms and Conditions," Kindle Direct Publishing.
84 Striphas, "Algorithmic Culture."
85 Jenny Sundén, Katrin Tiidenberg, and Susanna Paasonen, "Platformed Sex Lives," *AoIR Selected Papers of Internet Research*, October 5, 2020, https://doi.org/10.5210/spir.v2020i0.11151.
86 "Adult Content," Tumblr, https://tumblr.zendesk.com/hc/en-us/articles/231885248-Adult-Content.
87 Katrin Tiidenberg, "Playground in Memoriam: Missing the Pleasures of NSFW Tumblr," *Porn Studies* 6, no. 3 (2019): 363–71, https://doi.org/10.1080/23268743.2019.1667048.
88 Carolyn Bronstein, "Pornography, Trans Visibility, and the Demise of Tumblr," *TSQ: Transgender Studies Quarterly* 7, 2 (2020): 240–54.; Alexandra Cho, "Default Publicness: Queer Youth of Color, Social Media, and Being Outed by the Machine," *New Media & Society* 20, 9 (2018): 3183–3200.
89 Katrin Tiidenberg and Emily van der Nagel, *Sex and Social Media*, (West Yorkshire, UK: Emerald Publishing Group, 2020).
90 Alex Hern and Jim Waterson, "Why OnlyFans Had Second Thoughts on Banning Sexually Explicit Content," *The Guardian*, August 29, 2021, sec. Technology, https://www.theguardian.com/technology/2021/aug/29/why-onlyfans-had-second-thoughts-on-banning-sexually-explicit-content.
91 Interview with Axelrod.

Chapter 4: From Platform to Print

1 "About Us," Wattpad WEBTOON Book Group, https://books.wattpad.com/about-us.
2 Tarleton Gillespie, "The Politics of 'Platforms,'" *New Media & Society* 12, 3 (2010): 348.
3 Aarthi Vadde, "Platform or Publisher," *PMLA/Publications of the Modern Language Association of America* 136, no. 3 (2021): 456.
4 Bruno Latour, *Reassembling the Social: An Introduction to Actor-Network-Theory*, Clarendon Lectures in Management Studies (Oxfordshire, UK: Oxford University Press, 2005); John Law, "Actor Network Theory and Material Semiotics," in *The New Blackwell Companion to Social Theory*, ed. Bryan S. Turner (West Sussex, UK: John Wiley & Sons, 2009).
5 John Ellis, "The Literary Adaptation," *Screen* 23, 1 (1987): 3–5.
6 Interview with Ivey Choi, October 9, 2020.
7 Simone Murray, *The Adaptation Industry: The Cultural Economy of Contemporary Literary Adaptation* (New York: Routledge, 2012).
8 Alexandra Dane, "Eligibility, Access and the Laws of Literary Prizes," *Australian Humanities Review* 66 (2020): 122, 133.
9 Interview with Sol Tuberosum, February 25, 2021.

10 Joy Buolamwini and Timnit Gebru, "Gender Shades: Intersectional Accuracy Disparities in Commercial Gender Classification," *Proceedings of Machine Learning Research* 81, no. 1 (2018): 15.

11 Alexandra Dane, *White Literary Taste Production in Contemporary Book Culture* (Cambridge, UK: Cambridge University Press, 2023).

12 Interview with Tuberosum.

13 Robyn Caplan and Tarleton Gillespie, "Tiered Governance and Demonetization: The Shifting Terms of Labor and Compensation in the Platform Economy," *Social Media + Society* 6, no. 2 (2020): 1–13.

14 Ivey Choi, "Leaving Wattpad Stars," Twitter, November 18, 2020, https://web.archive .org/web/20201123200254/https://twitter.com/iveychoi/status/1330963133335126022.

15 Em Slough, "My Statement from Wattpad," Twitter, November 23, 2020, https:// web.archive.org/web/20201123193825/https://twitter.com/emslough/status/13309 53734893944834.

16 Lisa Nakamura, "The Unwanted Labour of Social Media: Women of Colour Call Out Culture as Venture Community Management," *New Formations* 86, no. 86 (2015): 106–112.

17 Aja Romano and Constance Grady, "Romance Is Publishing's Most Lucrative Genre. Its Biggest Community of Writers Is Imploding.," *Vox*, January 10, 2020, https://www .vox.com/2020/1/10/21055125/rwa-what-happened-resignations-courtney-milan -damon-suede-backstory-2020-ritas-conference.

18 Grant Patterson, "'Tone Police' This, Wattpad," *Grant Patterson* (blog), July 16, 2020, https://grantpattersonbooks.com/2020/07/16/tone-police-this-wattpad/. Page no longer available.

19 Interview with Demi Abilon, April 29, 2021.

20 Daven McQueen, *The Invincible Summer of Juniper Jones* (Toronto: Wattpad Books, 2020).

21 Interview with Daven McQueen, November 25, 2020.

22 Interview with McQueen.

23 Interview with Claire Kann, April 2, 2021.

24 Interview with McQueen.

25 David Craig and Stuart Cunningham, *Social Media Entertainment: The New Intersection of Hollywood and Silicon Valley* (New York: NYU Press, 2019).

26 Interview with McQueen.

27 Interview with McQueen.

28 Interview with McQueen.

29 Bengtsson, Maria, and Sören Kock, 2000, "'Coopetition' in Business Networks—to cooperate and compete simultaneously," *Industrial Marketing Management* 29 (5): 411–26.

30 "About Us."

31 Interview with Simone Shirazi, November 23, 2020.

32 The remainder of interview quotes in this section are anonymized to protect the identity of one author who requested quotes from this section of our interview remain anonymous.

33 Melanie Ramdarshan Bold, "The Return of the Social Author: Negotiating Authority and Influence on Wattpad," *Convergence*, 2016, 117–36.

34 Claire Squires, "Taste and/or Big Data?: Post-Digital Editorial Selection," *Critical Quarterly* 59, no. 3 (2017): 24–38.

35 "#PUBLISHINGPAIDME," Google Spreadsheet, https://docs.google.com/spreadsheets
    /d/1Xsx6rKJtafa8f_prlYYD3zRxaXYVDaPXbasvt_iA2vA/edit?usp=embed_facebook.
36 Anamik Saha and Sandra van Lente, "Re:Thinking "Diversity" in Publishing"
    (London: Goldsmith's Press, 2020), 1–40, https://www.gold.ac.uk/goldsmiths-press
    /publications/rethinking-diversity-in-publishing-/.
37 Dane, *White Literary Taste*, 4.
38 Anamik Saha, "The Rationalizing/Racializing Logic of Capital in Cultural Produc-
    tion," *Media Industries* 3, no. 1 (2016): 2.
39 Jodie Archer and Matthew L. Jockers, *The Bestseller Code: Anatomy of the Blockbuster
    Novel* (New York: St. Martin's Press, 2016).
40 Claire Parnell and Beth Driscoll, "Institutions, Platforms and the Production of
    Debut Success in Contemporary Book Culture," *Media International Australia* 187,
    no. 1 (May 1, 2023): 123–38.
41 Anne Gray, *Unsocial Europe: Social Protection or Flexploitation?* (London: Pluto
    Press, 2004): 3.
42 Jan Zwar, David Throsby, Thomas Longden, "Authors Income," (North Ryde, AU:
    Macquarie University, 2015), 1–7, https://researchers.mq.edu.au/files/122625541/3
    _Authors_Income.pdf.

Chapter 5: The Entertainment Ecosystem

1   José van Dijck, *The Culture of Connectivity* (New York: Oxford University Press, 2013).
2   Gillian Doyle, "Multi-Platform Media and the Miracle of the Loaves and Fishes,"
    Journal of Media Business Studies 12, no. 1 (2015): 51.
3   Graham Murdock and Peter Golding, "Beyond Monopoly: Mass Communications
    in an Age of Conglomerates," in *Trade Unions and the Media*, ed. Peter Beharrell
    and Greg Philo, Critical Social Studies (London: Palgrave Macmillan, 1977), 93–117.
4   Julianne Shultz, *Reviving the Fourth Estate: Democracy, Accountability and the Media*
    (Cambridge, MA: MIT Press, 1998).
5   Daniel Schiller, *Digital Capitalism* (Cambridge, MA: MIT Press, 1999).
6   Thomas Schatz, "The Return of the Hollywood Studio System," in *Conglomerates
    and the Media*, ed. Erik Barnouw and Patricia Aufderheide (New York: New Press,
    1997), 73–106.
7   Simone Murray, "Brand Loyalties: Rethinking Content within Global Corporate
    Media," *Media, Culture & Society* 27, no. 3 (2005): 415–35.
8   Gillian Doyle, "From Television to Multi-Platform: Less from More or More for
    Less?," *Convergence* 16, no. 4 (2010): 431–49.
9   Van Dijck, *Culture of Connectivity*, 41.
10 Dan Runkevicius, "How Amazon Quietly Powers the Internet," *Forbes*, September 3,
    2020, https://www.forbes.com/sites/danrunkevicius/2020/09/03/how-amazon
    -quietly-powers-the-internet/.
11 Aubrey Rose, "I Just Turned Down a Publishing Deal with Amazon," Aubrey Rose,
    2013, https://aubreyrosewrites.wordpress.com/2013/08/06/i-just-turned-down-a
    -publishing-deal-with-amazon/.
12 Jim Milliot, "Amazon Publishing Turns 10," *Publishers Weekly*, May 17, 2019, https://
    www.publishersweekly.com/pw/by-topic/industry-news/publisher-news/article
    /80098-amazon-publishing-turns-10.html.

13 Nathan McAlone, "Amazon CEO Jeff Bezos Said Something about Prime Video That Should Scare Netflix," *Business Insider Australia* (blog), June 2, 2016, https://www.businessinsider.com.au/amazon-ceo-jeff-bezos-said-something-about-prime-video-that-should-scare-netflix-2016-6.

14 Claire Parnell, "Mapping the Entertainment Ecosystem of Wattpad: Platforms, Publishing and Adaptation," *Convergence* 27, no. 2 (2021): 524–38.

15 Terry Flew, Xiang Ren, and Yi Wang, "Creative Industries in China: The Digital Turn," in *A Research Agenda for Creative Industries*, ed. Stuart Cunningham and Terry Flew (Northampton: Elgar, 2019), 164–78.

16 John Ellis, "The Literary Adaptation," *Screen* 23, no. 1 (1982): 3–5; Simone Murray, *The Adaptation Industry: The Cultural Economy of Contemporary Literary Adaptation* (New York: Routledge, 2012).

17 José van Dijck and Thomas Poell, "Understanding Social Media Logic," *Media and Communication* 1, no. 1 (2013): 2–14.

18 Parnell, "Entertainment Ecosystem."

19 Proma Khosla, "Netflix's Year-End Rankings Reveal the Most Binged Shows and Movies," *Mashable*, December 11, 2018, https://mashable.com/article/netflix-2018-year-in-review.

20 Jodi McAlister, Claire Parnell and Andrea Anne Trinidad, *Publishing Romance Fiction in the Philippines* (Cambridge, UK: Cambridge University Press, 2023).

21 AnakniRizal, *The Peculiars' Take* (Manila: Psicom, 2013).

22 Bianca B. Bernardino, *She's Dating the Gangster* (Manila: Summit Publishing Company, 2013).

23 AnakniRizal, *Wake Up, Dreamers!* (Manila, PH: Bliss Books, 2019).

24 Anna Cristina Pertierra, "Entertainment Publics in the Philippines," *Media International Australia* 179, no. 1 (2021): 70.

25 Pertierra, "Entertainment Publics," 70.

26 Pauline Gidget Resterio Estella and Martin Löffelholz, "Media Landscapes—Philippines," (Maastricht, The Netherlands: European Journalism Centre, 2019), https://doi.org/10.13140/RG.2.2.33091.76322.

27 Simeon Djankov et al., "Who Owns the Media?," *The Journal of Law and Economics* 46, no. 2 (2003): 341–82.

28 Estella and Löffelholz, "Media Landscapes."

29 Jason Gutierrez, "Philippine Congress Officially Shuts Down Leading Broadcaster," *New York Times*, July 10, 2020, sec. World, https://www.nytimes.com/2020/07/10/world/asia/philippines-congress-media-duterte-abs-cbn.html.

30 Tricia Abigail Santos Fermin, "Appropriating Yaoi and Boys Love in the Philippines," *electronic journal of contemporary japanese studies* 13, no. 3 (2013); Claire Parnell, Andrea Anne Trinidad and Jodi McAlister, "Hello, Ever After: #RomanceClass and Online-Only Live Literature in the Philippines in 2020," *M/C Journal* 24, no. 3 (2021).

31 Minjung Kim, "Gendered Migration and Filipino Women in Korea," in *Multicultural Challenges and Redefining Identity in East Asia*, ed. Nam-Kook Kim. (London: Routledge, 2016); Kristine Michelle L. Santos, "Disrupting Centers of Transcultural Materialities: The Transnationalization of Japan Cool through Philippine Fan Works," *Mechademia: Second Arc* 12, no. 1 (2019): 96–117.

32 Interview with Demi Abilon, April 29, 2021.

33 Richard Bolisay, "'Yes, You Belong to Me!': Reflections on the JaDine Love Team Fandom in the Age of Twitter and in the Context of Filipino Fan Culture," *Plaridel Journal* 12, no. 1 (2015): 1–22.

34 Porter Anderson, "Flirting With New Readers in The Philippines: Wattpad Presents," *Publishing Perspectives*, January 28, 2016, https://publishingperspectives.com/2016/01/readers-in-the-philippines-wattpad-presents/.

35 Patricia May B. Jurilla, *Tagalog Bestsellers of the Twentieth Century: A History of the Book in the Philippines* (Manila, PH: Ateneo de Manila Press, 2020).

36 Interview with Sol Tuberosum, February 25, 2021.

37 Interview with Tuberosum.

38 Interview with Tuberosum.

39 Agence France-Presse, "'Conservative' Romance Novels Attract Poor Filipinos," ucanews.com, August 24, 2011, https://www.ucanews.com/news/conservative-romance-novels-attract-poor-filipinos/28047.

40 Interview with Tuberosum.

41 Interview with Mina V. Esguerra, October 6, 2019.

42 Interview with Esguerra.

43 Laura Dietz, 2023, "Many Gates with a Single Keeper: How Amazon Incentives Shape Novels in the Twenty-First Century" in *The Routledge Companion to Literary Media*, eds. Astrid Ensslin, Julia Round, Bronwen Thomas (London: Routledge, 2023), 371–84.

44 Interview with Simone Shirazi, November 23, 2020.

45 Interview with Shirazi.

46 Interview with Shirazi.

47 Interview with Shirazi.

48 Interview with Esguerra.

49 Jodi McAlister et al., *Publishing Romance Fiction in the Philippines*; Claire Parnell, Andrea Anne Trinidad and Jodi McAlister, "Live Literature in the Philippines: An Ethnographic Study of #RomanceClass and Reading as Performance." *Creative Industries Journal* 16, no. 1 (2023): 56–75.

50 Parnell et al., "Hello, Ever After."

51 Interview with Shirazi.

52 Interview with Katrina Jackson, July 8, 2019.

53 Interview with Jackson.

54 Interview with Xio Axelrod, July 24, 2019.

55 Eloise Faichney, "Undisciplined Creation: Poetry on Tumblr as Autoethnographic and Authorial Practice," in *Post-Digital Book Cultures: Australian Perspectives*, ed. Alexandra Dane and Millicent Weber (Melbourne, AU: Monash University Publishing, 2021).

56 Interview with Axelrod.

57 Interview with Axelrod.

Conclusion

1 José van Dijck, *The Culture of Connectivity* (New York: Oxford University Press, 2013).

2 Kate Crawford and Vladan Joler, "Anatomy of an AI System," AI Now Institute and Share Lab, September 7, 2018, http://www.anatomyof.ai.

3 Emily Guendelsberger, "Amazon Treats Its Warehouse Workers Like Robots: Ex-Employee," *TIME*, July 18, 2018, https://time.com/5629233/amazon-warehouse -employee-treatment-robots/.

4 "Self Publishing," Amazon Kindle Direct Publishing, https://kdp.amazon.com/en _US/.

5 "About," Wattpad, https://company.wattpad.com.

6 Interview with Simone Shirazi, November 23, 2020.

7 "Book Covers," Leni Kauffman, https://www.lenikauffman.com/book-covers.

8 Ted Striphas, "Algorithmic Culture," *European Journal of Cultural Studies* 8, no. 4–5 (2015): 396, 397.

9 Anamik Saha and Sandra van Lente, "Diversity, Media and Racial Capitalism: A Case Study on Publishing," *Ethnic and Racial Studies* 45, no. 16 (2022): 233.

10 Richard Jean So, *Redlining Culture* (New York: Columbia University Press, 2020).

Appendix 2: Methodology

1 Helen Simons, "Case Study Research: In-Depth Understanding in Context," in *The Oxford Handbook of Qualitative Research*, ed. Patricia Leavy, 2nd ed., Oxford Handbooks (New York: Oxford University Press, 2020), 680.

2 Ben Light, Jean Burgess, and Stefanie Duguay, "The Walkthrough Method: An Approach to the Study of Apps," *New Media & Society* 20, no. 3 (March 1, 2018): 882.

3 Niels Brügger, "Website History and the Website as an Object of Study," *New Media & Society* 11, no. 1–2 (2009): 115–32.

4 Johanna Drucker, "Reading Interface," *PMLA/Publications of the Modern Language Association of America* 128, no. 1 (2013): 213–20.

Index

CLAIRE PARNELL was born in Canberra and received her PhD from the University of Melbourne, where she was awarded the Chancellor's Prize for Excellence and is now Lecturer in Digital Publishing in the School of Culture and Communications. She is coauthor of *Publishing Romance Fiction in the Philippines* (2023) with Jodi McAlister and Andrea Anne Trinidad.

www.ingramcontent.com/pod-product-compliance
Lightning Source LLC
LaVergne TN
LVHW041209050326
832903LV00021B/548